Presentiment—is that long shadow—on the lawn—
Indicative that Suns go down—

The Notice to the startled Grass
That Darkness—is about to pass—

EMILY DICKINSON

NIGHT HORIZONS

Gerard Casey

NIGHT HORIZONS

SOPHIA PERENNIS

HILLSDALE NY

Second edition, 2005
First edition, Phudd Bottom Press, 1997
© Sophia Perennis
All rights reserved

No part of this book may be reproduced or transmitted,
in any form or by any means, without permission

For information, address:
Sophia Perennis, P.O. Box 611
Hillsdale NY 12529
sophiaperennis.com

Library of Congress Cataloging-in-Publication Data

Casey, Gerard
Night horizons / Gerard Casey—2nd ed.

p. cm.

Includes bibliographical references.

ISBN 1 59731 034 4 (pbk: alk. paper)
ISBN 1 59731 035 2 (cloth: alk. paper)

1. Christianity. 2. Spiritual life. 3. Casey, Gerard—Correspondence.
4. Casey, Mary—Correspondence. 5. Casey, Patrick, 1932—
Correspondence. I. Title
BR124.C375 2005
230—dc22   2005051560

Acknowledgments

'Three Meditations on Prayer' first appeared in *The Woodbrooke Journal*, printed by The Society of Friends at Sellyoak, Birmingham, UK. The essays in the appendix on Ramana Maharshi and Jacob Boehme are slightly edited versions of those first published in *The Mountain Path*, a periodical of the Sri Ramanasramam at Tiruvanamalai, South India.

I wish to express my gratitude to several close friends: to Stephen Batty and Frank Kibblewhite for helping me in discussions to articulate more clearly the insights I seek to express in the postscript; to Louise de Bruin, who provided the biographical note, and whose sharp eye for detail and extensive knowledge of the persons, places, and subjects touched on in these letters proved indispensable in the editorial process, to which she devoted many painstaking hours—and who also, through many years of understanding and friendship, has never failed at opportune moments to direct my attention to the art of Rembrandt and Van Gogh; to Timothy Hyman for his portrait of me and his 'Night Flight'; to Jeremy Hooker for his kindly foreword; and to James Wetmore, for his encouragement, help, and support.

This book
is
dedicated
to
The Church of St. Peter and St. Paul
at
Mappowder
where for many years
whenever I was in the village
I rang the bell...

Village Church

men built ships in England ever to stay
in quiet anchorage of green fields
to withstand storms of sky of winter weather
unmoved ships of gray stone
with pillars of centuries old
gold sun bound underground
quarried carved to carry
roof wood
vessels to hold holy rood
God's Word to take in hold
all souls
mark of Emmanuel
God with us God with man
that man
labouring avails to build
temples of God

MARY CASEY

See 'A Note on the Headstone', page 255.

Contents

Editor's Note xv
Foreword xix
Letters to Patrick 23
Letters to Mary 105
Postscript 219

Appendix:

Jacob Boehme 235
Ramana Maharshi 245
Three Meditations on Prayer 251
A Note on the Headstone 255
Biographical Note 257

Editor's Note

The poets Gerard and Mary Casey, in the course of their companionship in marriage, developed an interest in and concern with the cultural roots and background of the Christian faith they shared. At times they found themselves separated—he in Africa, she in England—and during these periods they exchanged letters in which they often found themselves discussing the differences in emphasis that arose from their respective points of view. The letters collected in this book reveal the wide range of their reading and concerns. A number of letters written by Gerard to his brother Patrick are also included as essentially preoccupied with the same subjects. The reader will find in the appendix further writings of Gerard Casey that deal with the same general themes found in the letters, thus serving to throw more light on the whole. In view of the lapse of many years between these disparate writings, and the need for a unifying thread, the editor requested that the author provide a supplemental essay, which he has done in the form of a postscript.

Both Gerard and Mary Casey had arrived at an acceptance of the necessity of acknowledging the "transcendent unity of religions" as it is vigorously advocated and defended by the group of metaphysical thinkers associated with René Guénon and Frithjof Schuon. However, at certain levels, they remained critical in their response to this school of "traditionalist" thinkers. They found themselves advancing searching questions that seemed to arise from positions they felt might be oversimplified. For this reason alone the letters cannot fail to demand the close attention of all interested in these questions.

The title of this book derives from a passage in Mary Casey's "visionary recital" of the life of Plotinus, *The Kingfisher's Wing*, where, looking out to the horizon from "the shore of the sounding sea" at nightfall, Plotinus and Origen try to formulate the common essence behind the apparent differences in their points of view.[1] As Jeremy Hooker mentions in his foreword, Gerard Casey would sometimes characterize his and Mary's positions as similar to those of Origen and Plotinus. Lest this raise a smile, or seem unduly abstract, I should like to mention that, in conversation, Gerard described to me how, as a comparatively young man, he became preoccupied with Neoplatonism and Vedanta. Throughout his life he maintained his conviction of the importance of this mode of thought, which recurs in an extraordinarily clear form in the traditionalist school; but he came to feel that it could in practice lead too easily to a denial of popular religion and of the significance of *this* world, as opposed to *that* (the distinction is Plotinian).

Throughout the time he was writing these letters, Gerard was trying to "re-enter humanity" while Mary was running the risk of becoming a ghost; he was plunging into the path of the suffering and lost individual—who could be

---

1. See 'Epigraph', p. 106.

saved only by persevering through the wilderness of apparent alienation from tradition—just when, through his own influence, Mary was "setting out into the deep." These characterizations are of course overly schematic, and, as Gerard never tires of pointing out, Mary's poems display a deep understanding of the Christian emphasis on incarnation and redemption. But it remains true nonetheless that the poignancy, even urgency, to be sensed behind these unusual love letters, was fueled by Gerard's desire to draw Mary back, not only to him, but to the world—a world seen not as the antipodes of spirit, but as the stage for the transfiguration of matter through the individual spirit, the Exemplar of which was Jesus Christ.

After Mary Casey's death in 1980 a poem was found among her papers, summing up her responses and reactions to her shared inner journey with Gerard. We reprint this poem here as it provides a keynote to understanding the depths of their relationship and their problematic response to the traditionalist thinkers, who had so influenced them.

'It is Hard for Thee...'

now my dear comrade in invisible arms
I who have kept close to you from youth
am outwardly old and all the harms
and thorns in the flesh we have shared
have lost point but the inmost pains
pierce to the heart of truth—
without your word for this sharpness
I could not stand

in this new dimension of age—
strange to me for I am young
to sorrow and heartbreak—
I want to speak to this quiet page
of my closest companion
in the hardship of living
the wrestling being

to tell it is well to be strong in suffering
the torrent of words of St. Paul
to run into all the caverns of mind
let that spirit struck by the power
of its own lightning lighten there
and find
the hidden things of God

Foreword

A reviewer said of John Cowper Powys's novel *Wolf Solent* that it was "as beautiful and strange as an electric storm, and like the thunder on Sinai, it is somewhat of a sermon." This storm image, with its suggestion of darkness as well as light, has frequently hovered at the back of my mind while reading the letters Gerard Casey wrote to his wife, Mary, and his brother, Pat, from Africa. One obvious reason for this association is that the letters contain elements, as in Gerard Casey's denunciation of the doctrine of hell in his letters to Pat, that constitute a sermon. Another reason is to be found in actual stormy conditions, in which Gerard writes, or to which he refers. It is Africa, the land and its weathers and creatures, and Gerard's activities as a farmer, that give to his letters a natural elementalism, which corresponds to the Biblical and Homeric aspects of his thinking.

A man who speaks prophetically, and who on occasion will sermonize; an elementalist, close to nature and the basic conditions of life on earth; a poet for whom those elements and conditions are the source of his imagery: these are aspects of Gerard Casey that call to mind the thunder on Sinai. The association with John Cowper Powys's novel is also germane to Gerard Casey's relationship with the Powys family, through his wife and her mother, Lucy, and his friendship with Lucy's brothers, John Cowper, Theodore, and Will. All were exceptionally strong-minded individuals to whom Gerard owed, intellectually and, in the case of Will, practically, a great debt. They provided, one feels, formative influences upon the young Gerard Casey, who also, to some degree, shaped his own strong vision in loving difference from their visions.

The storm imagery has another meaning, too. Experience of darkness pervades Gerard Casey's poem *South Wales Echo* as well as his letters. It is, as it were, the medium of his vision. As a child he felt "the sense of an invading darkness." It was a religious experience, a personal contact with the dominant symbolism of Christianity, and it came with fundamental religious questions, about guilt and innocence, the redemption of suffering, the "restitution of all things." It was experience that could only be understood in terms of the Christian tradition and its symbolism of darkness, which means suffering, unknowing, but also that everything is possible with God. Waiting in darkness, with the presence of Christ, is central to Gerard Casey's thinking. Only thus are the ravages of time to be restored, and the divine image in all things realized. I speak here of a mystery, of course; and not in a futile attempt to explicate it. My aim is to indicate that it is knowledge gained through suffering that gives authority to Gerard Casey's religious vision. At this point, I should say that if I have a qualification for writing about these letters, it is that, belonging to a generation that questioned *all* authority, I have recognized, over a period of twenty-five years, the authority that sounds in his voice. It was a poignant moment for me when I came upon the following words in a letter to Mary: "Any influence, however small, I have, especially with young people, will be exerted to help men return, however falteringly and doubtingly, to traditional influences...." I recognized myself as one of those Gerard was referring to: such knowledge as I have of the Christian tradition, as a living experience of "keeping faith with the dead and through the dead with God," owes a great deal to him.

The thunder on Sinai that sounds in a man's voice can only be validated by humility, by recognition of his vulnerability and human neediness, by what he is in the sight of God. So it is with Gerard Casey, who writes: "I feel, I know myself to be under divine judgement. Not in the sense that God advances on me like the Cerne Giant with a club and threatens, no, in the sense... that God in His pure Presence reveals to us just what we really are.... One just sees oneself *in his Presence*." In another letter he writes: "I have come to trust in God simply because I have discovered I cannot trust myself." Speaking as one who is suspicious of all human claims to authority, this is why I trust Gerard Casey when he speaks of ideas and beliefs that are God-centered. While I do not always agree with him when he denounces the man-centered suppositions which, for him, define the evil of the modern world, I know that he writes with compassion and generosity of spirit, and condemns most vehemently sickness that he diagnoses in himself.

Imagery of storm will belie what is to be found in these letters unless it is understood to imply, not only prophetic thunder, but the flickering light of uncertainty, and darkness of unknowing, and divine hiddenness. It is not a symbolism that can be separated from light, and it is grounded in love. One of the most moving passages in the letters is that in which Gerard tells Mary that his love for her has changed the direction of his mind. "After I met you I found I was seeking love and a peace beyond all understanding." For many years before, he had been seeking "what is, humanly speaking, an ultimate emptiness, even though it be in itself a divine fullness." But in loving Mary he has worked his way back from seeking to dissolve all limits in approach to the sacred (the way of the East and the way of Plotinus' philosophy) to acceptance of the limited. But more than acceptance is involved in his change of direction. "To move beyond all distinctions into the unlimited would be to lose you, and this I found I *would not do*." Now, his spirit wills "to save into an eternal life, beyond the circles of this world, our loving relationships—and what is the Resurrection of the Dead but the symbol of this achieved, the restoration by God of the limits dissolved by death, those limits that constitute the very reality of those we have learnt to love?" Here speaks the religious thinker, but also the lover. It is true to the spirit of these letters, and to the characters of Gerard and Mary Casey, that what they think, in utmost seriousness, relates directly to what they feel. The implication of this, however, is that, as Gerard wrote to Pat, "to be alive is an expression of the fact that in you the search for truth is being carried on." In simpler terms, that vision springs from love. Not to dissolve the unique being, the divine image, in the limitless, but to restore the person: this is the passion Gerard Casey shares with the Russian religious thinker, Nicolas Berdyaev, and in each case, the strenuous and complex thinking is rooted in love of the particular, which extends to the whole of creation, and is grounded on faith in the ultimate "restitution of all things."

It would be wrong to see a conflict between Gerard Casey's thinking and Mary Casey's Plotinian metaphysics, not least because both serve a Christian vision. There is, however, a tension. This is between different directions of the mind: Gerard's mind, as he writes, from Africa, to the wife he misses, and Mary's mind, as, in Dorset, she pursues her deep involvement with Plotinus' thought (one fruit of which is her novel, *The Kingfisher's Wing*). It is a tension between the minds of husband and wife, "we who live so intensely in our inner visions." But it is also a tension in the mind of the man who is at once drawn by Eastern and metaphysical wisdom, and bound in love to "the mystery and utter value and uniqueness and wonder of realized personality."

Insofar as there is an issue between Gerard and Mary, within what are essentially their complementary religious visions, it turns, I think, on their different valuations and experiences of aloneness. Gerard's letters to Mary are love letters, in the usual sense of that word, as well as in the meaning on which the Christian religion is founded. It is most moving when Gerard writes to Mary: "You say, 'I do not choose to be alone but I am.' You are my dearest of dear friends, not alone unless you choose to be. The last, and perhaps *only* word of Jesus (rather, all He said implied this) to us was that what we ask for we receive. You are not alone unless you choose to be. I love you, and not I only; and love demands not understanding but acceptance." Acceptance of the person, the being known by his or her limits. Gerard is speaking here under compulsion, as a man for whom love has turned the direction of his mind. He is seeking "to return," from his quest for the unlimited, to personal communion, and feels that perhaps he should "remain silent." He finds, however, that "in relation to you a strong inner compulsion seems to force some utterance."

In his most impassioned thinking Gerard sometimes speaks as Origen to Mary, in the position of Plotinus who, in her depiction of the philosopher, "had realized the unlimited ground of his own existence." The difference at issue here is, perhaps, that between the flight of the alone to the Alone, and the man who, alone, waits in darkness, in the belief that "realized personality" will be restored. The crux, I think, is this: "Origen taught... the final restoration of all beings in God to their inherent divinely-willed natures, and those beings who will and realize the unlimited return to the same Divine Real that wills the restoration." Yet, "from within the limits of the finite there seems to be an inherent and utter apartness between the two ways."

It seems to me that it is Gerard's compulsion to speak, born of his love, and addressed to Mary in her aloneness, that is at the heart of his letters to her. The danger for a more sceptical, and less philosophical, mind is to conceive of this correspondence in sentimental or exclusively "romantic" terms, and, in writing about the visionary concerns of Gerard and Mary Casey, to identify easily recognizable "human" needs and elevate them above that which is "abstract" or metaphysical. In a sense, nothing is abstract that concerns religious truth. A sceptic may also surprise in himself some imp that winks mischievously at the identification of a man and a woman with Origen and Plotinus. I acknowledge the imp only to dismiss it. What we have here, in Gerard's letters to Mary, are love letters, in which the feelings of a man keeping in touch with his wife, and concerned above all with the wonder of her person, cannot be separated from the Christian vision founded on the conviction that "God is Love." The darkness in the letters is the ground of that light, in which God saves "into an eternal life... our loving relationships." The passionate, and sometimes violent, stormy feelings are ultimately a source of peace, as well as power.

JEREMY HOOKER

LETTERS TO PATRICK

Christianity is suffering for the Truth

KIERKEGAARD

The Beale Farm
25 October 1953

My dear Pat,

    I am grateful to you for writing this letter, in which you express so forcibly and movingly your present point of view on religious matters. You have suffered and are suffering, but I rejoice in this; for as with the suffering of love so with the suffering of thought—a man cannot grow spiritually unless he experiences these sufferings. All growth is bound up with suffering. Birth is a suffering, and the child being born may well, in some dim way (as psychologists assure us), wish rather to return to the comfort of the womb than enter into the sufferings of life. And most of us cling passionately to life, with all its sufferings, rather than face the suffering of death. We all wish to evade sufferings—it would not be suffering if we could enjoy it—yet, willy nilly, we have to go through with it.

    The only thing that distresses me in your attitude is its intolerance. I cannot agree with you that intolerance is a virtue. You say that your intolerance springs from your absolute certainty that you are right, and that that justifies it. But surely such absolute certainty must arise from intellectual and spiritual pride. You scorn human reason and the human mind—you perceive its limitations. But is not your own mind a human one? And if you perceive its weakness in others, how can you honestly attribute to your own thinking processes such absolute infallibility? I can sympathize with—but not agree with—the anti-rational tendency of much Christian thinking. It arises, I think, from the very impatience and eagerness to arrive at and possess the truth. It seeks to avoid the sufferings and contradictions of reason. But can Truth be won cheaply? Does the figure of Christ on the Cross promise an easy victory?

    You will notice that I said "much" Christian thinking, not "all." There are and always have been Christians *who put their whole trust in reason*; but I fear that they have in most cases been the persecuted ones. But what will you? What is reason? It is, we have been told by a fine Christian theologian, "the only faculty we have wherewith to judge concerning anything—even Revelation itself. It is in essence the God-given power to pursue the truth." If this be so, it seems that any refusal to meet the challenge of reason can only spring, in the final analysis, from intellectual laziness or cowardice. Now what you attack as "liberal" thought is the thought that has always insisted on the priority of reason in deciding the truth of any matter. Revelation is itself subjected to the test of reason; that is, liberal thought is concerned absolutely with the truth, and *is not prepared to accept emotional or traditional substitutes for it*. If, as you say, Christianity is incompatible with liberal thought, then so much the worse for Christianity. It simply is another way of saying that Christianity is not the truth.

But is it *true* that Christianity is incompatible with liberal—that is, free—thought? Very many of the finest Christians would certainly deny it. I agree that (as far as I can see) Roman Catholic Christianity does, but is Roman Catholic Christianity true Christianity? Millions of Christians deny it. Of course they can all be dismissed as "woolly" thinkers; that is the traditional Roman Catholic attitude to any thought whatsoever that in any way criticizes their Church. In the mouths of Roman Catholics *all* thought, except their own, is described as "woolly" or "superficial" or "sinful" or "human." But the reaction of honest thought to criticism is, not to fob it off as "woolly," but to examine it carefully and produce fair reasons for rejecting or accepting it. I admit to little patience with the kind of laziness that dismisses the thought of men with fine minds, who may have spent years in hard study of a question, simply as "woolly." Why not rather produce exact reasons for dismissing it, proving thereby that one has at least paid it the attention of examining it?

Here is a simple example: Christianity is fundamentally a belief (as you say) in the fact that a certain man, Jesus, has lived who was also the incarnation of God. *This belief is based on certain historical documents that purport to give an account of the life and sayings of this God-Man.* This being so, these documents are of absolutely fundamental importance. The Christian believes that his eternal salvation depends on the absolute and unqualified truth of this. To him therefore it must be a matter of terror if any error has crept into the records.

Now in the case of historical documents there are well-attested methods of examining them; of discovering just how much in them may be put down as factual truth, how much as uncertain, and how much as mythical, symbolical, or as interpolated by later writers. Historians have applied these methods to all historical documents in their efforts to arrive at historical truth. "Liberal" thought takes it for granted that it is good to strive to arrive at the truth. It has devoted much thought, of a kind that is very "unwoolly," and the most painstaking research, to the authenticity of the New Testament documents. *The New Testament (as a foundation for a dogmatic historical religion) does not, to put it very mildly, come out of the examination very happily.* Now a "liberal" thinker would perhaps innocently think: "that will give them something to think about; they must at least examine this criticism and meet it. It is vital to them." But what happens? *It is ignored.* The priests, who have never opened a book dealing with biblical criticism, blandly assure their congregations that, though the Gospels have been battered by years of criticism, they have come out stronger than ever. To "liberal" thought that sounds suspiciously like a bloody lie, but to the Roman Catholic it sounds the "note of faith." The more honest among them simply ignore the subject.

I have here on my shelves some volumes called *The History of the Primitive Church*, by Lebreton and Zeiller. It comes from the faculty of theology at the Sorbonne. It claims to be a dispassionate and scientific work of history. It is written to meet the desire of Pope Leo XIII, "who wanted to see a universal Church History brought into line with the progress of modern critical research." Well now, thought I, here we have it; they have at last realized the need to meet this criticism honestly. Having myself read some of the modern critical research, I knew it to be very destructive. I opened the book in high hopes of a first class intellectual battle. Remember, the authors conceive their eternal salvation to depend on the truth of the New Testament *as detailed fact.* They are historians, their lives are devoted to historical research, they are trained for the work, they cannot be unaware of the existence of this criticism. For a century men of the highest intellectual calibre have been examining these documents. They have raised grave doubts on many matters. Yet what do we find in this authoritative Church history "brought into line with the progress of modern research?" A seemingly complete ignorance of what in fact the "progress of modern research" has done, and the kind of problems it has raised. What are we to think? Is such criticism irrelevant? If so, why not say so and show it to be so? Can ignoring criticism of this kind be considered "bringing things into line?"

What is your personal reaction as an individual Christian to this? Do you say, as a Roman Catholic, that your spiritual superiors assure you all is well, and therefore that you personally need not consider the subject? If so, is this honest?

I want to get this straight. It seems—to my possibly "woolly" thinking—to lie very near the heart of the matter; yet I have thought about it as honestly and clearly as possible with the brain I find myself in possession of. I am still open-minded about the possibility of meeting such criticism. I know great non-Catholic Christians have striven honestly to meet this criticism. In the process they have been forced to modify their Christian beliefs. I have a great respect for them. But what am I to make of the Roman Catholic attitude of completely ignoring honest criticism? Can I retain my intellectual honesty and continue to respect them? Is there not such a thing as the intellectual conscience? Is the factual truth of history to be considered as irrelevant? How can it be irrelevant when dogmatic Christianity places all its claims on the evidence of factual history? If this kind of Christianity teaches the truth, why should it fear honest inquiry? If it is the truth, honest inquiry could only strengthen it. Can I be quite wrong in thinking that possibly such evasions indicate *a fear of the truth* or deliberate intellectual dishonesty?

You will notice that the works I refer to claim to meet the modern criticism; that is, they falsely attempt to make readers who have not the leisure to pursue the subject for themselves believe that the criticism has in fact been met. That seems to my liberal woolly thought sheer dishonesty, because I happen to know that the criticism has in fact been completely evaded.

I do not want to labor this point. The example I have made is only one among very many that people who have the time and interest to devote to these subjects are familiar with. You say: "I think everyone should be given the chance to know what Christianity is and that people should be frighteningly honest with themselves about their reasons for rejecting it." I agree absolutely, but I would add: "and they should also be frighteningly honest with themselves about their reasons for accepting it." And as regards what Christianity is, which of the hundreds of different sects represent the true Christianity? *You may say the differences are unimportant*; if they are, the Christians themselves have never thought so. They have considered these differences so important that they have always been ready to persecute on the strength of them. And then Christianity has varied much in its various teachings down the ages. The great representatives of Alexandrian Christianity, Origen and Clement, who taught a free and liberal interpretation of the Christian tradition, believed for instance in the *preexistence and future rebirth of souls*: "every soul has existed from the beginning, it has passed through many worlds already, and will pass through many more before it reaches its final consummation [Clement and Origen were second century Christians—no infallible pope then to correct their thinking for them]. It comes into this world strengthened by the victories or weakened by the defeats of previous lives." They reckoned among the angels the spirits of the sun, moon, planets, and stars. They taught that all souls would eventually reach salvation—to doubt this was to doubt the power of God's love. (How do these beliefs square with Roman Catholic dogma?; yet they are Christian beliefs.) They stressed the love of God rather than His justice, for what is justice but defeated love? Of course all these ideas they held in common with the great religions of the East; they were followers of the great *philosophia perennis*, the great central truths contained in the best of all the great religions. But all this implies of course that Christianity is no unique revelation, but is one historical manifestation of the universal religious impulse; it reveals, at its best, the same great insights and, at its worst, sinks (as do the others) to rigid, inflexible, intolerant dogmatic systems.

Why is it so difficult to accept the fact that men of all races and times and religions have arrived independently at certain great central truths? They are all created by God and have the same faculties. That they have expressed their insights in different ways is only to be expected, and yet there is a startling resemblance in spirit between the "sayings" of all the great religious teachers. It is their followers who work out the rigid systems, and damn and blast all who do not express themselves in exactly the same way.

It is the weakness of dogmatic Christianity that it has based its teaching of eternal truths on the shifting sands of vague historical uncertainties. Any thinking that perceives this is denounced as "woolly." *Is an omnipotent, loving God likely to have revealed Himself in such a vague way that honest men can spend a lifetime studying the subject and then, in real perplexity of spirit, discover that the Jesus of the Churches never existed; or perhaps that no Jesus existed at all?*

I am not here expressing any opinion on this historical problem; but the mere fact that honest enquiry can land a man in such a position on a matter essential for eternal salvation is surely a revelation of the uncertainties on which the Churches have founded their dogmatic systems—*and then to be intolerant!*

This is not at all to detract from the eternal truths taught through the New Testament, but in honesty to admit that these same truths have been taught—and less ambiguously—in other places by other minds, and so dispose of Christianity's claim to be a *unique revelation essential for salvation*. It has led the Churches into an impossible position, antagonistic to reason; and remember that many of the greatest Christians have insisted on reason. So have they seen it to be, in the words of a Moslem saint: "Reason is the shadow cast by God: God is the Sun. This Shadow is the Light of God in the Heart." Thus spoke one of the heinous Saracens—Jalaluddin Rumi—whom the "idealistic" looting Crusaders set out to murder. Have you never realized that the Holy Sepulchre was as precious to the Saracens as to their Christian antagonists? Islam has always honored Jesus as one of the great prophets of God. They conceived themselves (they were just as certain as you that they were right) as the true followers of Jesus. But to them it was a blasphemous idolatry to worship Jesus as God. They honored Jesus, but honored God more. Do you know that the Fourth Gospel has been rejected almost in its entirety by even the most conservative of free-thinking *Christian* theologians as in any sense a true historical account of the words and actions of a living man? And does not most of Roman Catholic dogma rest its claims on this very gospel?

Nietzsche says (and I agree with him): "A rainbow of compassionate love and peace appeared with the first radiant rise of Christianity, and under it was born Christianity's most beautiful fruit, the Gospel according to St. John."

But observe: the Gospel is born of the rise of Christianity, *not* Christianity of the Gospel. And how the Roman Church has managed to deduce the ugly inflexibilities of its dogmas from this radiant myth is one of the wonders of history.

Of the Fourth Gospel the greatest living New Testament critic (Schweitzer) has written simply: "What matters for the historical study of the life of Jesus is simply that the Fourth Gospel must be ruled out."

And that brings me on to one sentence in your letter: "Liberal thought is incompatible with Christianity and moreover incompatible with any progress or worthwhile action whatever."

Now Pat, that sentence is just bunkum. You can forgive me for putting the matter so bluntly when I admit that you'll have to write many more such rubbishy sentences before you catch me up in that respect. Nevertheless nonsense it is. And if it requires any answer, no answer could be more conclusive than for you to study the life and work of Albert Schweitzer. I ask you, as a special act of love and friendship and trust in your present difficulties, to turn to the thought of possibly the greatest living Christian, who is certainly a saint if that word has any meaning, and who has experienced all the agonies of spirit possible to one who is a real Christian and a great liberal thinker. I am going, as an introduction, to ask Francis to send you a biography of him by Seaver, and then you can turn to some of his own works. I suggest first his autobiography, which you will find full of wisdom and help, then his *Mystery of the Kingdom of God*, and then his *Civilisation and Ethics*; and after that you can tackle his great works of love and research: *The Quest of the Historical Jesus* and *The Mysticism of Paul the Apostle*. You should be able to get all of these books in any good library.

The life and work of Schweitzer is indeed the complete answer to all who think Christianity need fear freedom of enquiry in all matters. And that he will help you I know, as he helped me through similar sufferings of the spirit.

This letter is growing too long and wordy. But I do not often write to you, and as I feel you have in some way gained a false idea of my beliefs, and are in distress, I must make some kind of answer. Perhaps you will remember how in one of our conversations at Kisima you attacked Christianity, or, rather, Roman Catholicism, as "balls." I attempted to defend it, although you were then so intolerant of it that I could not say much. I have never thought Roman Catholicism "balls." It contains much of greatness and beauty, and has been a tremendous historical force. My distrust of it rises purely from its intolerance. It contains much truth, but is unwilling to have the dross purged away. Can any great historical organization evade the accumulation of some rubbish through centuries of striving and difficulties among many different nations and lands and climates of opinion? I do not think it can, and, as Roman Catholicism has always been averse to sweeping out the house, it has accumulated a vast amount of rubbish. I know it fears to lose what is precious in its tradition, but I do not believe that the truth can ever fail to survive a spring cleaning.

We liberal thinkers are the most resolute enemies of any kind of woolly thinking, wherever it may be found, simply because we believe in the truth and in free enquiry and have the faith that in the end, through whatever dark corridors it may lead, the pursuit of truth will lead to the Truth, the Intelligible Light beyond the Cosmos.

You seem to have the notion that I am hostile to Christianity, that is, to all and every kind of Christianity, and even to belief in God. I do not know who has given you the idea that I am so. I can understand and sympathize with many of the attacks on and criticisms of these beliefs, but nevertheless I have found that certain great modern religious thinkers are the ones who seem to me to have made the profoundest and most illuminating studies of the nature and destiny of man. In fact one of them, Reinhold Niebuhr, an American Protestant Christian, has written a remarkably fine work with that very title—*The Nature and Destiny of Man*—which has influenced me tremendously in my thinking. I gave it to Dada as a present some years ago and think you will find it at home; if so, you would find it extraordinarily good to read during, say, the Christmas holidays now your mind is on these problems.

But the modern thinker who comes nearest to my own way of thinking (that is, I find myself more in agreement with him than with anyone else) is Nicolas Berdyaev, who was a Russian Orthodox Christian. I will ask Francis to try to find you a copy of his *Destiny of Man*, with which, in general, I agree. If you can find the time to read any of his other works, particularly *Solitude and Society*, *The Meaning of History*, or *Freedom and the Spirit*, you will find them worth the effort. Bill has Berdyaev's *Slavery and Freedom*; perhaps you could ask him to lend it to you, it is very good.

The other great modern I find myself in deep sympathy with, but who, like you, is intolerant and thinks along the lines on which you do at present, and to whom I stand in a relation of what I can only call love-hate (that is, I feel for him a sympathetic antipathy and an antipathetic sympathy), is the Dane and Lutheran Christian, Sören Kierkegaard. If ever intolerant Christianity has found a great champion of first-class intellect and high courage and humor, it is in this man. He would indeed support you in our present difference. But his was certainly, in my opinion, one of the finest minds and saintliest characters modern Europe has produced. Do try to read some of his work. *The Sickness unto Death* is probably the best, but you should perhaps read his aesthetic works, such as *Either/Or* or *Stages on Life's Way* first.

Well! There you have it. You have tended to regard me as a woolly headed antagonist of Christianity. Yet the men who have most influenced my thought among modern thinkers are all Christians: Schweitzer, Berdyaev, Kierkegaard, Niebuhr. These men, with Whitehead (thinking of his *Adventures of Ideas* and *Science and the Modern World*) and Nietzsche, are the men from whom I have learnt most. Nietzsche, to whom you probably feel unsympathetic at the moment, has been the subject of a well balanced and appreciative study by Father Copleston, S.J., which has been published by Burns and Oates; you would find this book an excellent introduction to a more sympathetic understanding of him.

I mention these men because I feel that if, as an act of friendship to me, you could read some of their works, you would know something of the background of my own thought. I, on my side, would love to read any books you have found particularly illuminating. It is probably the best we can do to approach a clearer understanding of each other's point of view, as we have, neither of us, either the time or perhaps the ability to write long letters accurately expressing our thoughts. I find letter-writing difficult on these subjects, for I am conscious always of how much I am leaving unsaid, or saying obscurely, or without sufficient modification. The essential meanings I strive to convey seem to escape in a lot of words; and as many of the things I would like to say have been said by other men far better than I can say them, I am content to let them, to some degree, speak for me.

There is just one more point on which I must take up the cudgels with you. You say you couldn't care less what the Bishop of Barcelona did to some heretic some hundreds of years ago. I do not think you can honestly say that, if you think hard enough. The anguish of all beings, in all times, has to be redeemed. God is Love. To God it is not indifferent. God is as intimately concerned in the fate of that man as in yours. But man, as a collective whole, has, with the help of God, to work out his own salvation. To fail in compassion for the sufferings of another, even though you be separated from him by great spaces or many years, is to be at the least hard-hearted, or at the most to range yourself with his persecutors. Man cannot make merry on the graves of his tortured ancestors. This is to fail in love to them. You may say you cannot help them or alter the fact of their suffering. How do you know that? All moments in time are equidistant from the eternal, and we can, we believe, regain contact with and redeem the past; in fact if the creation is to be redeemed we must do so. A man can be spiritually closer to a man who lived thousands of years ago, or who lives on the far side of earth and whom he has never seen, than to a man who lives in the same house with him. His religious obligation is to fail in love to no one, and the fact that another lived long ago is irrelevant in eternity. The belief in God as Love is incompatible with the belief in eternal damnation. To believe that God could fail in love or power to a single being He has created is to fail to believe that *God really is Love and really is all powerful.* It is not beyond the bounds of belief that you yourself are the reincarnated spirit of either the Bishop or his victim. Read Origen regarding this possibility.

God suffers in the sufferings of all beings, the animals not excluded.

The suffering of each and all is God's suffering. God suffers in you. He suffers in the heretic burnt three or four hundred years ago, in the slave flogged to death in chains crossing the Sahara a hundred years ago, in the spiritual degradation of the inquisitor, and of the slave owner. He suffers in the suffering of the child chopped up "like a lemon" by the Mau-Mau, in the suffering of the child's mother as she was slowly strangled, watching her children being chopped up. In the suffering of the women who were strangling her. In the suffering of men who will have to shoot or hang those women. In the suffering of the women as they are being hung, the suffering of the priest as he administers extreme unction to the broken-necked dying man or woman in the hanging-pit. In the suffering of the woman's husband as he revenges his wife and children. In all the endless intertangled sufferings and horrors of existence in all places and ages, both physical and spiritual. In the shudder of lonely horror and despair of each dying heretic He suffers. In the shudder of lonely horror and despair of each girl simultaneously raped and strangled by the executioners of Tiberius. He suffers in the soul of Tiberius. Where track the beginning or end in the agonies of the sideless world? This is the individual suffering of each man, and the accumulated suffering of God... can you remain indifferent? Has not each of us to repent what we have all done and are capable of doing? Listen to the wind at night blowing over the planet—is it not burdened?

It is in its insight into the horror of the world's suffering that Christianity has penetrated deeper than all other religions. It saw in the figure of Christ Crucified that God too shares this suffering. God is not protected by space and time, as each individual man is. William Blake said, beautifully and profoundly, "Time is the Mercy of Eternity.... Eternity is in Love with the Productions of Time.... The Ruins of Time build Mansions in Eternity." But pause here. Man is protected by time from sharing the complete suffering of God; but has, as the price of his entry into eternity, to share that suffering: to enter the eternal is to become "open" to all the agonies of time. The agony of that man "you couldn't care less about" is an agony you will have to endure in eternity—before, with the aid of God, you can help redeem it. We may well pray.

Can you remain indifferent?

Only the vision of God, the Alpha and Omega, the Beginning and the End, the eternally present at each instant of time, the undefeatable love, the central sweetness and glory, the Intelligible Light "shining itself in silent stillness" of Eckhart, the "Sparkle in the eternal dark" of Boehme, the divine Freedom rooted in the Eternal Nothing, the Accepter and Redeemer of all suffering, the Zodiacal Light at the Heart of the World—only God can give us the strength to endure what must be endured before the end.

> Be shelled, eyes, with double dark
> And find the Uncreated Light.

With love,
Gerard

P.S.

St. Teresa speaks somewhere of the terrible suffering of the approach to God.

"The God in Whom we live and move and have our being," and "to Whom all things are possible"; our "Cape of Good Hope."

Lux est Umbra Dei.

"For to save man from vengeance, that deem I is the bridge to the highest hope, and a rainbow after long tempests."

The Beale Farm
6 December 1953

My dear Pat,

Your letter has made me happy. No! I do not think you have or could say anything that would upset me in the way you fear. I express myself rather extremely at times, I am afraid. But always remember that, whatever I say, I am always aware that there is much to be said against my view—and also that what I think is very much limited by my own mind and insights. If I say a certain way of thought is "absurd" or "fanciful" or "thoughtless" it only means that the way in which it presents itself to me suggests such a judgement—which is an entirely personal one. It does not at all mean that I necessarily consider the person who thinks in that way is dishonest or thoughtless, for I know that the thought must present itself to him in a different way, so that he has a different understanding of it. We have said much to each other about Roman Catholic belief. Certain strands of that belief strike me as fundamentally thoughtless, yet I know that many thoughtful men and great thinkers—witness Jacques Maritain today—accept those beliefs. I do not think Maritain is a fool, or a humbug. I think he has an exceedingly fine mind. Yet certain beliefs of his, *in my mind*, seem thoughtless; and the probability is that I am simply failing to penetrate fully into the depths of his thought. Nevertheless, in honesty, I have to say what I think of his thought; but in revealing what I think, I realize it is possible that I am simply revealing the inadequacy of my own thought. Heavens! What a prolix fellow I am. I seem unable to say the simplest thing in a simple way. *Whatever* I write or say I immediately feel the need to modify it!

How I do appreciate and entirely agree with what you say about longing for simplicity! Yet the simplest things are the strangest and often the most difficult to express. Again, it is at least partly true that "oversimplification is the original sin of the intellect," as Aldous Huxley, I think, said. I am going to enter into some of my thought in detail in this letter; but, whatever I say, don't think I am just being arrogantly dogmatic. It is tedious to be always inserting "it seems to me" or "this is of course only a partial view," etc., etc.

Your letter set going in my mind some old problems I thought I had dealt with, and now they lift up their heads again. It may be that the shrill indignant note that creeps into my statements is simply my attempt to shout down my own objections to my belief. My inward attempt to accept the Roman Catholic form of Christianity has been the inner splendor and misery of my life. It has been an object of love and of loathing to me—and also of simple intellectual curiosity. It is in my destiny to be at once its champion and its deadly antagonist. I sometimes feel I understand it too well; at others, that I have no understanding of it. I have—and not so long ago either—defended it just as vigorously as I have attacked it in my letters to you. Because I know what it is to defend it in love, I know what it is to attack it in anger—as I am going to do in this letter. Roman Catholicism has never been a matter of indifference to me, and it is my love of what it is and could be that makes me hate what it is and has been. Of it I think with beats of my heart's blood; and that, I think, is the only kind of thought that ultimately counts. Here are some observations on some of its doctrines, over which, if you can help me—and say stoutly what you really think—I will honestly be grateful. Fresh insight is always a help.

The Infallibility of the Pope.

I don't wish to spend much time considering this question for two reasons: (1) the notion of infallibility, of any objective general kind, among men seems to me just fantasy thinking; (2) I have not the least desire to place myself under the spiritual authority of the Roman Church, and so I have not felt bound in any strict sense to investigate this doctrine insofar as it applies to the pope. I can see of course that any organization has the right to make its own rules and expect its members to accept them—and in the final event someone has to make the final decisions and enunciate rules binding on its members. It is reasonable that the head of the Church should expect his ruling to be considered final... as far as his Church is concerned. But the Roman claim goes far beyond this, claiming a general infallibility on all matters concerning the relationship of God and man and asserting its authority even over those who are not, and never have been, members of the Church. In this respect the *Syllabus of Errors* of 1864 contains many revealing items. One part of this "irreformable" (heaven help us!) utterance runs: "It is an error that every man is free to embrace and profess the religion he shall believe true, guided by the light of reason.... that the eternal salvation may (at least) be hoped for of those who are not in the True Church." This of course runs parallel with the article in Pope Pius IV's Creed, in which the doctrinal decrees of the Council of Trent were summed up: "This true Catholic faith, outside which no one can be in a state of salvation."

Well! It is an odd experience to find oneself, with the great majority of the human race, so complacently damned—or considered damned—by the "irreformable" decrees of these infallible ones! I am glad your heart has more kindliness; for, although it is rank heresy (you must remember that the above little pleasantries are strictly binding on every member of the Roman Communion), you stoutly say that you have "no opinion on the fate of non-Christians," and that a "mortal sin is a great rarity." You must rejoice that you live in an age when your Church has no power to take you to task physically—otherwise you would either have to retract those statements or burn. That is the unpleasant fact, admit it or not. Even today—try it—you will be excommunicated if you express that opinion publicly.

From my school days I remember well the questions and answers regarding going to Mass on Sundays, and that "if I die in a state of mortal sin I shall go to hell for all eternity." Puzzling teachings and abominable, coming from a religion professing to represent on earth the God of love.

But a few more remarks on the infallibility question. The Roman Catholic church is fond of pointing to the unanimity of its opinion. Have you read any accounts of the proceedings of the Vatican Council of 1870, which discovered that the pope was infallible? It makes curious and illuminating reading, even from Roman Catholic sources: the long careful secret preparation... no modern dictator ensuring his success in an election could take more trouble to achieve the desired result. Yet even so, 150 of the delegates—among them great churchmen and theologians of the highest authority whose devotion to their Church was not in doubt—bitterly opposed the motion, and rejected the *placet*. They opposed it on doctrinal, religious, and historical grounds; but no, Pope Pius IX and his Central Commission had already made up their minds as to what they wanted and were determined to get it. In the general debate Bishop Hefele pointed out that Pope Honorius I had been condemned as a heretic by the Sixth Ecumenical Council—this in reply to the claim that belief in infallibility had always been implicit in the Church teaching. Another bluntly called the proposed dogma sacrilege. In the special debate each item was met with vigorous and repeated repudiation.

Nevertheless, once the motion had been steam-rollered through, the critics accepted the dogma—under threat of excommunication, which, to them I presume, meant damnation. Döllinger was left to face his old friend the

Archbishop of Munich (who in the debate was one of the most vigorous denouncers of the dogma) with the words: "As a Christian, as a theologian, as an historian, as a citizen—I cannot accept this doctrine...." And for this he was excommunicated. Döllinger was, I may say, one of the highest authorities on Roman Catholic theology and history, which fact of course was denied after his excommunication—as it will be to you now if you make enquiries about him. This is what is termed unquestioned tradition!

What of the row caused among "the faithful" in France, Austria, and Germany by the promulgation of the notorious *Syllabus of Errors*? There was no dogma of infallibility in 1864 to keep the mouths of the faithful shut, but arrangements were soon made... and by 1870 we find the pope had become infallible.

Pius IX "irreformably" declared the Immaculate Conception to be a dogma necessary for salvation in 1854. Yet St. Bernard declared it a scandal, and St. Thomas Aquinas denied it: two of the highest Church authorities were... heretics! The position is fantastic... As one of the French priests who had opposed infallibility said when this monstrous dogma was approved by the Vatican Council in 1870: "Pius has said to Mary: 'Thou art Immaculate!'; Mary has replied to Pius: 'Thou art Infallible!'" And two thousand odd years of this kind of nonsense is proclaimed as an "unbroken and unquestioned tradition"?

The claim that communion in the Church of Rome is necessary to salvation was unknown in the first thousand years of the Church's history. Many saints— recognized as saints by Rome—died out of communion with Rome, such as St. Meletius of Antioch; not to mention that *Buddha* (whom it is difficult to claim as a Roman Catholic) was canonized under the name of St. Josaphat in the sixteenth century. In the year 1054 the Church at Constantinople excommunicated the Church at Rome, which hardly indicates that the Roman claim to be head of the Church was in those times universally recognized. Well! It would be easy to go on in this vein for many pages, but it does not prove anything except that the tradition we are told of is a rather confused one. And it was not until the Council of Trent (1545-63) that tradition ("unwritten tradition," that is) was discovered to be on a level with Scripture as a source of dogma. That is to say, when the Church found itself faced with informed criticism that could show that much of its dogma could not be deduced from Scripture, it fell back on "unwritten tradition." And it is this tradition that now "knows" the New Testament to be completely true, even though no historical scholar outside the Roman Church can possibly believe this; and the Church hasn't attempted to meet the criticism in any serious sense. It just "knows"; and if you don't "know"—then *anathema sit*. But of course one has to admit it is not possible to discuss any question with an "infallible" authority: you see, it "knows," and that is all there is to it!

I remember learning from my catechism that one of the six sins against the Holy Ghost was "resisting the known truth." Now the Church is, I believe, guilty of this sin in its blind resistance to even the most widely accepted results of biblical criticism, biological science, detailed studies of geology, history, and mythology. The Church, in its infamous syllabus of 1864, openly proclaims itself to be based on thoughtlessness and antagonism to thought, and defiantly admits itself to constitute the largest number of organized people in the world whose lives and spiritual strivings are based on thoughtlessness. Remember: every member of the Church has given up all right to think for himself on religious and most other matters. If you dispute this, read again the syllabus.

You may here object, "consider the great libraries of theological learning, the many great thinkers and scholars among the Church authorities." One has to admit all this—the superstructure looks imposing enough; but what of the foundations? It is here that the persistent determination to refuse to think, to remain in the realm of fantasy—which is underpinned by an infallible assertion of infallibility—is observed. Yet it is at this level that it requires most courage to remain thoughtful; it is the thought at this level that determines the value of the thought built on it. If the foundations are thoughtless all the superstructure is at best a kind of thoughtful thoughtlessness. Of course the claim is made that the foundation—where all attempts to think have ceased—is in some topsy-turvy way more thoughtful than thought.

Again (and I wish to stress this to avoid misunderstanding), to admit all this—if one does—is not to assert that Roman Catholicism (lock, stock, and barrel; inside and out; past and present) is a lot of nonsense. It is not. But what is valuable in it—*and much is*—is founded on a great past (to admit this is not to retract from the damnableness of much of its past) when the Church did not refuse to think, and did not tie itself up in absurdities like "infallibility," or, if you like, "irreformability." These particular criticisms I am making apply mainly to the modern Catholic church (since the Council of Trent), which was a counter-reformationary movement. At this moment in history, decisive for its future (when it could have saved itself and probably united Christendom if it had had the courage to subject itself to a profoundly honest and thoughtful self-examination and self-judgement), it plunged, at the Council of Trent, into thoughtlessness and indefensible dogmatic assertions of absurdities that had their inevitable culmination three centuries later in the doctrine of infallibility, which had become necessary in order to defend the position it had adopted. People like Döllinger could, even in the nineteenth century, have helped the Church to recover itself; but no, the movement was to an ever-deepening antagonism to thought, with all that this implies. And Döllinger was sacrificed to the God of Thoughtlessness. It is a melancholy story, and has left the Church in a state of divorce from Thought. I know a few fine thinkers like Pascal and

Newman have managed in the intervening centuries—at the cost of a continuous suicide of reason (the famous "crucifixion of the reason" in "imitation of Christ," though what evidence we have that Jesus crucified his reason I don't know)—to swallow Roman Catholicism. I am afraid they are the exceptions that prove the rule; and in this way I have no desire to be a similar exception. It is hard to know in what way the Church can extricate itself from the mess in which the infallible ones—particularly Pius IV and IX—have left it. To simply accept its position shows no true devotion to the Church. Döllinger and his companions were those who, in the Vatican Council, had the true interest of their Church at heart. Today there is a tremendous amount of goodwill towards the Church (I mean on the part of those outside it), and people with such goodwill are prepared to go a long way to meet it; but alas!, the insistence is on "crucifixion of the reason," and the Church has placed itself in a position where the very notion of self-criticism is accounted heresy.

I think the two main obstacles are the doctrine of infallibility (which means the Church is completely right and every one else completely wrong—see again the syllabus regarding this) and the doctrine of the damnation of all men outside the Church (which, whether one likes to admit it or not, is what that famous article in Pius IV's Creed I have quoted means—if words have any meaning). It must be strange to live in a world surrounded by men whom, we are infallibly certain, are damned to an eternity of torment—to such lengths can the refusal to think lead us! And then also to announce that the object of existence is happiness—strange happiness, this, that was shared by Nero fiddling while Rome burned!

Here is a little problem in dogmatic theology: What happens if a later pope infallibly declares that earlier popes were not infallible? History has before now brought stranger consummations to pass!

Persecution

Let us go over this again. Here it is claimed that men's beliefs cannot be judged by their actions, etc., etc. What is the utterance of Jesus on this very problem?: "By their fruits ye shall know them." In the case of the Church persecutions the train of thought is clear: (1) there is an eternal hell of torment; (2) all men are destined to enter this hell—it is their eternal destiny—unless they hold right belief, that is, Roman Catholicism; (3) therefore it is better that some men should suffer torture and death than that many should, by their influence, be corrupted into false belief and so go to hell.

Well! The argument is a reasonable one once you admit its premise. It is an example of ecclesiastical mathematics. It is a sad necessity..., it hurts me more than you..., etc.

Here is a clear case of evil doctrine leading to evil practice, as it always must. "Contrariwise," as Tweedledee would say, when you find evil practice it issues from some evil belief. It is for this reason that it is quite fair reasoning and comment to point to the fact of persecution.

But here a defense is made. We are told that the Church cannot be held responsible for the actions of its members. This defense is not valid for two reasons. One is that persecution was the result of official Church policy: far from issuing reprimands, she issued orders and encouragement (if you doubt this, make a study of H.C. Lea's *History of the Inquisition*, which even Roman Catholic historians quote as an authoritative work). The second reason is that even if the Church had not officially encouraged it she would still be responsible for actions her members committed in the belief that they were essential to salvation.

Here another defense is produced. We are told that the Church today cannot be held responsible for actions of its members many centuries ago (and not so very many centuries ago; heretics were burnt well into the eighteenth century— witness Gaundier in France). This is again no defense, for two reasons. One is that, since the Church now claims that she has, and has always had, infallible guidance, she does not and cannot believe her policy in the past to have been wrong. That is, she can only approve of it. Secondly (and I am deadly serious about this), the Church would still today persecute if she had the power. She does not do so simply because she no longer has political power. Indeed, the articles of her belief must of necessity force her to it. She has always persecuted when she had power to do so. If you read the *Syllabus of Errors* carefully and honestly you can come to no other conclusion than that there has been no change of heart. In fact she makes no secret of the fact, but blatantly announces it— and bewails the fact that "the temporal power" as it is put, has passed from her.

The fact that she has not changed is shown too in that she has never, as a Church or in any official pronouncement, condemned the persecutions or repented of them. This means she commits every one of her members individually to the same position. You cannot as a good Catholic condemn the policy of your infallible authorities. This means in turn that each Catholic is individually responsible before God for these persecutions, just as each of us is responsible before God for executions carried out on criminals in the name of the state we belong to—unless we personally repudiate them and their necessity. The only way in which an individual Catholic can escape this responsibility is to publicly emphasize to the Church that he considers that she has sinned in this and should repent. But how long would he remain in the Church if he did this?

A final defense made by Catholics who are ignorant of their own doctrine is: "You are quite wrong. This is not the teaching of the Church. You exaggerate. The Church does not teach the damnation of all save her members." One can only tell such ones to re-read their catechisms—and at the same time to think. For my part, I remember my catechism only too well (and my time spent in a Roman Catholic college being "educated" for the priesthood, and many sermons preached from church pulpits) and I have spent the last twenty years thinking about it.

Christianity in general

Most of my remarks refer to the Roman Catholic church and not to other forms of Christianity, such as Greek Orthodoxy, Protestantism, etc. However, I wish to say something about any and all forms of Christianity that teach a doctrine of *hell as eternal*. This belief is based on Matt. 25:41. This is one of the sayings of Jesus that, so far as can be discovered, is very probably genuinely historical. It is understandable historically if one believes Jesus was a man, and that His mind was conditioned—as are the minds of all men to a large degree—by the climate of opinion of His age and country. However, considered from the point of view of orthodox theology, there is this to say. We are told that Jesus proved to us the divinity of His Nature by the loftiness of His character and teaching. Therefore, because He was God and said this, it must be true. My answer to this is: if these words were in truth uttered by Jesus, they prove to me conclusively that He was not God. They appear to me as, not "lofty" in any sense, but evil and cruel, and an example of how even the noblest of men are conditioned by their time.

St. Augustine (along with a whole line of Christian saints and mystics) tells us with the utmost emphasis: "God is in the heart," "enter into yourself to seek God," "God is the ground of the soul," etc.—all of which sayings are strikingly re-echoed in Islamic and Hindu religious thought. They say in effect—if you do not find God within you, you won't find Him anywhere. Well! If this be so, I can only affirm that the God within me rejects absolutely, without any faintest furthest suggestion of any kind of hesitation, the notion of hell as eternal punishment. If a man believes this then I cannot believe him to know, or even to suspect, what I think of as God.

As this is so with me, the words of Jesus cited above are enough to settle finally and completely all Christian claims as to the divinity of Jesus. For me to accept and believe these words would be spiritual suicide; I know them to be false, and not all the theological arguments in the world can alter that conviction. And I have always so known them to be false. As far back as I can remember I have always just "known" that any religion that could teach such abominable doctrine was not the whole truth.

Not all Christians have believed in an eternal hell. There is nothing essential to Christianity in this belief, rather the contrary.

It is not much good now exhorting me to think again, to be cool and logical, to examine the claims of the Church objectively, etc. I believe I am quite capable of so doing, and that I have done so. I have in my whole conscious life been inwardly and intensely preoccupied with religious problems. As a child this was so, and I remember as a child quite calmly and quietly within myself "finding the Church wanting" on the sole grounds of belief in eternal hell. I have not altered, and cannot and must not alter, that judgement. It is me. I would not find it at all difficult to believe the possibility that I am a reborn inquisitor and burner of heretics who had repented so utterly of that kind of cruelty that nothing could drag me back to it. What do we know of ourselves? I am coming to the feeling that most of our Western thought is immature and childish. Only in recent years have I slowly been discovering in the thought of the East the kind of philosophical and religious background my mind needs. These discussions with you have to some extent brought me back into the old parochial atmosphere, but I have no desire to stifle. I do not mean I have learnt nothing from Western thought. As I have told you, Western religious Christian thinkers have been the main influence on me. But they do not satisfy me—with very few exceptions—in the way I already am satisfied by the "logoi" of the East. In the last analysis I feel more at home with that wise whimsical old pricker of balloons Chuang Tzu than with any modern Western thinker—except perhaps John Cowper Powys. This cool quiet still wisdom—yet whimsical and humorous—is the wisdom to live with, and to die with. No Christian prayer or invocation is likely to leave my lips as I move deathwards. No Western man can fail to be moved to wonder and heart-searching and loving regard by this most tragic and agonized of the great world-religions, with its worship of Christ Crucified and its desperate desire to pluck the heart out of the mystery of things. It cannot fail to rouse tears and love in the heart of any man not wholly stupefied by the modern dullness. And yet... in me another voice sounds deeper and stranger still, and, who knows?, truer:

> There is a thing inherent and natural,
> Motionless and fathomless,
> It lies in the bottom of man's mind like still water...
> It may be called Tao...
> Peace, peace, peace...

God and Evil

I want to say something about this, as it is hardly fair to expect you to understand my thinking about hell, unless you have some general idea of the background of thought I am thinking against. But before I go on let me say this. I do not think I "know all about God" (in fact I know very little), and a large part of my thought about God is that He is for the most part "unknowable." He is an iceberg that floats on and in a fathomless sea of mystery. This means that I am very aware that anything I say of Him must be inadequate and even, in a sense, impertinent. And I have no desire to join in the thoughtless chatter about God that seems to have become rather common these days among men who imagine the projection of their own pet notions into the infinite to be God—and are therefore convinced they have an intimate "inside" knowledge of God. As you know, I at first refused to discuss God with you simply because I know that usually such discussions lead, at best, to misunderstanding and, at the worst, to bitterness. Also, it seems a hint ridiculous—two very fallible and limited human beings gravely "arguing about God." However, there is more to it than that. From your letters I am not now afraid that any discussion between us will lead to unnecessary bitterness, and I feel too from your letters that you make a genuine effort to understand your opponent's way of thought, and that though you may disagree you do at the same time try to be fair. So I'll take the plunge, on condition you always remember that my views are tentative and limited, and that I know they are. Still I can only try to express something of what, after much thought, I have come to feel. Having said so much I hardly know where or how to begin. But let us take a bold plunge. First:

God is beyond good and beyond evil

This obviously needs some elucidation if it is to be understood in the sense I write it. Perhaps I should say "beyond all human ideas of good and evil." And yet that is not quite it. There is a clear danger here that one may be just playing with words..., but let us go on a little. I will say: Evil is the limited, the temporal, or, rather, the element of resistance, of confusion, in the becoming of the world. It is the persisting shadow of the unreal haunting the real. Yet in its way it is real enough in the world of becoming—the temporal world. Good is the infinite, the eternal—that is, in its essential "itness"; but as we find it in the temporal world it is always shot through and through with evil—that is, with the conflict of becoming. In the world of becoming we cannot separate good and evil in any absolute sense: to have done this would be to have already attained salvation.

It may perhaps be said in this way: evil is the suffering in the strife of becoming, good is the joy in the strife of becoming. But in a deeper sense suffering brings about ever more comprehensive realizations of the good. In the effort to overcome suffering and to transcend it the spirit arrives at a truer and deeper level of the good. In this sense evil is not "evil" in the usual sense, nor is good "good": they are part of a deeper process that unifies and transcends them both. The objection here that this view leads to "immorality"—or, if you like, "amorality"—is met by the fact that evil is suffering, and no one wishes to suffer longer than necessary. (Again it is met by the fact that in every man is also the principle of the good, which cannot finally be resisted; but that leads us too far off the track for me to follow just now.) The situations in which we say a man "likes" evil—that is, in a certain temporal sense derives pleasure from it—lead eventually to a gradually intensifying conflict between the evil and good in the man, and this is suffering. He does not in fact, and cannot, evade suffering; he merely increases its ultimate intensity—either in this life or another.

Even if one can admit the validity of this way of viewing good and evil one cannot draw any hard and fast line. The "Goodness" of God is beyond any kind of good we can know. Our good and our evil are equidistant from it. Our "evil" is as necessary as our "good" for the realization of the "Good" of God.

Again, evil is by definition (in this attempt to state the problem) the transitory, the vanishing, the suffering in the process. It cannot in the nature of things coagulate into an eternal form—hell. To speak of eternal hell is (in this mode of thought) a contradiction. It would be the same as to speak of an eternal transitoriness or changefulness. But the eternal is by definition the unchanging. Whitehead was indicating this line of thought when he wrote that "the instability of evil is the moral order of the Universe." This view may be made more clear by saying that in the world of becoming evil is the labor pains; good is the implicit unknown end. The eternal world is being born from and in the suffering of the temporal world. Just as a child being born may, in some half-conscious way, recoil from the suffering of the birth-process and wish to relapse into the comfort of non-being (since for the child the pain is an "evil," yet one that is simply the process of entering into existence), so the "evil" of this world is simply the process of entering into the eternal.

God is conceived as both immanent in the temporal process and as transcending it. This is orthodox theology. God, as the eternal Ground, precedes the process as Non-Being; God, as the eternal Light, completes the process as Being. God is also eternally present in each moment of the process. God as the *ground*—the eternal dark; Non-Being—and God as the *result*—the eternal light; Being—is one and the same. And this God, both as the preceding Dark and as the resulting Light, is in each moment. This metaphysical concept may be perhaps more clearly understood with the help of a geometrical figure, after the manner of the "mandalas" used in the East in preparation for meditation on metaphysical truths:

WORLD CYCLE

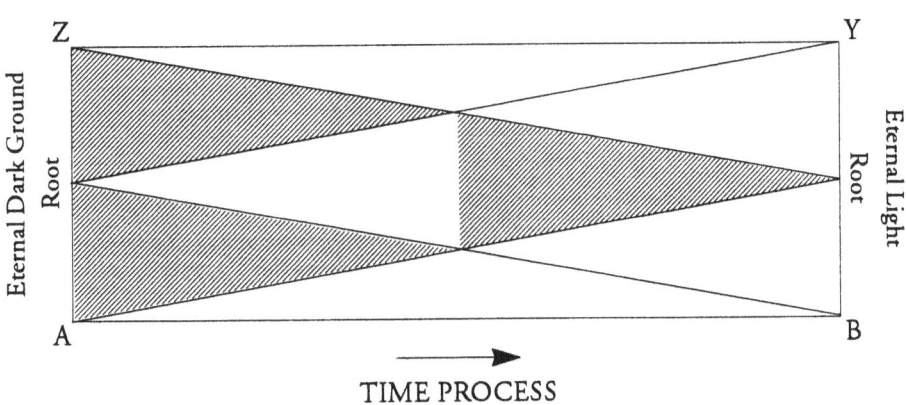

Here the dark cone standing on the eternal dark ground is what we call "evil"—the strife of the becoming. The light cone standing on the eternal light is what we call "good"—that is, the divine light present in the process that brings the becoming to pass. "In the beginning," as is said in Genesis, is represented by line AZ: the Light is implicitly present as a point, the apex of the light cone. At the end, the dark is implicitly present as the apex of the dark cone—it is but a point swallowed up in the base of the light cone. In the earlier half of the process the Light is enclosed in the Dark. In the later half the Dark is enclosed in the Light.

Now, if you cut out the figure ZABY and form a cylinder of it, so that AZ and BY become one and the same line, you have exemplified the fact that the preceding dark and the ensuing light are one and the same ground, while the cylindrical form represents the curve of the cycle. The dark root in the light, and the light root in the dark, are seen as *one and the same root.*

I don't want you to take this figure too seriously. It is simply a rather naive attempt to express something that is simple in itself but difficult to describe adequately in words. In the figure the whole cosmic epoch is represented; but the point is that all this exists in each moment of each man's existence as the underlying eternal reality—and this the figure cannot represent. The whole "life" of each man (which may include many "lives," or also each instant in a man's life) can be represented by the figure, though here the dark ground represents the inner depths of the spirit and the light represents the immanent "God as Light" in each instant. More generally, it must be remembered that the dark ground is shared with all men—so is the Divine Light. This is the expression of the fact that in my ultimate ground I am one with all men, as I also am in the eternal Light. It expresses the fact that all suffering is one suffering, all history one history. (If an eternal "hell" can be fitted into this picture—as it cannot—the spirits in hell are fundamentally one with my spirit, so that I have left part of myself in hell; but, as I am part of those in hell, part of them remains in heaven—therefore it cannot be hell in the orthodox sense. But all this is nonsense, as the orthodox hells and heavens are purely illusory.)

All this is no more than an attempt to bring out the full content of St. Paul's God "in whom we live and move and have our being." I do not here mean the full content of God, but the full content of St. Paul's saying about God; and that brings us on to God as the Unknowable. This can only be expressed in the figure by giving to the ground—to the (for us) eternal Dark—an infinite and unknowable depth, while to the Light is given an infinite and unknowable Light. And the Dark and the Light are One.

The Unknowableness of God remains the infinite question mark against all we can know of Him. It remains as the question mark—and the question mark against the question mark—against all definitions, notions, and dogmas. It remains as the Question Mark against all Thought and forms of Thought; and yet as the ultimate justification for the infinite adventuring of thought. And Thought is Spirit.

When I was reading Eckhart last year I wrote the following thought as an expression of this: thought as adventure, as a striving to understand that which it yet understands to be essentially unknowable, thought as speculative rejoicing—this is spirit. Thought as cowardice, as a seeking to reduce the mystery of things to the realm of the knowable—this is the death of spirit. Spirit is the freedom of the unknowable, the breath of the unknowable blowing into the misery of the knowable. God is the Unknowable—the Question Mark against the knowable.

Whether this seems too paradoxical or contradictory to you I do not know, but it is the nearest I can come to expressing my thought—my last and highest and deepest and most inward and most precious thought—about God. This thought is God in me. God in me is the unknowable in me, and the unknowable in me drowns the darkness of the knowable in me in its unknowable Light, which is yet Darker than all the Darkness of the knowable.

Mary pointed out a few evenings ago a sentence in Whitehead's fine work *Religion in the Making*: "Religion is what one does with one's solitariness." This is profoundly true. In solitude one becomes aware of the eternal, and of the eternal Unknowable; and the true religious life is a plunging into ever deeper solitude, a solitude though in which we approach ever nearer others insofar as we all share the eternal ground... And death is a solitude, the last and complete solitude: and "solitude is full of God."

I want you to come to a closer understanding, if not agreement, of my understanding of what the New Testament is, and, for that matter, what all sacred traditional scriptures are. I will try to express it by telling you some of my own inner history.

For a long time when I was a boy and young man I had lying in the back of my mind an image, which, at first, was just there (I cannot remember how it first came there), but which very slowly acquired a symbolic meaning. The image was that of a skull lying on an ash-tip. The skull lay among refuse—cigarette ends, old broken bottles, empty tins, ashes—and a thin gray rain was always falling. This image recurred to me at odd, unoccupied moments. I did not much question its presence, children perhaps rarely do. But after some years I had become aware that I identified myself with the skull. And then slowly came a sense that I—the skull—was waiting; but I did not know for what. This went on until about five years ago.

Then one day the image had changed, and yet I "knew" it was the same. In the new image a human head was rising out of a perfectly still sea. There was no land; it wasn't dark or light, but twilight. The eyes of the head were closed. I "knew" this head was identical with the skull on the ash-tip. The sense of waiting had grown stronger. Later I understood that the head knew there was a sun below the sea-horizon, and was waiting for that sun to rise. The image stayed like this for a long time, except that light grew over the horizon and the sense of waiting grew more and more intense. The eyes were still closed. Then one day the eyes had opened and the sun was exactly half-risen—pale reddish gold—over the horizon. The eyes were watching the sun and there was an even more intolerable sense of waiting, and the sense also that the head did not now know whether the sun was rising or setting—and waited to know.

This stage of the image lasted a long time. I was most of the time more or less conscious of it, though at other times I would forget it completely. The sense of waiting had reached breaking point. In all these images was a sense of deep eternal actuality combined with a sense of immense aeons of time slowly passing. Also, I could never decide when a change had taken place. When I became aware of change I became aware that it had happened long aeons ago.

Then some months ago the image had changed again. The head was gazing at a great iceberg floating on an unfathomable sea; and the sun, now risen, threw a far glitter and glory over the motionless sea around the innumerable pinnacles of many-colored translucent flashing ice; and a white bird was flying swiftly sunwards from the iceberg.

This image is still with me, except that the bird has gone and the sense of waiting is stilled.

I have tried to relate this history as simply as possible, and without comment. It was and is always accompanied with a sense of untellable significance, but I cannot hope to convey that significance in any other way than by telling the story.

But let me try to get "outside" it and say what I think may be its nature.

Firstly, I think all or most of us have similar inner experiences. I do not mean similar in detail, but in kind. And I think they represent a kind of inner "mystical language" in which the spirit is striving to convey to itself, and to understand in itself, its own inner history. The spirit seeks to reveal to itself its own inner meaning in an "image-language."

In the same way we find that the writings of the mystics are full of curious, unearthly images, or of language that often seems meaningless, yet full of meaning; that is, meaningful for those who have had inner experience in part corresponding to that of the mystic. Ordinary human language has been developed in the struggle of countless generations of men to deal with the brute fact of the material world. Most of its vocabulary and its structure are determined by this long striving. Most men, during very long ages, have had little or no leisure to pay much attention to, or try to express in language, their inner mystical life. They have had to worry too much about the next meal, or illness, or the attack of a merciless enemy. The result is that language is a poor instrument for expressing inner experience, whether religious, aesthetic, or speculative. This has led to the rise of what may be called "mystical languages" in the case of religious experience. Man, finding his everyday speech inadequate, is forced to express himself in images, or to force mere words to express meanings for which they were never intended. This it is that makes the language of the mystics often approach unintelligibility, or renders certain poems, paintings, and music "obscure" to those who have not experienced something corresponding to them in the depths of their own consciousness.

Now these deep obscure spiritual insights, working darkly in the collective consciousness of generations of men, issue in the formation of myths, which, in a world-deep, huge, only half-articulated way, express to men the deepest levels of their own spiritual experiences. And these myths usually concrete around some measureless imagistic symbol—or object or man symbolized. Round this (in the deepest and most real sense) sacred symbol will center all the darkest, furthest spiritual strivings of many generations.

I think that the Sacred Scriptures of the human race in this way contain symbolically the essence of the inmost spiritual experience of man. They are authorities. But only secondary authorities. The first authority is always, and can only be, for each man his own spiritual experience. He comes to the Scriptures with a sense of discovering what in some obscure way he has already known. Were this not so, they would be meaningless to him. Accordingly, he can only profitably interpret them in the light of his own prior knowledge; but of course they can help him to clarify and understand and deepen this prior knowledge.

If you want a long, arduous and exciting quest, find out all you can about the words *Aum Mane Padme Hum* and then write and tell me what you think about it!; though I warn you, it will take you some time, perhaps indeed the rest of your life. You could end up with a work of several volumes on Eastern religious thought!

The New Testament

Here Schweitzer has gone far to establish that Jesus really lived and was a great religious teacher; he has also gone far to show that much of the detail is not strictly historical. Robertson and his school of thought have gone far to prove the mythological character of the unhistorical concretion around the figure of Christ. Robertson himself tends to the conclusion that Jesus did not live, but I think he has not given sufficient weight to the evidence against that view. Though he has obviously made a profound study of mythology, Robertson does not seem to have penetrated into its deeper significance; however, he has done valuable work as a historian.

This concerns the New Testament viewed simply as a historical problem. Considered as a spiritual document, it is obviously an authority in the highest degree. The great Christian mystics have always treated it in this way, and have shown themselves rightly unconcerned with its historicity. Clearly, something tremendous in the spiritual history of the world happened at that time, and expressed itself in the rise of Christianity as a world religion. One wonders if ever again men can look at the world without seeing the terrible and tragic signature of Christ Crucified stamped in and across all things.

But I believe the time to be coming when men of all races will be forced, by the inner spiritual destiny of the human race as a whole, to enter into and strive to understand and take into themselves, the most secret spiritual traditions of alien cultures. Not until this has been done on a world-wide scale will humanity as a whole be able to take its next great spiritual step forward. Such a process will very probably take many generations.

I have tried briefly in my figure and comments on it to indicate the kind of general metaphysical scheme I believe may be the truth of things. It is a mode of thought that has arisen in many countries and times widely separated from each other—wherever men have developed the capacity for speculative metaphysical thought. When we turn to the utterances of the mystics of all these different sources we find the same thing—a mode of religious experience that presupposes the truth of some such metaphysical ground to the world as I have attempted to describe. Mystics have, in general, not been metaphysicians also; and it is of extraordinary interest that the utterances of so many of the mystics have unknowingly presupposed a metaphysic that contradicts, or is not harmonious with, their orthodox religious creed. Tragedy arose when—as in medieval Europe—the mystic was metaphysician also, and felt impelled by inner necessity and his vision of the truth to challenge the accepted orthodoxy.

This mystical tradition is, I believe, the great central religious tradition of man. The superficial differences due to historical and geographical influences cannot deceive anyone who shares (even in part) the same immediate religious experiences—if he once takes the trouble to honestly penetrate into the inner meaning of seemingly alien traditions. In Western mythology we find references to the great World-Tree with its roots in the earth and branches in heaven; in Eastern mythology we find the World-Tree with its roots in heaven and branches on earth. They are both One World-Tree, with roots and branches intertangled at both ends—the Great World-Tree of Tradition. And on this Tree Christianity is one of the great root-branches, with many lesser branches and twigs shooting off it. The great root-branch of Christianity is the great central Christian mystical tradition, and Roman Catholicism is part of that branch insofar as it remains true to that tradition. The trunk of the World-Tree is (I believe) found in the south central Asiatic religious tradition of the Hindus, running from the "men of long ago," who instructed the seers of the Upanishads, down to the Vedanta of Shankara, and on to the mysticism of Sri Ramakrishna in modern times. India is the Great Mother of Religions.

Lux est Umbra Dei—Ex Oriente Lux

Esoteric Tradition

I would like very briefly to go into this question here. Is there an esoteric tradition in Roman Catholicism? This is an important question, yet probably unanswerable in any decisive sense for laymen. Most great religious (and countless minor) cults have had a secret teaching that was only divulged to an elect—those who in some way had proved themselves capable of assimilating higher doctrine. René Guénon, the French thinker and interpreter of Vedanta, has hinted that there may be some such doctrine in the Roman Catholic church. He is very sympathetic to the Church and states clearly that he considers that the only hope of saving Western civilization is to be found in the Roman Catholic tradition. He does not go into any detail, but he has certainly a most acute mind, and was probably (I should guess from his writings) brought up in the Church. This is the only hint I have ever come across of any esoteric doctrine in the case of Roman Catholicism, and I have no doubt the Church would publicly deny the existence of any such thing, though we must remember here that for a doctrine to be truly esoteric its very existence should be a secret except to the initiated. Guénon seems convinced that some doctrine of this kind existed in the Middle Ages, but fears that it may have since been lost or misunderstood.

Now this is an extraordinarily valuable hint. I have often been puzzled as to how men of the intellectual capacity of so many Roman Catholics have been able to assent in full to its exoteric teaching. The existence of an esoteric doctrine would go far to explain this. Most religious authorities in the past have considered the ordinary "unregenerate" man as incapable of grasping and assimilating the profounder religious doctrines. They have thought that such teaching was highly dangerous if given to ordinary men; both dangerous for the men as individuals and dangerous for society as a whole. Men should reach a high degree of spiritual development before such doctrine could with safety be entrusted to them.

In the case of Eastern religions the belief in hell as eternal has been taught as popular exoteric doctrine, while to the initiated all hells and heavens have been revealed as subjective states. The *Bardo Thodol*—the Tibetan Book of the Dead—contains much very interesting evidence on this.

I have been puzzled for some years, since reading his horrific vision of hell, that Dante allows himself to escape from it, not by re-ascending the circles, but by penetrating to the lowest pit, then clambering along the body of Satan and passing through the center of the earth at his navel, along a rocky vent. He emerges then in a cavern on the banks of Lethe—the River of Forgetting—which he follows until it brings him to the island of Mount Purgatorio.

Now here we have some very profound symbolism and teaching of a kind hard to square with orthodox Roman Catholic doctrine. From the bottom-most pit of the Inferno we find an escape-vent to Purgatory and Paradise! We must remember that in Dante we have perhaps the greatest intellect of the Middle Ages—an orthodox Christian believer, and a man who may well have been initiated into secret doctrine, supposing such to exist. I have been puzzled by this, and by many other curiously suggestive sayings in the works of the Church mystics. Again, Jung in his psychological works has thrown suggestive light on the works of the medieval alchemists—though in their case it seems they chose to express esoteric doctrines in an obscure form to evade prosecution for heresy. Boehme also seems to have been working in the alchemical tradition, as his *Signature of All Things* clearly shows. All these considerations, together with what we know of similar developments in other religions, certainly point to the existence of such a doctrine.

If we assume that there is such a secret tradition, it certainly throws light on many obscurities; but it also raises new problems. I have tried to show that, as I think, the belief in hell as eternal was the root cause of the persecutions. But if the esoteric doctrine of the Church taught that hell was not eternal, what then? Here the following considerations may lead to persecution. Firstly, heresy may have been conceived as a betrayal, or attempted betrayal, of the secret doctrine: the initiated always consider pure religious doctrines as terribly dangerous if put into the minds of men unprepared for, or incapable of, receiving them. If a man cannot understand a doctrine it is no good teaching it to him, as he will not receive the true doctrine but a misunderstanding of it. Heretics were probably often laymen who by sheer spiritual insight had inwardly arrived at a truer and deeper doctrine than was considered good for them. They were also uninitiated and not bound to secrecy. It is possible to understand how dangerous all this would appear to the medieval churchmen: they saw that such public teaching of hitherto secret doctrine would tumble down the medieval world and the Church—as it eventually did. And I do not know that in this they were not right. If we have in truth lost such a tradition, through misunderstanding and perverting it, we have lost something more valuable than all our modern improvements and accomplishments. Well! This is a line of thought I cannot pursue very far here, though I frankly admit that, if it were true that there was an esoteric teaching that admitted even the possibility that hell was not eternal, then I could go most of the way with Roman Catholic teaching, for then very many things that repel me would appear in a very different light. Even the doctrine of infallibility, which, without such an esoteric doctrine, is a mere absurdity, would be eminently acceptable and reasonable. As things are, I can only say that I cannot accept the exoteric teaching of the Church in its entirety; and that I hope and pray there is in fact a deeper esoteric understanding among the Church authorities than appears on the surface. This whole question of exoteric and esoteric teachings raises difficult moral and religious problems. It means that the popular teaching of the Church is not the whole truth but only as much truth mixed with untruth as the Church considers good for the laity—and even perhaps for most of the clergy. One can of course rise up in righteous indignation and demand the whole truth and nothing but the truth for each and every man. But here we have the undoubted fact that most men are so spiritually and intellectually immature that they cannot in fact assimilate the whole truth. If it is given them they only misunderstand it, and therefore do not in fact receive it. And there is no doubt that misunderstanding of this kind can lead to the most terrible results—results of the kind that have brought the modern Western world to the extreme edge of measureless catastrophes. It is precisely because modern men have, in general, misunderstood the truth given them that they are proving themselves incapable of using it. I cannot here doubt the possibility that, as Guénon indicates, the Roman Catholic church as the repository of the most secret and precious traditions of the spirit—held esoterically—will prove eventually the saving factor in Western civilization, or else will build a new civilization—and a saner—on the ruins we leave. I have a full and humble consciousness that this may in truth be so, and pray that it is so.

It is a strangely moving and hopeful discovery, this matter of finding the hints of a saving central spiritual tradition flowing down under many disguises from the headwaters of our world-age—the Upanishads, the Tao-Te-King, the Eleusinian Mysteries, the New Testament. Why did old Plato write, almost word for word, teachings written centuries before him in far away countries by "the men of long ago" who taught us of the Upanishads? And Christian mysticism from the days of the great Greek Fathers on—what does it not owe to Plato and Plotinus? But this is to "dive deeper than Ishmael can go!" *And all these things are not without meaning.*

It is also worth some thought that the three great English metaphysical, or, if you prefer, philosophical, poets—Milton, Wordsworth, and Shelley (three great "heretics")—should, when the final tide of their high poetic inspiration carries them away, give utterance to visions seen so long ago by the seers of the Upanishads. Listen to Shelley expounding the central doctrine of the Vedanta:

> The One remains, the many change and pass;
> Heaven's light forever shines, Earth's shadows fly,
> Life, like a dome of many-coloured glass,
> Stains the white radiance of Eternity,
> Until Death tramples it into fragments.

And Wordsworth, writing of the pilgrim soul "wandering on from world to world":

> Our birth is but a sleep and a forgetting:
> The Soul that rises with us, our Life's star,
> Hath had elsewhere its setting,
> And cometh from afar...

Or, with the vision of Lao-Tze, he writes of "the central peace at the heart of endless agitation." 'Adonais', 'The Prelude', 'Intimations of Immortality', and 'Tintern Abbey' are as good an introduction as any to the study of Eastern thought!

And then the solitary one, sitting in the dark, a darkness more enduring than any enclosing a Tibetan hermit entombed in his remote cave among the Himalayan snows—what splendid hymn of praise and adoration is this, breaking from the lips of a blind man? Oh listen:

> Hail, holy Light, offspring of Heaven first-born,
> Or of the Eternal coeternal beam
> May I express thee unblamed? since God is light,
> And never but in unapproachèd light
> Dwelt from eternity, dwelt then in thee,
> Bright effluence of bright essence increate.

I see your point when you say I cannot believe that God can inflict punishment simply because I don't like the idea. This is true and a just comment. But there is, as always, more to it than that. My whole conception of God rejects it. Yet I do allow it as a possibility in that, as I have said, God is largely unknowable and the question mark against all human ideas of Him. There is this also to be said. We believe each human being is created in the image of God. And I cannot believe, except as an abstract possibility, that the eternal image of God in any man can be obliterated, however much it may be defaced. As I have said elsewhere, to believe this seems to imply lack of faith in the final power of God's love. I certainly cannot believe that it will be obliterated merely because of the acceptance or non-acceptance of Roman Catholic doctrine in its entirety, which seems to be the meaning of the passages I have quoted from the *Syllabus of Errors* and the Creed of Pius IV. I know that the love in me cannot tolerate such an idea. How then could the infinite love and power of God do so? I have imagined the most frightful things happening to a person I love and to myself, yet I cannot bring myself to feel eternal anger against any one who might perpetrate this against me. Were I to allow this the world would be a darkness to me. If God were not infinitely merciful, who could bear to live? Are the human differences in vice and virtue between the greatest saint and most abominable sinner so great as to appear great in the eyes of an eternal merciful God? Our greatest saints are not so very fine and our worst men not so very bad. To understand all is to forgive all; and God does understand all.

Here your case of the man who resolutely turns his face from God is to be considered. It is a case of a man punishing himself. But I cannot believe a man can so completely do this: he has the divine image within him, and this image constitutes his own deepest reality and being. Most men are pitiably immature at death. And the most mature man is pitiable alone before God. All religions have allowed a period after death in which the spirit may mature. I think myself—for many reasons I cannot here go into without writing a book—that the belief in rebirth in other human or non-human forms of existence is the most satisfactory form of belief to meet this necessity. Most modern Western men seem to find this idea fantastic, though in what way—religious or philosophical—I do not know. Even among Westerners in modern times such men as Whitman, Emerson, Wordsworth, Melville, Goethe, and others have at least accepted the possibility of it. And of course throughout the whole ancient world and the modern East it is an accepted commonplace and considered as a necessary metaphysical doctrine. Empedocles said, "I have been a boy, a girl, a bush, a bird, a scaly fish in the ocean." The old Welsh *Triads*, J.C.P. showed me, are full of similar utterances. They are more than mere poetical fancies. No being can develop depth of understanding in only one experienced form of being. Each man, as St. Paul says, is to work out his own salvation; and he may need many lives to accomplish this. The idea of the eternal decision being decided on the result of the meagre experience of one life in the vast complexities of the universe is intolerable. The loss of even one unique God-like soul would be a failure and challenge to all the rest. If you can do get hold of a small work by Radhakrishnan called *The Hindu View of Life*, in which he deals clearly and convincingly with the necessity and rightness of this idea. But for my purpose here it is sufficient to say that, granted this belief, the man who resolutely turns his face from God faces an endless prospect of intensifying suffering in other lives, until he is forced by the very intensity of his suffering to turn at last to God. The suffering is inevitable, for in turning (or attempting to turn) from God he is, as it were, attempting to sever himself from himself. And yet this frightful thing cannot be done. He can only go on miserably and endlessly trying to do it, an endless and fruitless striving in pain to accomplish the impossible. Meanwhile, ever and always, God as Love stands over against him and inside him waiting to heal and restore him. But I cannot myself conceive of a man so monstrously perverse.

Are men as bad as we sometimes think them? I do not think so. I am a faithful champion of Pelagius against Augustine in this matter. Insofar as Augustine lacked faith in the goodness of man he seems to me to have disbelieved in the image of God in man. I know this is a great simplification of a difficult question. All I can say here is that I believe the Church took one of its wrong turnings when it allowed itself to be dominated theologically by Augustine rather than Pelagius. Pelagius was the man of greater faith—in man and in God.

Your question about the claims of Jesus to be God seems to me to depend on a very great over-simplification of the whole matter. We would for instance have to know far more about the true nature of the Gospels than we do to put the question in that form. I do not believe the choice is between believing that "Jesus was either God or a knave." Or between believing that the Gospels are literally and absolutely true factually, or believing they are a "pack of lies." These alternatives depend on what seems to me a false idea of the nature of sacred scriptures. Similar unreal alternatives can be posed about the Buddhist canon. I have tried to indicate my approach to these problems in other parts of this already too-long letter, so I won't plunge into it again now.

Well, I must stop this letter some time, and yet I feel very dissatisfied with it. I feel I should be able to say something simple to harmonize our thinking. Yes, but how? I write here among my books in the quiet night with darling Mary asleep upstairs. I think of the immense background of my thinking, of all human thinking; of the endless procession of the world-cycles born from the Eggs of Brahman being swallowed by the great World Snake—the world-swallower. I consider the vastness of even this one universe with its multitudinous worlds and beings, hanging in space—and the endless diversity of creatures inhabiting the worlds. I think glancingly back along the innumerable generations of sea-gulls that have lived their time over one bay on the coasts of this one world, of the innumerable generations of sea-gulls yet to emerge into being, creatures remote from all human strivings and interests darting, diving, swooping over the ancient sea—a sea itself filled with beings strange, strange, strange to us and all our thinkings. I touch too with a faint far flickering of the imagination the endless forms of life, unimaginable to human thought, that must inhabit other worlds; see too the Sherpa tribesman pause beside his yaks on the high desolate pass in the Himalayas and reverently utter the words *Aum Mane Padme Hum*, words he will again breathe out with his last dying breath lying perhaps under some softly-accumulating snow drift—the peace at the heart of the world-lotus. I see the fierce whaleman pause in the still center of a great armada of whales and, gazing down through the translucent deeps at the inscrutable monsters of the sea, say to himself, "Even so, amid the tornadoed Atlantic of my being do I myself still forever centrally disport in mute calm; and while ponderous planets of unwaning woe revolve round me, deep down and deep inland there I still bathe me in eternal mildness of joy."

Think too of the child, dead now nearly two years after the atrocious agony of tetanus, for whom my prayer of assurance was "Child of God: God is Love"; of the unmoving skeleton lying so quietly locked up in the multitudinous abyss of the worlds—this child of the stars and elements and the deep beyond the earth, lost in the world flow... Think of a footprint under the glaciers of Mt. Kenya; of a weeping, a wave, a flower—"the wild gander leads his flock through the cool night"; of a small child with a toy telescope standing beside his mother looking up at the stars; of the strangeness of Heraclitus, or a many-gloried iceberg floating in the Polar Sea under the far-flashing Aurora Borealis, or the paw of a Polar Bear; of the signature in all human countenances of a divine source and destiny, of the hangman carefully setting his noose, of an ash-tree growing on the bank of the Dee near Corwen, the River of Life flowing always swiftly to the sea; of old J.C.P. striding out over his Berwyn Mountains "like a giant about to run his course," chanting *Pen-glog-babany-yaur*, or Theodore, the gentlest of men, dead; "the wandering swan everlasting journeying on from world to world"—see the wandering swan remotely shadowed forth in the eyes of all men, and death. Think of a black camel kneeling in every man's path; a shell, a cloud, a smile, an empty space, a silence, a stillness resting on such pieces of the world with a light momentary moth-like alighting of thought: what uncertain light of suspended judgement and sense of inadequacy cannot but fall across my thought?

>All this is Brahman.
>Brahman is beyond being and beyond not-being.
>Peace, Peace, Peace.

Evolution

Don't be misled here. I am no biologist or historian or geologist, but I think we owe it to our intellectual conscience to accept the opinion of men who have devoted their lives to the study of these subjects. With the exercise of common sense the ordinary man can fairly decide whether a man is talking nonsense or not. Of Darwinism, and evolution in general, Julian Huxley writes (and he seems a fair choice to represent the consensus of biological opinion on this subject): "It is often asserted that 'Darwinism is dead.' This is very far from being the case. Insofar as Darwinism was a reasoned assertion of the fact of evolution, it is much more firmly grounded today than it was in Darwin's own time, and every year brings fresh evidence in its support.... The anti-evolutionists find some weak spot in a widely detailed theory as to the method of evolution [the fact is not in doubt] and at once proceed to state the whole idea of evolution is false—a procedure only to be explained as the result of weakness of logic or lack of intellectual conscience."

I have copied this passage from his long, detailed, and excellent essay on the subject in the *Encyclopaedia Britannica*. I have never been able to understand why this theory has aroused such antagonism from Western religions. Eastern religions as long ago as the Upanishads had propounded the metaphysical basis necessary to account for evolution, and had accepted the fact in broad outline. All philosophies that view the world as a process of becoming are evolutionary in their outlook. Darwin produced, as Huxley says, a reasoned, detailed description of a process recognized in the most ancient philosophies. The doctrine of pre-existence and rebirth go far to account for the philosophical difficulties experienced in attempting to produce a metaphysical basis for the modern biological description of the process.

I cannot account for the antagonism, which seems to me quite unreasonable. Can *Genesis* still be the root of this trouble? But surely we can accept *Genesis* as the religious and profound myth it so obviously is. Why has every word of scripture to be interpreted in this literal way?: "the letter killeth, the spirit giveth life."

I have always felt friendly to biological evolution because it establishes so clearly—if such a thing needed establishing—our close relationship to the animal creation. I cannot accept the notion that animals have no spirit. I have had perhaps too much to do with them. Even plants and minerals are beings, or, if you prefer, becomings—or both. I have the deepest sympathy with Origen when he reckons among the angels the spirits of the sun, planets, and stars; and with the ancient polytheistic animism that saw streams, crags, hills, waterfalls, pools, winds, clouds, and seas as each haunted by indwelling spirits. Modern dullards write condescendingly of such beliefs as "primitive simple-mindedness," but I suspect the "simple-mindedness" lies rather with these 'superior' ones. The eternal spiritual reality of the cosmos presupposes the spiritual reality of all its parts. Many of the most precious moments of my life have been moments of communion with the elements... touching great rocks, diving into cool clear water, looking into the heart of fires on winter evenings, walking at night under a wet sky, wind and rain flowing over the face. How calculate the loss—the spiritual loss—if such moments and memories were obliterated? How do we gain our profoundly intimate knowledge of what it is to be a pebble, a wave poised to fall upon a pebble, a star, a wind, a flowering grass bending before the wind, a tree, a thin tracery of twigs quietly moving or perfectly still against a gray evening sky, a gull, a flying fish in the beak of a seabird, an iceberg, a headland jutting into the sea? Do we not in truth meet all these, in fact or imagination, with an untellable and unbreakable sense of ancient kinship and recognition? Listen to a voice three thousand years grown silent on this planet:

Who sees all beings in his own Self, and his own Self in all beings, what delusion and sorrow can ever be near him?
O Life-giving Sun, offspring of the Lord of Creation, solitary seer of heaven! Spread thy light, withdraw thy blinding splendour that I may behold thy radiant form: that spirit far away within thee, is my own inmost spirit.
Aum! Remember, O my soul, remember past strivings,
Remember, Remember!

I do understand many of your doubts, difficulties, and values. I think from your letters we are very alike in many ways. You write: "Where is God? Is He?" Often and often I have, alone in desert places of Kenya and Somaliland and Abyssinia, on the pebbles of Chesil Beach with a night wind blowing chill from the dark sea, in the snow at the edge of glaciers on Mt. Kenya, in the sand edging the brilliant sea near the Straits of *Bab-el-Mandeb* (the 'gate of tears' in Arabic), in the dust near *Habas Wen* (the 'great dust' in Somali), in the water of streams on Margam—written just those words: "Where is God?" And often, later, I found I just traced out the one syllable GOD, as the Eastern hermit utters the one word AUM.

"O the depths of the riches both of the wisdom and the knowledge of God! How unsearchable are His judgements, and His ways past tracing out!" exclaimed St. Paul. And Chrysostom comments: "We wonder at the greatness of the sea and its measureless expanse, but terror and fear only seize on us when we gaze down into its depths: dizzy before the unfathomable main and gazing down into its yawning depths, he [St. Paul] recoils precipitately and cries aloud in terrified wonder: 'O the depths of the riches both of the wisdom and knowledge of God....'"

I will like to think of you walking over our South Wales hills during these next weeks. I read not long ago Giraldus Cambrensis' *Welsh Itinerary*; it is very good. He has some quaint stories about Margam and fairies living under the moor. I long to walk over Tondu Mountain and down to the Aberavon reservoir again.

I entirely agree with you about Chesterton. I never forgot his splendid essay on a piece of chalk. The best study I have on Blake was written by him. I admire his courageous and whimsical refusal to be browbeaten by the modern Dullards (Bertrand Russell, etc.) into backing out of, or rationalizing away, his beliefs.

I like too the words of your friend the priest; he is tolerant and wise. I say unreservedly: if your belief gives you a sense of freedom and joy and infinite perspectives and compassion, then defend it to the death. The only right I deny is the right to impose by force one's belief on another.

I rejoice that you too appreciate the greatness of Whitman; he has, I know, brought strength and courage and the free spirit to unnumbered "queer ones," and are we not all queer when alone? I think his 'Out of the Rolling Ocean, the Crowd' one of the supreme love-poems in our literature.

I wish I could read your story about the three-legged lion. For heaven's sake don't be scrupulous over accepting money for honest work.

You needn't feel overwhelmed by my learning. There is nothing prodigious about it; it is simply that I have had many more years than you have had yet to read widely on subjects that interest me.

Soon you will see the white candle lit on Christmas Night. And go to Midnight Mass with Dada and Mama and Anne, and perhaps Mary. I would like to be with you all. I may have uttered harsh criticisms of Roman Catholicism in these letters; and yet, when I consider it, I find that what divides me from it is not much—though it is to me vital. I cannot (and do not wish to) escape its influence and the fact that it moulded my spirit in years that I cannot now remember. I feel sure that it does introduce into the minds of the young the seeds of a true spiritual growth, perhaps more certainly than any other form of belief traditional in the West—though I hesitate a little over this, as there is no doubt that we are all prejudiced in favor of what we have known intimately and loved in childhood. I have loved, and still love, the Church's sturdy and resolute insistence on the truth of the supernatural world, on the fact of God's certain existence; its emphasis on the first and last things: birth, death, hell, and heaven; its unwavering defense of the "degrees of knowledge," and its calm certainty, nourished by its long and rich tradition, in facing the often irrelevant criticisms of the modern Know-all Dullards.

I have entered churches in odd places and been comforted by the lights of the Real Presence. Yet the way in which I interpret the doctrine of the Real Presence would probably be anathema to the Church. The life of the spirit cannot be founded on anything but absolute sincerity, and this leads to developments that make it impossible for some of us to remain in the Church. But that does not blind us to the wonder and strangeness of the birth of Jesus into the world and the unimaginable impress this birth has left on the religious thought of the world.

When I was returning across the Mediterranean Sea in a troop ship at the end of the war I felt I penetrated far into the mystery of Christianity. This ancient sea, the nurse of so much we value most in the past, has always moved me to deep insights. I had at that time been reading widely about St. Paul and the origins of Christianity. But nothing in my reading and my absorption in the story of this extraordinary man could have prepared me—in the early sunlit afternoon, when the high ridges of the mountains of Crete were rising over the horizon, with a thousand soldiers thronging the decks all round me, with the brilliant sunrays slanting down into the shadowy waves, with the disturbing knowledge (for disturbing it is and must be to any man of imagination and baptized as a Christian) that just over the eastern curve of the horizon lay the Holy Land, the land where Jesus lived and taught and died in atrocious agonies of body and spirit—; nothing could have prepared me, sailing the ancient sea, the dark unharvested sea of Homer, the same sea that Paul so often voyaged across on many and many such golden afternoons as this, bearing the message of Christ Crucified and Risen Again that was to enter with such terrible power into transvaluing all the values of the Western world—; nothing of all this, though my imagination was at that time obsessed with such thoughts, could have prepared me, I feel convinced, for a sudden falling away of so many piled-up centuries, so that for a still moment I knew myself to be contemporaneous with the Crucifixion: the glorious golden afternoon darkened around me, and the black shadow of the Cross lay in me and over and around me. There was no time or space between me and the Death of Christ, and this black shadow was so dazzling it darkened the glory of sunrays falling on our planet nineteen centuries afterwards.

But here, at Christmas time, let us think of another moment in the history of our tragic planet:

> But peaceful was the night
> Wherein the Prince of light
> His reign of peace upon the earth began:
> The winds with wonder whist
> Smoothly the waters kissed,
> Whispering new joys to the mild ocean,
> Who now hath quite forgot to rave,
> While birds of calm sit brooding on the charmèd wave.

With love to you and all at home,
Gerard

"Seek the Intelligible Light beyond the Cosmos," said Plutarch.

"Peace and Peace and Peace be everywhere and with all men." *Katha Upanishad.*

The Beale Farm
26 December 1953

My dear Pat

Thank you for sending me this splendid poem by Dylan Thomas. I have not read many of his poems. I must get his published collections. The poems I have read by him I find in anthologies, and I have been deeply moved by them. Mary said that his 'And death shall have no dominion' is Shakespearean, and she is right. I do not know of any other poet of our time who could be described so.

I wrote you a longish letter some time ago which I now feel rather guilty about. I was rather "kali." I hope you will forgive me for this. The subject of hell (eternal) always brings to light a rather unpleasant streak in me. As I do not believe in it, I should not worry about it—except that I cannot bear to think of children being taught this, and know what monstrous results have flowed from this doctrine in history.

I am glad you feel as I do about the futility of arguing! I have not thought about our letters in this way. I like to think of them as discussions in which we may help each other to think more clearly about difficult problems. You are thinking and wrestling with problems that have long occupied me, and that has lead me unfairly to attack in you doctrines I have come to detest, although you have not indicated you believe them in any detailed and positive sense. Boehme says, "all rising, swelling contending about opinions is an image of the proud self." In all discussions we should always remember we are "seekers," and not "defenders and attackers." We should welcome honest criticism. It forces us to modify our thought in the direction of truth and to think out our belief in a deeper and truer way. Nietzsche has done a great service to Christianity in the modern world if he has forced individual Christians to think more deeply, particularly on ethics. But declaring *anathema sit* and leaving it at that is evasion. Kierkegaard was the pre-destined antagonist for Nietzsche. Unfortunately he lived before Nietzsche, and the great German never read the Dane's works. What would not one give to be able to eavesdrop at a conversation about St. Paul between these two lovers of the intellectual lightning! Is there a man alive and writing today with the capacity of mind equal to writing an 'Imaginary Conversation' between them in the way W.S. Landor did so splendidly for others? I do not think so: Landor himself could not have done it.

Kierkegaard makes much of the fact that Christ had to appear on earth *incognito* if he was to elicit a purely spiritual response from men. This, if correctly developed, is the true Christian answer to criticisms of New Testament obscurities, contradictions, etc. It is true that a man only reveals his true nature and what he truly believes in face of the possibilities of the world. There is no possibility of self-revelation in the face of indisputable fact. In this sense, doubt is that in faith which is the mark of its sincerity. The fact that a man is aware of alternatives and is in constant anguish of spirit lest he be mistaken, and yet believes a certain doctrine—this fact is at once the mark of his sincerity and also a revelation of his spirit. I have said before in these letters that what is called atheism is (in the case of honest men) but a moment or stage in the development of the spirit. When a man rejects old conceptions of God he does so, perhaps unconsciously, in favor of new conceptions that seem to him truer. At a moment in this process of rejection he may say that there is no God, but a close, sympathetic analysis of his subsequent thought reveals the fact that he is moving toward a new apprehension of the unknown God. This is certainly the case with many of the great minds dubbed atheistic. The essentially religious striving in their thought is revealed in the supreme importance they attach to the idea of Truth. It is, I think, true that many men called atheists are more religious than the majority of the supporters of some religious orthodoxy—that is, if we define (as I think we should) religion as the pursuit of truth. Remember that the New Testament insists that the godly man is the "witness for the truth" and "suffers for the truth" as did Jesus. If this be accepted, it is an indisputable historical fact that great numbers of men in all ages and countries, and outside the Church and in antagonism to it, have so suffered. I have probably said all this before *ad nauseam*. Yet I say it again because I think it of fundamental importance, and because as yet you do not admit it. (This was written before your last and best letter came. I now withdraw this statement.)

Looking back through your letters, I feel I must also say rather more than I have said about suffering. Let us take as a starting point your observations on the Plymouth Brethren. You say that, in your observation, they do not appear to be suffering. They are, you say, complacent, self-satisfied, etc. Let us look into this a little more closely. First, I would again ask how you can possibly know the facts of their inner experience. The answer is (if I am right) that their whole attitude, facial expression, way of speech, etc., signifies this. That is not a sufficient reason. I will here again become personal, though I wish in general to avoid it. Nevertheless, certain subjects we can discuss only by an appeal to the most convincing evidence we have. You have suffered inwardly. I think I can without presumption warn you that you will continually suffer more the longer you live. But the present fact we have to consider is that *you have suffered*. How many of your acquaintances, or even friends, do you think have perceived this fact in you? Do you show it in any very obvious way? Again, I may consider here facts of my life. I have suffered. Let me say this. I have had by human standards a happy life so far. I have had good friends, the joy and light of my life. I have had work to do that interests me. I have had good health, no financial cares. I have had leisure to do many things that delight me. I have, I think I can say, a stable, quiet, even temperament. When I look around me, when I read history, I know with deep gratitude that I am, as they say, "one in million" in the sense that I have enjoyed, so far, an extremely fortunate life. All this is true, and it is much. Yet, in simple truth, I must tell you that for long periods of my life I have lived, moment by moment, day and night, on the edge of self-destruction. I have experienced, and still do, an inner anguish and horror of spirit, and a dull ugly unendable loathing for myself that has brought me to the continual contemplation of suicide. This is not a pretty thing. And yet this inner despair of myself is child's play compared with certain other things I have suffered as possibilities within me. I know now too that in a sense I cannot hope for release from this kind of suffering. I can only look forward to an intensification of it, and perhaps, in hope, to more strength to deal with it. I have come to trust in God simply because I have discovered I cannot trust myself. It is the trust and hope arising from despair. I tell you this and it is true. Yet when I am shaving I do not see any desperate wild suffering countenance in the mirror. I only see what I see in most of the faces around me: a rather round, dull, complacent looking, more or less contented countenance. Yet I know of at least one case, and have read of many others, in which a man with just such a dull complacent face surprised his friends one evening by calling for a drink all round and then quietly, unfussily going outside to hang himself. It is statistical fact too that the suicide rate increases with the degree of comfort and ease enjoyed by men. I have sometimes thought that insofar as suffering becomes externalized and visible it is mastered. This is at least partly true. Have you looked into the faces of many inmates of mental hospitals? There is no need to make too much of this line of thought, but it should at least caution us against too quickly deciding that we know what any other human being may be suffering. I think all living creatures suffer, and suffer increasingly, as they grow in spirit. If a man really is contented (that is, if he experiences it so in himself) and more or less complacent, it is simply that his spirit is for the time being vegetating, resting from growth. But always remember, in compassion, that this seemingly unattractive vegetating is necessary and right for him while he enjoys it. He has suffered, he will suffer; now he is resting. And for all any outsider can know, he is resting with inner knowledge and patience; although it doubtless also often happens that a man so rests away a lifetime in something approaching complete quiescence of spirit—it may be several lifetimes. Yet all this is but a moment in his long pilgrimage.

This brings me to a question I left unanswered in my last letter but one, as that letter was already overlong. You questioned the fact of there being Eastern "religions" at all. They are rather, you claim, speculative philosophies. It is true that the philosophical implications of their religious beliefs have been highly developed among the Eastern peoples. They have a deep genius for contemplation and speculation to the degree that their great metaphysical systems make Western metaphysics seem childish. Nevertheless, these religions are true religions in every sense of the word (excepting possibly the Chinese systems); that is, if one takes Christianity as a norm. They have sacred scriptures, incarnations of the Deity, systems of ethics, elaborate rituals. A good introduction to this immense subject is to be found in Radhakrishnan's *Eastern Religions and Western Thought*—it is an excellent work, which you'd find in any good library (I hope).

The idea of an "avatar" is completely Eastern in origin. The idea of the possibility of an avatar is of course the foundation and possibility of

Christianity. In Eastern thought an avatar is a descent of God into Man, into human form, to help men in times of great distress. The orthodox Hindus recognize ten avatars. The last two were Krishna and Buddha. Modern Hindus recognize Jesus as another avatar. In the *Bhagavad Gita* (the Song of God) Krishna is presented as a complete manifestation in human form of *Isvara*—the Supreme God. He says to Arjuna, "Whensoever righteousness languishes I create myself. I am born age after age, for the protection of the good. Quickly I come to those who seek me, who worship me only, I shall save them, here and hereafter." In many sayings Krishna announces himself as the incarnation of God on earth far more clearly and unambiguously than did Jesus in the Synoptic Gospels.

Buddha also, in Mahayana Buddhism, is believed to be a personal God and Savior. It is important to realize that Hindus who believe Jesus to be an avatar believe just what the Christians believe of Him. The difference is simply that Christians believe in the possibility of only one avatar, Christ, while the Hindus believe that different ages need a fresh message, a new descent of God into man, because their spiritual problems differ.

I have said that Krishna was conceived to be the incarnation of *Isvara*. *Isvara* is the Supreme Deity, the One of the Hindu Trinity: *Brahma* the Creator, *Vishnu* the Preserver, and *Shiva* the Destroyer. Krishna was more particularly believed to be the incarnation of the second person of this Trinity, Vishnu. Beyond Isvara is *Brahman*, the ultimate ground and all embracing reality. Brahman is at once the Godhead of Eckhart and the phenomenal world of appearance. Radhakrishnan says that all the six Brahmanical Systems accept the view of the great world rhythm. An endless procession of universes issues from the Eggs of Brahman. These island universes, floating in the sea of the Absolute, rise into being, endure to consummation, and pass away into Brahman. Vast periods of creation (Brahma), maintenance (Vishnu), and dissolution (Shiva), follow each other in endless succession. This is not the doctrine of the "eternal recurrence of all things," as taught by Nietzsche. It is strange that Nietzsche, with his acute mind, did not realize that his doctrine of an eternally recurring world—the same down to the smallest details—is meaningless. It does not require great insight to assent to the doctrine of the identity of indiscernibles. In the Hindu system, the world systems are each a unique and precious effluence of the Divine Spirit, just as each human spirit is. They rise gloriously into being and find their unspeakable consummation by re-entry into Brahman. They constitute the eternal activity of the Absolute. It seems to me that this idea corresponds to the idea of the agony of the Unmanifested Godhead in Boehme, that element of necessity in the Godhead that issues in the creation of the worlds. It has been instructive to me to note how, whenever Christian thinkers adventure freely in thought, they arrive at conceptions closely paralleled in the Eastern systems.

All these Eastern religions aim at the practical end of salvation: complete poise and freedom from the discords and sufferings of life, which no rebirths can break into. The systems believe in rebirth and pre-existence. Radhakrishnan says, "Our life is one step on a road, the goal of which is lost in the infinite. On this long road death is never an end or an obstacle, it is a fresh opportunity. The development of the soul is a continuous process broken into stages by the recurring baptism of death.... The cause of bondage to the wheel of rebirth is ignorance, and release can be achieved only by insight into the truth. We are like children stranded in the darkness, in illusion (samsara), imagining fears and clinging to false hopes in the gloom of ignorance (avidya), striving to realize our true nature.... Man's eternal destiny carries him beyond this unending World Rhythm and the Wheel of Rebirth into the Peace of Brahman, Who is beyond being and beyond not-being.... He is helped to this destiny by the descent of Avatars, incarnations of God in human form. In Sacred Scriptures we find the revealed eternal word of the Avatars...."

Surely all this may fairly be described as truly religious? And these systems of belief, so noble and free and lit by infinite eternal perspectives—may they not be called religious? Or is the arrogance of Western man to deny not only civilizations, but religions also to the rest of mankind? For myself I see in them a grandeur of outline and depth of insight that I search for in vain in Christian theology. You may ask, why this endless rise and fall of teeming universes? Sri Aurobindo replies, "for the joy of the dancing." Each universe, just as each spirit, is a separate adventure of the spirit. Brahman so realizes His infinite potentialities. The ground is freedom; the becoming therefore cannot but include conflict, and therefore suffering. Each individual spirit is rooted in Brahman, nay, *is* Brahman. The whole adventure is His adventure. I note two attitudes with regard to the peace of Brahman. Some see it as escape, rest from suffering. The more robust see it as simply rest between adventures, and below adventure. These differences are probably decided by temperament, and the stage each spirit has reached. Men and universes grow weary and long to return to the peace of Brahman. Healed in the peace of Brahman, they issue out in new adventures. Below all the conflict within you and around you lies the peace of Brahman; by true knowledge and insight you may realize this unutterable peace that is your own deepest self, *Atman*. The realization of this peace constitutes your deep-rooted central strength when engaged in the strife of becoming. It has been said that the Hindus are deficient in joy. Yet somewhere they write of "Brahma the Enjoyer hurling His worlds." With them joy is rooted in peace. Joy flowers out of peace. Before joy may grow the soil of peace must be found and the seed of resignation planted. Joy cannot be found in the flux of becoming unrelated to its ground, which is peace. The peace and joy are there all the time within you, but you have to "realize" the fact. You have to realize the deepest levels of your self: Atman, Brahman. *Tat tvam asi*—thou art that—say the seers of the Upanishads. The phenomenal you, your personality in its suffering and conflicts and joys, stains the white radiance of the eternity within you. To be conscious of the eternal is to overcome suffering. Kierkegaard said, "despair is lack of the eternal." The ancient thinkers of the Upanishads would agree. It is not that the suffering of process is wrong or evil or unreal, but it should not be given undue emphasis; it should always be seen by the white radiance of the eternal, as Shelley knew.

The most tragic and intense sufferings appear muted, softened, transcended from the perspective of the eternal. To know truly that, come what may to us or to those we love, we are in truth rooted in the eternal peace of God—this is salvation here and now. No need to look further. Here is peace, rest, stillness, joy, love, the ground of the suffering and the fruit of the suffering. Life and death, joy and sorrow, are seen with an eye freed by the eternal perspective. Hear Spenser:

> What if some litle paine the passage have,
> That makes fraile flesh to feare the bitter wave?
> Is not short paine well borne, that brings long ease,
> And layes the soule to sleepe in quiet grave?
> Sleep after toyle, port after stormie seas,
> Ease after warre, death after life does greatly please.

I do not think that only Eastern thinkers have arrived at these liberating conceptions. It would be quite untrue to claim this. Human minds in all ages and countries have done so. But in the East I, at least, find them lit up and clarified and enriched with a particular effulgence and depth of certainty that is not found elsewhere. This is probably due to the fact that the East has the older and richer religious tradition, and a tradition that has not tended to deny freedom of thought. *Anathema sit* is unknown in the East. In the East religion and metaphysical speculation have nourished each other and intimately influenced each other in a way unhappily unknown in the West. For this tragic fact I believe the Roman Catholic church is primarily responsible. Western secular thinkers, like Bradley in his *Appearance and Reality*, who arrive at metaphysical conceptions similar to those of the East, are not nourished by a profound, all-embracing religious tradition. They think, as often as not, in antagonism to the religious culture of their own society, in a kind of spiritual vacuum, and this leads to an undoubted impoverishment—a kind of spiritual anemia—in their work. This is felt in the curious bleakness and thinness that seems to invade their thought. They are largely dependent on their own individual insight, and it is astonishing how far they get, in the circumstances. Their thought suffers in depth, in richness, in completeness. This is the tragedy of Bruno, of Spinoza, of Eckhart, of Bradley. It is a tragedy indeed not only for them but for Western civilization, as anyone who knows the issues involved—and what metaphysical thought is and can be and should be—cannot doubt.

I have just read a most interesting study of Boehme by the Danish Lutheran Bishop Martensen. It is instructive to read a criticism of the inspired cobbler from the point of view of orthodox Protestant theology. Martensen does, I think, bring out the impoverishment Boehme experienced in his thought insofar as he did not fully absorb the whole richness of the Christian tradition. He also very fairly indicates that the whole Protestant thought of Boehme's time was similarly impoverished. He sees clearly the loss as well as the gain occasioned by the Reformation. In reading this book two points occurred to me in connection with our discussions. Firstly, Martensen brings out in a masterly way the extraordinary complexity and subtlety of Boehme's doctrine of God. Here we have a simple, almost illiterate, shoemaker speculating on himself, the world, and God day-by-day as he bends quietly over his last. In the result we have a religious vision of the world and God of surpassing splendor and truly unfathomable depth. We find in the small skull, poised over the upturned leather, of Boehme (who would have been an "untouchable" in India) one of the most profound and far-ranging intelligences that has appeared on this planet. And this simple honest old Jacob, this all but inarticulate man, finds that in order to articulate his thought of God he has to develop a doctrine far more complex than the orthodox Trinity. His God, in its barest outline, is a Seven-in-one rather than a Three-in-one. This fact struck me forcibly in connection with your remark about simplicity, in which you imply that thought of God and eternity must necessarily be simple and easy to understand. I know your feeling and sympathize with it and have shared it. But does it reflect the truth? Over-simplification can very easily become falsification. Here we have a simple man, and a good man if ever there was one (no man was less likely to want to make a mark in the world by cutting intellectual capers), who, in striving to give utterance to his vision of God in simple words and homely expressions, produces a system of thought staggering in its sheer complexity, in which too the man's massive integrity and depth of insight force one to concede that this complexity of expression is necessary. We must remember also that Boehme, in his ignorance of formal theology and metaphysics, thought he was producing a highly simplified edition of orthodox theology! Yet this "simple faith" was so astonishingly complex that the vast majority of orthodox theologians could make nothing of it, or so misunderstood it that Boehme was subjected to the usual persecution with which orthodoxy attacks whatever is beyond its understanding.

In connection with simplicity and doctrine, it should also be remembered that the orthodox doctrine of the Trinity is anything but simple and easy to understand. It has been attacked as blasphemy by the champions of simplicity in all ages simply because they could not understand it.

The second point I wanted to refer to is Martensen's discussion of the doctrine of eternal hell in Boehme. Boehme, there can be no doubt, believed in a well-populated eternal hell. Martensen, a Lutheran Bishop, subjects the notion to a most destructive analysis, an analysis based on Scriptural evidence and a wide knowledge of orthodox theologies. But what really interests me is that Martensen points out that even Franz von Baader, *who was a Roman Catholic theologian* and at the same time a disciple of Boehme, utterly rejects the doctrine of eternal hell on both Scriptural and theological grounds. I can only think that either there is indeed an esoteric doctrine in Roman Catholicism, or that von Baader was fortunate in living in an age when the pope did not imagine he was infallible.

Von Baader and Oetinger both think that the Church doctrine on this point rests upon a misinterpretation and mistranslation of the word "eternity" in the New Testament. They point out that the word αἰώνιος has a double meaning. It means primarily that which is *indefinite* in duration, that of which one *cannot predict* any definite end. They claim (I think fairly) that this word cannot be construed in the same sense when one speaks of eternal life and eternal damnation. "Eternal" life must be without end because *it is grounded in the eternity of God*. But "eternal" death can only mean that of which the end is *undefined* and unforeseeable; it cannot be eternal (in the sense of *aeternitas*) because only God is eternal, and hell is by definition separation from God. The punishments of hell are not infinite but *indefinite*. It is important here to remember that we have to concede that the true original meaning of the Greek word αἰώνιος is "unending," in the sense of indefinite. It acquires its right to be translated as "eternal" only when it is tacked on to the idea of life in the eternal God. Von Baader says that in Hades *Grace goes before Justice*, and that it was universally believed in the first three centuries of Christian life that the descent of Christ into hell after the Crucifixion was *redemptive*. He says that those who came just after the Apostles held this view: Irenaeus, Tertullian, Cyprian, Chrysostom. But in hell proper (as distinct from Hades), *Justice comes before Grace*.

The duration of punishment in hell is indeterminable. But death and hell must be vanquished at some time or other, or else the last enemy is not destroyed and Scripture remains unfulfilled. The restoration of all men is "an article of secret hope," held in virtue of the power of the eternal love of God, that the words of Scripture, "in that day all thy creatures shall praise Thee," be fulfilled. It is interesting too that these theologians believe in the existence of many stages and states of the soul after death before it achieves the beatific vision—along lines essentially similar to the Eastern beliefs in pre-existence and re-birth in different grades of being and universes. They claim rightly that most of the Greek Fathers accepted such beliefs. These Greek Fathers were in their turn influenced from the East through Plato and Plotinus; and here as always, if we have eyes to see, we see the World Tree: Ygdrassil—the Tree of Tradition.

But what particularly interested me in Martensen's fine treatment of this subject is that he brings out the criticisms arising from Scripture and Tradition rather than criticisms arising from purely metaphysical reasoning. I do not know how all this (my resumé is only a brief summary, but does, I think, contain the main points) strikes you. I would like the opinion of an intelligent Catholic priest on this subject.

I have also in the last two days been reading an excellent book Lucy sent us as a Christmas present. It is called *Waiting on God*, by Simone Weil. She was a magnificently intelligent French woman who had been discussing the possibility of her entry into the Roman Church with a Catholic priest; and this wonderful book consists of letters and papers she sent him in the course of their discussions. I do wish you would read this, as she brings out so clearly many of the difficulties intelligent people, who are separated from the Church, feel. I am astonished and humbled by the absolute honesty and great knowledge of this woman. I have never read a word by her before, but I can already say unhesitatingly that she is a prophet—along with Kierkegaard and Berdyaev and Schweitzer—of a Christianity refreshed and cleansed from the accumulated rubbish of centuries. Of a Christianity humble enough, honest enough, great enough, to see itself as but one expression of a great world religion of the future. She stands as a European prophet of the religion of the future foreshadowed in Persia by Abdul Baba of the Bahai branch of Islam, and foreshadowed in India by Sri Ramakrishna, Sri Aurobindo, and Radhakrishnan. We are moving into a new and terrible world age, but this coming world age is not without its great teachers and prophets. And among them Simone Weil will have an honorable place. I will send you a copy of this book. It has, among other precious things, an essay entitled 'Reflections on the Right Use of School Studies with a View to the Love of God,' which I would like to make compulsory reading for all teachers and students.

I asked Francis to send you some books two months ago: Berdyaev's *Destiny of Man*, Jones's *Studies in Mystical Religion*, Huxley's *The Perennial Philosophy*, and Seaver's *Albert Schweitzer*. All these should be quite easy to get, and if he has not sent them I think he must have forgotten. If you have not had them call on him at Better Books of Charing Cross Road, not far from Foyles (on the opposite side), and inquire about them. Also, get any other books you particularly would like. He has a deposit from me. If you see him, get a copy of this book by Simone Weil. It is of surpassing interest and value.

Night Horizons

29 December

I left this letter a few days ago and had no chance to finish it. Your letter has just come. It is a precious letter. I don't think we differ very much in what we believe, as I hope to show you. But I find it difficult to accept what you think of as Roman Catholicism as the real thing. I find I am discussing two separate, or rather three separate, points of view. There are your point of view and my point of view, which I now feel are not very different in essentials, and there is also the Roman Catholic view which, although you cannot see it, I feel is different from both our points of view. I find that the parts of your letter that reflect Church opinion don't ring quite true to me, while the parts that reflect your own private thoughts I can nearly always accept in their entirety. This is not to say we are necessarily right and the Church wrong. It may easily be the other way. Nevertheless I do not think your way of thought is a true reflection of Church Doctrine.

I must make another effort to make clear my attitude to certain historical questions. I won't return to the historical angle in later letters because I think that, fundamentally, it does not make much difference to our basic attitudes. I will just try to clarify my points before leaving the subject. I know you will come to an honest conclusion if you give yourself time for impartial study. You will forgive me for saying that your approach so far can hardly be called impartial. History, of course, is a tremendous complex of heterogeneous facts; and all our formal history is, and can only be, a selection—usually tending to establish the private presuppositions of a particular historian. It is quite possible for a historian, wishing to emphasize a certain viewpoint, to so select his facts and so present them that, although each detail in itself is perhaps indisputable, the final result is a blatant distortion. This selection of particular facts on the part of the historian may or may not be conscious. But allowing for all this, I still feel some histories impress me as more honest and comprehensive than others in their attempt to present the truth. In a sense, a layman, as against the professional historian, is helpless. He cannot personally check all the evidence, documentary and otherwise, for himself. If he is honest, he is (I hope) finally most influenced by the account that seems to him to make the whole process intelligible. I cannot say more than this. History is the realm of the temporal, and therefore of the relatively unimportant. It is for this reason that I think final religious problems cannot be solved on a historical basis. That is why, in the final analysis, I cannot accept historical and traditional evidence as more important than reason. I feel sure, for instance, that a man born on a remote island among people who have had no contact with outside culture and traditions should be able to save his soul. If this be admitted, it seems to prove all organized religious thinking to be unessential to salvation. Consider the generations on generations of primitives who have lived their lives quite unconscious of the existence of Christianity, Islam, Buddhism, or any other "ism." All this seems to be laboring the obvious, yet it has implications that seem to me habitually ignored among the devoted adherents of the major religions of the world.

However, let us return to a consideration of some of the particular problems we have been discussing. First infallibility: this question is essentially a historical one. I liked and was impressed by all you said on this subject. Yet frankly I must say that your interpretation is barely tenable. In effect you reduce the dogma of infallibility to your agreement with the popes. You rightly stress the condition that only when the pope speaks on a matter of faith or morals is his utterance to be accepted as infallible. But you interpret this in a private sense insofar as you say that what you happen to agree with is a question of faith or morals. What you disagree with you reject on the ground that it is merely a private opinion of a particular pope. I will only take a few examples for examination to show you what I mean.

You believe salvation to be possible outside the Church. So do certain Church theologians. So, I know, in practice do the majority of thinking Roman Catholics. Nevertheless, in discussing Roman Catholic doctrine I am discussing not your private opinions but the officially enunciated dogma of the Church as laid down by Ecumenical Councils, Papal Bulls, Proclamations, etc. *You* and the particular theologians you quote (and some of your friends), I do not dispute, believe a man may be saved outside the Church. Yet the Church most decidedly teaches that a man *cannot be saved* unless he accepts the Catholic Faith. I cannot withdraw a word I said in this connection. I *know* the Roman Catholic church officially teaches in effect the damnation of those outside the Faith. I quoted to you in my last letter an article of the Tridentine Profession *of Faith*. I should have thought the quotation finally settled the question beyond any shadow of doubt. I quote again: "I believe in... this true Catholic Faith *without which* [my emphasis] no one can be in a state of salvation." Your reply to this is, "this I take to be an expression of the private opinion of Pius IV. It is not a question of faith or morals." That is your private opinion, but it is not the opinion of your Church.

These words are taken from the Bull of Pius IV, 1564. It was issued after the Council of Trent, to be publicly recited by all bishops and clergy *with their congregations* as a profession of *faith*. It is an official creed of the Church. In fact, it is the creed that distinguishes the Roman Catholic form of Christian doctrine from all others. Other churches accept the Apostles' Creed—the Athanasian Creed. But this is the distinctive Roman Catholic Creed *imposed to this day on all converts to Roman Catholicism*. This cannot be denied. It is this article in this creed that made me clearly understand that I could no longer honestly accept the Roman Catholic Faith. It is this creed that has prevented any possibility of the re-uniting of Christendom in the last four centuries. As you probably know, since the time when the Lutheran Protestant philosopher Leibniz approached the Church with proposals for discussions with a view to re-uniting the Christian churches, Reformed churches have many times sought a reunion. They have always been told, without one exception up to the present day, that the first condition of reunion was the acceptance of this creed. This no honest historian can deny.

As this is so, how can you, or the theologian you quote, possibly claim that this article is not a question of faith and morals? Numberless Christians willing to go a very long way to meet the Church have been turned back because they could not in honesty accept this article (it is not the only one, but is sufficient for our purpose here). These Christians and would-be converts have always had it insisted to them that this *was* a matter of "faith" to be accepted by decree of the pope.

Now read the article once more. What does it plainly say? I have read the dishonest interpretations of it. They disgust me. The words have a plain meaning and are obviously meant to have a plain meaning. Let us be honest enough to accept that meaning.

Now you will perhaps then ask why the Hierarchy in England did not condemn the obviously heretical opinion of Sheed: "A man who does not accept the Catholic church may be saved, that is, he may enter heaven."

I can only here point to the truly detestable duplicity of the Roman Church on such matters in modern times. They cannot now call in the Inquisition. They have to tread warily. They can excommunicate (and that is a cruel enough punishment for men who believe their salvation depends on communion with the Church), but even here they have to be careful. If they draw too much attention to these doctrines they may find that they have to push half their members out of the Church. Excommunicating people attracts attention to them and to the doctrines they dispute. The truth is that a modern Roman Catholic has to force the issue, as did noble Döllinger at the Vatican Council. They have to make it impossible for the Church to ignore them before the position can be clarified on a certain issue by excommunication.

As a practicing and honest Catholic today there is only one way of getting a clear ruling on the above article of faith. I would ask of my bishop that he supply me with a clear-cut rejection of the above article of the Tridentine Profession of Faith—with the clear-cut permission to send on his rejection to the cardinal for affirmation; and from the cardinal in turn a clear-cut permission to bring his rejection to the notice of the pope. Nothing else would satisfy me on this score, as I do not think, from my experience of Roman Catholic "apologetics," that any other action would clear the humbug out of the way. Of course I know in fact that if I made it impossible for them to ignore me they would be forced to publicly excommunicate me. These are hard words; it doesn't give me pleasure to write them. But I know now that you trust me to be honest in saying what I really think. I say also that Sheed would have been burnt at the stake if he had written that in centuries when his Church had the power to silence him. Men, many men, were burnt for far less.

This brings us to the Inquisition again. The attempts of the Church to evade responsibility for the Inquisition are utterly dishonest. You produce their edited version of history in everything you write. The Inquisition in its entirety lasted from at least the sixth century to the nineteenth. It was not until 1814 that the Papacy abolished, under civil pressure, the right to torture in the tribunals of the Inquisition. The Inquisition is simply a name for ecclesiastical jurisdiction and courts. It was not confined to Spain but was present wherever the Church had legal power. Can you absolve the government of a country from responsibility for its system of administering justice? This is a fair and strict parallel. The activities of Innocent III in particular are of interest in connection with the development of the Inquisition. Pope Honorius III and Gregory IX: a study of their papacies is vital for a true appraisal of the nature of the Inquisition. In general it is a historic fact that in the worst centuries (13th, 14th, 15th) each individual inquisitor was appointed by the pope and could only be removed by the pope.

The Inquisition was simply the official legal machinery of the Church for dealing with heresy. It is one of the most abominable phenomena in history. There is an immense documentary evidence covering many of its activities. The popes were directly involved again and again in the arrangements of its organization. If you read H.C. Lea's *History of the Inquisition* you will find it sickening and, alas!, convincing. And if you read the *Syllabus of Errors*, and think out all its implications, you will see that the Church has not changed her mind. You say the *Syllabus of Errors* is not a matter of faith and morals. This was just one of the points Döllinger made—that the dogma of infallibility would turn the *Syllabus of Errors* into an Infallible Pronouncement. The Council did not contradict him.

I honestly cannot see where a man has any room left to think for himself on any scientific, political, or social problem once he has inwardly accepted that Syllabus.

This brings me to another point. We have heard so much of this question of faith and morals insofar as it affects infallibility. We are told that certain pronouncements are *ex cathedra* and others are not—in private discussion. But consider that many honest men have refused to enter the Church, others have left it, over this question. Yet the Church has never issued a clear-cut list of

Papal utterances that are to be considered as infallible, and others that are not. This again is dishonesty. We are told Honorius I was not speaking on a question of faith when he adopted the formula of Ecthesis in his attempt to reconcile the Monothelites. Yet the Sixth Ecumenical Council considered it to be so, and declared him a heretic; they were obviously laboring under no delusions about infallibility. As this dogma of Honorius I considered the nature of Christ in his relation to God, it is hard to understand how it could be anything but a matter of faith.

This is where we come to the Vatican Council. You must have read an extraordinarily well expurgated account of these proceedings if Döllinger was not mentioned. It would be analogous to a history of the Second World War with Churchill left out. One may not approve of Churchill, but it is hard to imagine a history of the war that omitted all mention of him as being truthful. You say that your "main impression" from your account of the Vatican Council proceedings was that the great objection to the dogma lay in the contention that the time was not opportune. No doubt your account was expressly intended to create such an impression. Nevertheless it is a sheer falsification. To say the dogma had always been implicitly held by the Church is another falsehood. The Council of Chalcedon and the Sixth Ecumenical Council sufficiently dispose of such a fantastic claim.

Again, your treatment of the Reformation. I admit that you mention some of the reasons for it. But you only mention the ones it suits Church histories to notice. There were other no less cogent reasons far less complimentary to the Church, which was corrupt to an almost unbelievable degree at that time.

Well Pat, you see now how it is between us! I won't go on like this, and I won't return to the subject. But I honestly believe your historical judgement is heavily biased in favor of the Church, to the extent that I hardly recognize your history as history. I do not believe I am wrong if I say this view of history you have is almost entirely drawn from Roman Catholic histories and sources. Here the accused is his own witness and judge. No contrary evidence is allowed.

You may ask, "Even if it be granted that all this is true, what of it?" I would say in answer that it does not lead me to believe the Church is utterly false, but it leads me to believe the Church should *publicly and unmistakably repent* of her past sins, and promise, with the grace of God, to try to evade such sins in the future. If she did this she might easily become the most powerful religious force in the world of the future. But will she?

Well, this seems an ungracious return for your letter. But you will see that in all this we disagree on the subject of history, church history in particular. We simply see it in different lights. But, this apart, I say unreservedly (except for one or two reservations, which I'll go into later) that I loved your letter and agreed with most of what you had to say, especially when you speak of what you yourself believe and not of what you consider that the Church expects you to believe. I liked particularly what you said about *Genesis*, and about evolution. I agree that you should be free to think in this way, imaginatively and poetically. But others too should be free to see it in their way, which the *Syllabus of Errors* does not allow. You must see that deciding to treat some parts of the Bible literally and others symbolically raises difficult problems.

Regarding evolution. You say there must be doubt about any theory. You are right. But that principle applies to all theories, theological as well as scientific. Again, the *Syllabus of Errors* does not allow this, nor does the whole structure of Roman Catholic dogmatism. I feel you do not realize how intolerant this dogmatism is. It is now, in modern expositions, far more tolerant than it used to be. But it is only so under extreme pressure from outside.

You misunderstand my assertion that "no scholar outside the Church can accept the New Testament as true." If I wrote it like that I was wrong, but I think the context should have indicated that I meant literally and factually and completely true in the sense the Church claims it to be. I agree that great numbers of people think it is true in quite another sense, including myself.

Now we must glance in the direction of hell again, and the possibility of *eternal* damnation. You will find my account earlier in this letter of Martensen's criticism of Boehme, which is of some interest in this connection. Let me add, before tackling this subject again, that I realize I am in this respect outside the main stream of Christian tradition, both inside and outside the Roman Church. Some of the Christian thinkers I most respect and have learnt most from, like Kierkegaard and Boehme, accept this belief. To me it lies like a blight across most Christian thought. I think Christianity is destined to pass beyond it. To me it makes nonsense of the doctrine of the eternal image of God in man. You say some souls are "too heavy"; and that is in effect what most other defenders of the doctrine of eternal hell say. Who made these souls "too heavy?" Everything comes from God. *God is responsible*. I do not think the doctrine of free will can be interpreted in the sense that the impossible becomes possible. I went into this as well as I am able in my last letter. The most I could agree to is that certain souls drop out of existence into non-being. This may be so. I remember that all these ideas are theories and that, as you point out, there is always some element of doubt. Nevertheless, Orthodox Christianity teaches that each soul is created in the eternal image of God and is therefore indestructible. The suggestion that no human souls are in hell does not alter the essential nature of the doctrine. *Any soul*—human, angelic, or of any other kind of being unknown to us; even one soul (Lucifer only, let us suppose)—in an eternal hell would constitute a judgement of failure on all the other beatified souls in creation. This I believe without any qualification. It may be we have to accept such a failure and judgement. I don't know. But it makes nonsense of the whole idea of Christianity that God is Love, is All Powerful, and wills to redeem the whole creation. If it is true that one soul is damned, then Christianity is a false religion, whether viewed mythologically or in any other way. I have never understood how the majority of Christians cannot see this. The number of souls damned cannot make the slightest difference.

My objection to hell is best put thus, briefly: hell is separation from God. Separation from God is non-existence. Nothing can exist apart from God.

Nevertheless, Roman Catholic theology as it stands, and in spite of the reassurances of individual Roman Catholics, implies the certain damnation of numberless beings. Leaving out of consideration all non-Catholics, I cannot forget that I had it drummed into my head for years as a child that if I failed to go to Mass on Sunday through my own fault, and died unrepentant, I would go to hell for all eternity! I have my catechism here and can easily find the particular question and answer. How many Catholics must be damned in this way alone? It is mere sophistry to pretend that they all may have made death-bed repentances. I have not myself been to Mass for years. I will not repent the fact because I feel no need to. In my mind it has nothing whatever to do with the possibility of my eternal salvation. You say a mortal sin is a great rarity. That is your private humanity and compassion speaking. On Roman Catholic dogma, as it stands at present, it can only be sophistry to pretend that it can be anything but common. If you say God can in every single case save each soul by a special act of grace, then you, to my mind, reduce the dogma to an absurdity. It ceases to have meaning. Kierkegaard, Boehme, Simone Weil (and of course the great majority of Christian thinkers)—all seem to view despair as a deadly sin. Once hope dies, salvation is no longer possible. I cannot fathom this notion; it makes a mockery of the power and love of God—and "God is not mocked." We are informed, on what authority or process of reasoning I do not know (I have not discovered it after years of reading and searching), that after death the soul cannot change the direction of its will. Why we should believe this I don't know. The great religions of the East teach the contrary. In my thought the essential will in a man, considered as an immortal being created as the image of God, is identical with the will of God. A man can only, in the end, experience the destiny God wills for him. He is in essence an expression of the freedom of God. Cannot you see the contradiction? St. Thomas Aquinas says that even the power of God cannot sustain a contradiction. In a sense, true contradictions are an absolute impossibility—to admit them reduces all our thought to nonsense. I grant that you have the majority of Christians, and most of the ones with undoubtedly great minds, on your side. However, we must remember that Christianity, viewed in its own understanding of itself, came into a fallen world where men had lost the truth and even, to a large degree, the capacity to understand it. If this be so, it is easy to believe that it may take humanity many thousands of years to develop a full understanding of Christianity.

It is fantastic to assume that men have from the beginning understood the full content and implications of Christ's message. Why should we presume fallen man to be immediately capable of understanding the Word of God?: Roman Catholicism, after nineteen hundred years, declares itself to be still eliciting dogma from Scripture. This seems to me an entirely acceptable idea; but on what grounds do they presume that they have never made any mistakes? This claim is based entirely on one passage, of doubtful authenticity, in the New Testament ("Thou art Peter..."), and on an even more doubtful interpretation of it. It seems to me the Church forgets it is composed of fallen men. If only the Church would honestly declare that the message of God is, in a sense, beyond the easy understanding of men; that it has made mistakes; that it repents of them and hopes to learn from them; that new generations armed with the acquired insight of the past generations might rise to new insights—what vast increase of rightful spiritual authority would it not then acquire? The very heart of Christianity is the doctrine of the forgiveness of sins, yet the great Christian Church trembles to trust to this truth. It is just as stubborn as any sinful man in not admitting its sins, yet until it repents them it cannot be forgiven them. This is only to apply fairly to the Church itself the truths it teaches to its individual members. Like a sinful man too the Church imagines that all criticism rises from hatred. This is not true. Numberless Christians who loved the Church (and, because they loved it, declared to it its errors), were abominably tortured to death with the full consent of the highest authorities of the Church. This is the truth. How sad for Christians to find their Church, betraying the spirit of Jesus and acting like the high priests of old, playing the worldly part of Anti-Christ. This is a terrible indictment. I believe it cannot be denied. My message to the Church, the message of an anonymous unknown who has yet seen a little way into the truth of things, is "Repent and be saved!" But the Church is proud, and stubborn, and self-righteous, and, it seems, far above listening to simple words of simple advice. You write, Pat, as though it has been a pleasure, a kind of childish naughtiness, for Christians to criticize their Church. This has no doubt been so in many cases. Things are very mixed up. But sympathetic love and insight would show you the incredible heroism of all the nameless ones who could, in the atmosphere of the Middle Ages, robbed of all the comforts of their religion, often (they were human) fearing that they had after all made a mistake and were perhaps accursed by God as well as man, dare to criticize their Church (and dare thereby death by torture) in the name of Truth. Centuries afterwards, it is easy to misunderstand. They were misunderstood in their own time, and in aftertimes. Their spirits were full of the worst of all anguishes: the fear that they were after all mistaken, that in human limitation they were casting away their lives for nothing, or in a blasphemous criticism of the Church of God. It strikes the darkest religious horror into the mind to contemplate the way the Church of Christ treated these people. It re-crucified Christ in them, in the name of Christ. I am on the side of these men, but that is not to claim I imagine I am made of the same stuff. In fact and truth my worst inward affliction has been cowardice—physical, moral, intellectual, spiritual. This can produce suffering in life that more courageously constituted people little dream of. But perhaps because I am a coward I can understand the anguish of these burnt, broken, strangled, "questioned" ones. Many of them were perhaps frightened too. Frightened of life, of death, of pain, of God. Yet they went to death in circumstances too pitiful to contemplate without tears. Something God-like (a new incarnation in truth, in each case) entered into them and they were able to venture far out as witnesses for the truth. These silent witnesses, tortured in thousands, generation after generation (this is but the literal truth) until their suffering cried to God for vengeance, achieved for us the more tolerant societies in which we live. They died for us. If they are in hell, then I will stay with them. The God who could cast such beings into hell is but a blasphemous caricature of a God. But I believe, I know, that in them God suffered, and that the force that tortured them was Anti-Christ. This isn't a pretty world. Is the Church possessed by a devil, that it cannot repent? What unspeakably evil twist has entered its thought that it cannot or will not see what it has done? The talk (like Chesterton's facile glibness and thoughtlessness) on this subject by believing Catholics, when they so easily absolve themselves and their Church of responsibility in these matters, is unutterably, cowardly, vile; *it smells of damnation*—but not, thank God, of eternal damnation.

Your question about God creating weights too heavy for Him to lift is an easy levity. Try rather to penetrate into the meaning of what we so lightly discuss as eternal damnation in a being created, in the image of God, for immortality. Do this, and you will soon feel the God within you utterly rejecting such a conception as a ghastly reflection of the evil in you, which, in essence, is but the emptiness, the poverty, the paltriness of spirit trying to empty itself of God. But it cannot empty itself of God eternally. The experiment is too painful to endure for more than an instant. God cannot empty Himself of Himself, and this constitutes our salvation. It seems to me that only a being that is a becoming, hardly as yet emerged from the not-being of God, can conjure up such fantasies as the possibility of emptying itself of God—that is, of emptying itself of itself. Man, a creature just emerging slowly and with infinite pain and difficulty from the not-being of God towards the being of God, indulges in fantasies conjured up out of his own nothingness.

I think that it is a tragic deprivation for a man to be forced to develop his religious life outside the tradition of his own culture. If he is truly developing in a religious sense, it is like depriving a runner of air to breathe. Take Achilles "swift of foot," afflict him with asthma, and you have the image of the religiously developing man deprived of the help and nourishment of his own religious culture. This kindly operation Churches perform when they excommunicate, or declare *anathema* those who breathe a word of judgement upon them. Or when they so mark time, and grow rigid and heavy in their dogmatic development, that many men feel suffocated in them and are forced to seek air, but a draught of pure air, in some alien religious tradition. Great numbers of such men have been so seeking a breath of air in Europe during these last centuries. It is their salvation that they find air in Taoism or Hinduism or Buddhism, or solitary mysticism; but they do not deceive themselves that their substitute atmosphere is an adequate replacement. It is but the best thing they can do. Their last resource. To live they have to breathe. The European races are living through a period of affliction in many ways, and not least through a period of religious affliction. Unhappily too they are infecting other civilizations with their spiritual disease.

But all this is not an accusation thrown at you. It is rather a quite inarticulate attempt at explanation. I loved your letter. The you in it I rejoice in. Your noble description of what the Church means to you moved me to acceptance. We all have separately to work out our salvation in fear and trembling. St. Paul knew what it was to be robbed of certainty in religious faith. Yet perhaps we may believe that to move beyond certainty is to move ultimately to higher certainties. One thing at least is certain—death. All else is uncertain. Theodore Powys, the most religious and the gentlest and the profoundest man I have known, said in his *Soliloquies of a Hermit*, "A belief is too easy a road to God." He also said to Mary and I one of the last times we saw him that "every prayer is a cry for help." He was a man afflicted in a terrible sense—the modern world in general is too superficial to even suspect the possibilities of such affliction. His life was a deepening movement into solitude of spirit. He spoke with a kind of whimsical savagery of his impending death—"obliteration" was the word that came to his lips. Well! now he is "obliterated," and a light has gone out of this world. The means of obliteration was a cancer in the rectum. A notice in the *Times* facilely called him a pagan. There is a fine stench under the ground in Mappowder churchyard. But is Theodore? Theodore is a name; it means "a gift from God." What does all this mean? There must be meaning in it. But how arrive at that meaning? Is it so easy?

In saying that your vision of the Church won my acceptance, I mean that I believe your vision is true and good. I think my vision is also true... and evil? Both visions are truth. Perhaps I see the invisible Church and you the visible, or the other way round. I don't know. I know that both visions are in some sense true. I feel at present that it is my destiny to be outside the Church, whatever that may mean for my eternal salvation. And yours to remain inside the Church. But I here and now, as my last word in these letters, cancel all prophecies I may have made on any subject. I am no prophet.

I am grateful to you for sharing your thoughts with me and don't believe I am unsympathetic. I have, I have found out, a complicated mind, and it has not been always easy for me. When I write letters of this kind my pen often runs away with me, and I find frequently that I have been unkind. I have only been able to write to or talk to very very few people as I do to you. It is a happiness to me to think of you walking "my" hills that I so loved and feeling on them the bliss (no other word will answer) of the awakening spirit, and its sorrow. Life is joy and suffering, suffering and joy. They cannot be disentangled. I feel suspicious of certainties. I suspect all certainties in this life are premature certainties. Be compassionate, strive not to be afraid, adventure freely, this I would like to claim as my wisdom; only I have not the right to claim it in practice.

With much love,
Gerard

P.S.

15 Jan. On re-reading your letter other points crop up that I haven't dealt with properly. As usual, they are historical. It is the historical that divides us. Here are a few more remarks about myth. First, although some scholars, and very fine ones too, have believed the New Testament to be entirely mythical, I do not. I think other historians have fairly revealed difficulties in this view that the "mythicists" do not fully meet. I say this emphatically because in this last letter of yours you seem to imply that I accept the mythical theory completely. However I do not agree that your point about martyrs at Rome so soon after the Crucifixion destroys the myth hypothesis. I have seen the process of myth-making, religious myth-making, going on in this country in the last two years. Jomo Kenyatta is believed by most of the Kikuyu to be a divine savior. The whole esoteric side of Mau-Mau, insofar as it has become known, is revealed, as a tribal religion of redemption, by a savior—Kenyatta. Rituals, oaths, ceremonies, prayers, hymns, are addressed to Kenyatta. Christian prayers and hymns and ideas are debased and parodied, and center round Kenyatta. That Kenyatta is imprisoned and persecuted increases his prestige as a martyr-savior. The whole thing seems to be a curious perversion and hotch-potch of primitive Christian ideas and ancient tribal beliefs and customs. It is this religious aspect

of Mau-Mau that makes it so difficult to deal with, and which is so little understood outside this country. Putting the Bible into the hands of primitives can have odd results. Remember, it was their only printed literature for many years. Add to this the fact that most of their later printed literature is subversive politically, as well as the whole complex of economic and social problems attendant on the disintegration of their old tribal culture under modern European pressures, and you have Mau-Mau. However, my point is that here we see the myth-making faculty in full swing among a primitive, almost illiterate, people. Already many martyrs are dying for Kenyatta. Once a Kikuyu takes the necessary oaths and is a member of this tribal Church he quite deliberately takes upon himself the fact that he automatically is under sentence of death by the government, just as an early Christian did under the Roman government. Remember too that the Roman government considered the Christians to constitute a secret, subversive political movement. The motives of the Roman persecutions were essentially political. The Romans were widely tolerant of religions—if they thought them harmless politically. Here you have a clear case of martyrs dying for a myth centered around a tribal prophet in modern times, when so much so powerfully militates against all such processes. It is true historically that people have always been ready to die for religious myths, and that such myths can crystallize around some spiritual leader or prophet with great speed. The Christian claim that the blood of martyrs is an evidence of the divinity of Jesus would establish equally the divinity of many others. The founder of the Bahai religion, the Persian Mirza Ali Mohammed, was executed in Teheran in 1850. Within two years, by 1852, thirty of his disciples had suffered death by atrocious torture as witnesses for "the Bab"! Here of course there was no claim on the part of the Bab or his disciples that he was a divinity. Nevertheless, within two years after his death we find people willingly dying for his faith. And today his movement has become a world-wide religion, with adherents among Christians, Moslems, Hindus, Buddhists, and free-thinkers. He said he was the prophet of a new world religion that embraced the truth of all previous historical religions. For this he was martyred by the Islamic orthodoxy of Persia. There are many other examples in the ancient world, in the medieval world, and in the modern world—both East and West. There seems no reason to doubt that a similar process was at work among the earliest Christians. There have been countless martyrs and witnesses for the truth quite outside Christianity. Socrates willingly died for the truth within him.

The truth about the New Testament probably lies in some combination of the mythical and real. Jesus did live, was a powerful and great religious teacher, was possibly what the Hindus believe him to be—an avatar. But there is little doubt that large legendary concretions have also collected around his name and teaching as presented in the New Testament. No other hypothesis can adequately account for the numerous parallels between the New Testament and other ancient scriptures (some of which precede it). And as for the historical fact, as Frazer in his Adonis section of *The Golden Bough* has clearly brought out, the whole religious complex of ideas of the New Testament—the Savior, His Death, His Resurrection, His Body and Blood, the Atonement, the Sacramental element, Sons of God sacrificed for men, the related legends of Attis and Osiris, the Eucharist—saturated the ancient cultures of the Mediterranean world long before the birth of Christ, especially in all the countries immediately around Palestine. The parallels often extend to the most unlikely details. The evidence that the New Testament is at least partly a reflection of these myths is overwhelming. What more natural than that men should seek to explain the astonishing character, life, and death of Jesus in religious terms long familiar to them, terms that were indeed part of their very mental make-up. It must be conceded and remembered that Christianity was in the main rejected by the Jews and accepted by the Gentiles, and that these mythic elements are largely non-Jewish. For the most part they reflect the religious mentality of the Gentiles; that is, of most of the eastern Mediterranean peoples of that age.

A few more words on the Roman Catholic claim so often implied in your letters: that Roman Catholic historians are necessarily the most trustworthy sources in matters connected with Church history. They have the only adequate sources, it is claimed. This is quite untenable. This has been the method employed in the attempt of the Church to prevent a true revelation of her history. But historians have immense resources for research in methods and directions that the Church cannot interfere with. Try to get and read carefully, with an open mind, some such great historical works as Ranke's *History of the Popes* or Harnack's *History of Dogma* or Lea's *History of the Inquisition*, and you will soon be convinced of this. Before these monumental histories appeared, we were told that only Church historians could present a fair, detailed account of their subjects. Well, these histories adequately refuted that claim and also revealed much that the Church would prefer to forget. And then, after a decent interval, we find Church historians quoting these men as authorities on the very subjects we were originally told they could not possibly deal with. Of course the Church historians take notice of, and quote from these men, facts that they have no objection to remembering—the rest they ignore. As the secular historians had striven to tell the truth, naturally much that they had to say was favorable to the Church and was welcomed by her. It is true that many of the "defenses" used by Church thinkers in many fields of thought were first thought out for her by secular thinkers who were anathema to her.

It is in the field of history that modern European thought has most revolutionized our thought. Not only Christianity, but the other great world-religions as well, have been subjected to a similar searching. They too have produced similar untenable arguments in their effort to preserve the traditional belief quite unchanged. There is not a single argument Christianity can use that cannot be used, and has been used, to defend the other religions. Why the historic religions should use so much energy to defend untenable positions can only be explained by realizing that the human mind is intensely conservative and stubborn to the emergence of truth. Christianity has always said this, but not seen that it applied to Christian thought as well as to the thought of other religions, and to secular thought. European free-thinking scholarship has done a tremendous amount, for example, in revealing to the Hindus the historical basis of their scriptures. Conservative Hindus claimed that Europeans from an alien culture, and in an age three to four thousand years afterwards, could not possibly discover more than was already known. Nevertheless, most Hindus now accept the results of this research, and the acceptance is by no means all a loss to them. Nor would it be so for Roman Catholics.

It is understandable that religious people fear to lose what is precious to them in the process of criticism. Yet they should strive to overcome this fear. If their love is for the truth, and if this constitutes the essential religious attitude, then they should have faith that honest criticism can in the end only elicit truth more clearly.

The True Catholic Church is an Invisible Church made up of all men, of whatever time or place or attitude, who have honestly sought the truth in their lives. The claim of the Roman Church to be "catholic" is manifestly false. The catechism says: "The Church is catholic or universal because she subsists in all ages, teaches all nations, and is the one Ark of Salvation for all." This is true, but it is an obviously false claim to apply it to the Roman Church. It can only apply to the "Invisible Church of those who seek the Truth and suffer for it." The Roman Church has often been in antagonism to the True Catholic Church. This does not mean that countless individual Roman Catholics, particularly the humble ones, have not been members of the True Catholic Church. They have, and so have even greater numbers of men who have never heard of the Roman Church, and others who have lived in antagonism to that Church. An atheist can be a member of this True Catholic Church if he honestly seeks the truth, as he usually does. A man becomes a member of this Church merely by "seeking the Truth." It is a Church of Seekers; it has subsisted truly in all ages, among all peoples, in all lands. It is the True Church; it is the Church that is our Ark of Salvation. The historic Churches are only branches of it, or members that often attack the parent body, not realizing they attack that which has brought them into being: the Search for Truth.

In this True Catholic Church you are a member, and I am a member, insofar as we honestly seek the truth. So are your Plymouth Brethren, so is old Chuang

Tzu. So is Giordano Bruno being burnt at the stake by the Inquisitors; so are the Inquisitors who tried him; so is some old stone age man, a pygmy in the Ituri forest, a follower of Kenyatta who has murdered his own son; so is a Red Indian alone with his Great White Spirit; an Indian "untouchable," his head bent, like Boehme's, over his leather; or the people of Herat slaughtered by Genghis Khan; or Genghis Khan himself.

One mixes up with odd church-fellows in this Invisible Universal Church. In fact, it is made up of all the men who have ever risen out of the dust of this planet. They have, one must admit, searched often in strange, unlikely places, and have not been too scrupulous over their treatment of their fellow men in the process insofar as the search has been a search carried on by barbarians (and this barbarism is reflected in the religious dogmas they have evolved)—but seekers have they all been. The most common mistake they have made is to imagine that they had found truth long before they had, to get the untruthful and childish notion in their heads that what they had found was the truth, and what other people found was rubbish—and on the strength of this to persecute them. The very rise of life into consciousness, the spiritual domination of billions of dancing atoms into the form of a human mind—this process is itself part of the search for truth, it is spirit seeking to realize itself, to rise from ignorance, *avidya*, non-being, into truth, *vidya*, being. To be alive is an expression of the fact that in you the search for truth is being carried on. A single hydrogen atom, if it truly exists (that is, if it is in being), is a search for truth. This is expressed by the fact that it exists. Untruth, ignorance, the dark: this is utter non-being; Truth, light: this is the summit of Being. All Becomings—from electrons, through men, to stars and angels—are creatures on the road to Truth.

If you in truth see this Church of Truth arising into Being as the eternal fact at the heart of the Roman Church, then it is indeed the True Church. But this involves clearly recognizing the same for other Churches, and also recognizing that all historic Churches in the World of Becoming are a large mixture of untruth retarding the growth of the Truth. And working from within your Church to purify it, to realize in it its central truth—that is an expression of the eternal True Church. When all Churches, historic partial embodiments of Truth, have achieved their task, they will find that they are all members of the True Catholic Church; and that will be the Day of Salvation. This I have expressed in a confused way, yet I feel you will understand it.

Theodore Powys said: "the soul is the waiting silence in us that is free." This silent witness within us, uncomplicated in the storm of the world-flow, this is the Atman of the Hindus, which is identical with Brahman. At odd moments in our lives we all, "as through a glass darkly," realize the presence of this witness. To attain peace is to become continuously conscious of this presence. This witness, Theodore says, is "waiting"; waiting for what? For the Consummation of All Things—the Unutterable Glory of the Kingdom of God. We all share this sense of still waiting (and below even the waiting, the still unwaiting), the motionless fathomless eternity of the Self that is identical with Brahman. This is the stillness of knowing at the center of the Cloud of Unknowing. When each spirit after death passes through hell—the image of the accumulated evil of its life—and drinks the waters of Lethe, the River of Forgetting, before its rebirth (as we see it shadowed forth, in the ancient mythologies, to our understanding), this silent witness remains a witness. It does not drink the dark waters of Lethe. It does not forget. Motionlessly poised in its still eternity, it remembers; and it reflects forward its remembrance into the next form of becoming, the next life. Here we have the explanation perhaps of that most mysterious fact of our spiritual experience, which Plato expressed by saying that all true knowledge is recollection. The spirit is healed of its wounds in the waters of Lethe, and it adventures, refreshed and strengthened, wrapped up in a cloud of forgetting, into its next existence. But the "waiting silence in us that is free" remains a silent witness. This is the man in us more ancient than the sun, more ancient than any of the revolving galaxies, more ancient than any of the universes that unimaginable ages ago rose and sank again into Brahman and "left not a wrack behind." And this ancient self in us lies in each particle of matter in the multitudinous universes; it is divided and yet not divided; it is the Eucharist, the real presence at the heart of all things; it is the Truth underlying the doctrine of the Real Presence. St. Thomas Aquinas, in 'A Sermon on the Body of our Lord,' says: "He gives us men for a refreshment the bread of angels. On the breaking of the Bread Thou art not broken, nor art Thou divided. Thou art eaten, but like the Burning Bush, Thou art not consumed."

This is the One in the Many, the Peace in the Conflict, the Life in the Death. A martyr broken on the wheel, or strangled, or burnt, or stoned, or crucified, is reduced to this: the Bread of Life. Foully mangled and smashed in his outward man, or reduced to a heap of ashes, the waiting silence in him that is free unwaitingly waits on. It is not mangled by the wheel, torn apart on the rack, burnt in the fire, or chopped up by the panga; nor is it strangled by the rope, or pierced by the bullet, or stupefied by vice, or forgotten out of existence by stupidity, or boredom, or madness.

To realize this essential self in us is infinitely the most precious and wonderful thing we can achieve; that is, to realize it in a continuous, unforgetting sense and not only momentarily, as most of us do. It is also the most precious gift we can give to others, to help them achieve it. Ancient civilizations were more intent on this task than in ministering to the outer man. Modern civilization is too much concerned with the outer covering of man's spirit. This is by no means an entirely wrong development: the ancients were perhaps too neglectful of the body, which is the visible manifestation of the presence of the spirit. However, I think we go too far in the other direction; we tend to be, or try to be, an empty outside. This empty outside we lovingly provide with comfort and ease, and are surprised then that, if we glance inwards, we see dark, neglected horror. We fill great mental hospitals with men who have glanced inwards once too often without the spiritual knowledge requisite to adventure into that dark inward confidently. It is more important to give a man the knowledge to enable him to enter into himself than to give him a loaf of bread. "Man does not live by bread alone." Nevertheless he needs bread too, and modern thought is right to stress the fact; but it is wrong to stress it at the expense of the Bread of Life.

I sense in you this conflict. I say that your first duty is to discover and realize yourself. You can only understand what your duty to your neighbor is when you know yourself. For your deepest self and his deepest self are one self. The main part of a man's duty to his neighbor is to leave him alone. The greatest privilege a man can have is to be left alone. This is freedom. It is almost nonexistent in the modern world. This is not callous self-regard and indifference to others. It is simply to give oneself—and them—the opportunity to realize oneself. We should provide simple food and clothing for ourselves. We should try to evolve an order of society in which it is possible, without soul-killing effort, for each man to provide himself, and those immediately dependent upon him, with the simplest, barest necessities. Our Church should simply utter the WORD. We have no duty, in an outward sense, beyond these simple duties to our neighbor. The rest lies with each individual man to become what he wills to become. It is his sacred privilege. He has an inward Mt. Everest to climb. He has an inward China Deep to plumb. He will need all his courage, all his intelligence, all his patience, all his energy of spirit, to achieve this inward task. Leave him to it. You can't help him until you have yourself performed your task—and that will keep you fully occupied. You cannot even utter the Word, except at second hand, until you have realized yourself. One man, Jesus, goes into the desert to pray for forty days and forty nights, and the history of the world is changed. One man, Buddha, sits under a tree for forty days and forty nights, and the history of the world is changed. Millions of other men bustle busily about for centuries, and things go on very much the same as before.

Listen in passive empty inwardness to the waiting silence that is free within you. Listen in obedience and deepening emptiness of waiting. *Become* the waiting silence that is free within you. You don't need to run to sea or flee to the desert—although that might help. When one is young, inexperienced, still tangled up in the demands of the temporal, it does help to flee to the desert, the physical outer desert. But it is dangerous. One needs to have already moved some degrees in an inward direction to even wish it, let alone do it. Move rather for short periods, lengthening them as you grow stronger, into the desert within you. Expect nothing. What you have to realize is, in a sense, nothing. Your task is to wait with the waiting silence within you that is free, to allow this silence to well up and flow out into the temporal. Don't be impatient, the very condition is still patience. You have a lifetime, if necessary an infinity of lifetimes, to realize your purpose. Wrap yourself up in mediocrity. You are not running for a prize in the temporal. You are waiting for a prize in the eternal. Be perfectly poised in your moments; though implicated in the temporal, be unimplicated. Be passive, be receptive. You cannot wrestle with a silence. The problem is to remain in the stillness while engaging in the temporal. It is the hardest task. The spirit gazes out at the same time as it gazes within. It gazes out from infinite depths at the phenomenal world of appearance. The world of appearance is also Brahman. The silence and light of the inner eternity flow into the spirit from the world of appearance, which is clothed in radiance. The silence and light of the inner eternity flow out from the spirit over the world of appearance. The difficulty is that the intellect arrives at understanding easily enough, but this intellectual understanding has to be translated into spiritual vision. The radiance of the waiting silence has to be "realized" and then allowed to flow forth to purify the vision. It has to be *allowed* to flow forth. It cannot be forced. In a sense, all spiritual growth is simply allowed to happen. We remove the hindrances, the clogging rubbish; that done (and that is hard enough), we can only *wait* for the growth to take place. Unless we have faith and patience we may believe we have landed ourselves in hell rather than heaven. This is because the growth takes place in darkness and suffering, yet this darkness and suffering we must not attempt to dispel. We cannot, if we will to succeed, jump up at this stage and visit the pub or go to the cinema. Yet we must be careful. If we feel our sanity imperiled we must move outward into daylight.

This threat to the balance of the mind does not in fact arise from the emptiness, from the still waiting. It rises from the lack of emptiness, the lack of relaxed waiting. We carry a tension of expectancy into the emptiness. This tension grows intolerable. The mistake is that we should have introduced the tension; tension is lack of poise, or, rather, lack of the poise that we have to attain here. There is a deeper eternal tension of waiting, but this invigorates and refreshes the mind. The maddening thing is to introduce a disguised temporal tension into the eternal, and to eternalize it—or to attempt to. If we make a mistake of this kind we must come to the surface quickly. In the beginning we should only take brief plunges, shallow dives; if we are to become leviathans swimming down into fathomless depths we should forget the image of the leviathan and think of ourselves rather as frogs—and later, as J.C.P. advocates, as newts, slowly sinking down through still clear water. But in all this the gaze of the spirit is directed outward; it sees the external world clothed in the radiance of the eternal as it slowly sinks away from it. As it sinks into its own eternity it perceives ever more clearly the white radiance of the outer eternity. In sinking from the world, it approaches it. Until the moment of death the phenomenal world appears (or should appear, if the movement can be maintained) in ever deeper brilliance and beauty. All this of course will inevitably be broken into, smashed up, fouled by eruptions of brute ugliness and pain surging up from within and without. The task is to retreat into the still waiting until the radiance re-flows to transfigure the temporal horror. The supreme achievement would be to retain this deepening radiance until it reaches its climax at the moment of death. We should strive to be conscious up to the moment of death, resting in the still eternity. If we can do this, many mystics in the East say, we can escape rebirth and enter the full peace of Brahman. If we can remain fully conscious in the still silent witness, we will save ourselves from drinking the waters of Lethe, and so from entering upon rebirth. It is perhaps for this reason that some men do not shrink from martyrdom: they can meet death as they choose rather than have it imposed on them by brute chance.

This inner mystical striving should not be allowed to turn into a retreat from the world. We have to transfigure the world in the radiance, not run away from it. Life should be greatly simplified, but this really is a concession to weakness. As we grow stronger we should be able to live full, complex, enriching lives while simultaneously deepening the inward movement. But the inward movement is the more important. The Inner transfigures the Outer. All moments of supreme value, of insight, beauty, love, joy, peace, are outflowings of the inner eternal world of spirit transfiguring the outer world. It is important to keep this in mind. Certain mystical schools have overstressed the inward journey. They turn right away from the external world. This is spiritual cowardice and desertion, and is probably a move into empty darkness without radiance. The true mystic darkness is radiant with light that transfigures the world. It does not desert it. Christ and Buddha did not turn away from the world. Nevertheless, beginners probably need an extremely simplified form of life, and long periods of physical solitude. We start to learn to play the piano with five-finger exercises. We cannot hope to play a Beethoven sonata at once. Most of us are too impatient. We feel the first stirring growth of the spirit in us and immediately try to force the pace. We hurt ourselves, and either enter a madhouse or retreat and try to forget all about it. Then entertainments, reading the paper, learning all-in wrestling, busying ourselves with our neighbor's business, gossip: these things become important activities to help us forget our failure. We are afraid to wait in patient persistence of spirit. It is painful. If we dodge suffering we cannot get far. We relapse into comfort and ease. And sometimes too put a bullet into our own brains. It is wise to spend time with the Chinese mystics; they instil a whimsical humor, a full detachment from our own efforts that is the saving grace in perilous moments. True humor toward oneself is the mark of maturity of spirit. Nietzsche says the Spirit of Gravity is the devil, and he is right. It certainly plays the devil with us if we indulge it too far. A humorous gravity is healthy; a grave gravity is a deadly spiritual disease. We have to learn to laugh at ourselves and try again. We should see our spiritual efforts in a ludicrous light. Man is the most spiritually advanced creature we know—he is also the laughing animal. When a man laughs after a tragedy to himself or after beholding one in another, we say "how hard-hearted." That is a shallow judgement. He is more probably recovering his balance. In man, spirit emerges to the prospect of the eternal. Humor is essentially the eternal in man. Humor is the refusal to take the temporal too seriously. Humor is eternity's own refusal to take itself too seriously. In the dog, which is the animal spiritually most akin to man, we find glimmerings of humor. We say despair is lack of the eternal. Despair is also lack of humor. Montaigne was a maturer spirit than Calvin. Rabelais than Pascal. In our day, Charlie Chaplin has helped to save more souls than Karl Barth. The inquisitors, the persecutors, the Pharisees—these are the grave, humorless men. Calvin couldn't relax into a chuckle at his own spiritual antics, so he had Servetus put to death. We read of soldiers with ghastly wounds dying with a joke on their lips. We are told of murderers about to be executed laughing with their executioners. So the eternal laughs at the grotesquerie of the temporal. A man who smiles at the horrors of his temporal existence so identifies himself with the eternal. When we are edging along under spiritual affliction it will go hard with us if we can't enjoy Chaplin in a film, or the humor of our friends in the pub. When my African workers had taken the Mau-Mau oath they could not laugh, as long as they were under its power. To get them to laugh, or smile ruefully, was to rescue them from the power of the spirit of gravity. You can't crack a joke with the Mau-Mau. Chief Elind, confronting hundreds of grave Kikuyu who had taken the Mau-Mau oath, knew he had won when he got them to laugh. The moment they laughed, the perspective of the eternal was re-emerging in them. Chesterton is a safer spiritual guide than Newman. William Blake takes us much farther than Cowper. The men who turn from the world to plunge ever deeper into the dark eternity have no sense of humor. They take their salvation too seriously.

We may hope with a smile that after spending long aeons gravely plunging into their dark eternity they may at last see the joke, and with a chuckle at their own absurdity re-emerge to the surface to start their essential task of transfiguring the world in the light of the radiant eternity.

Two extraordinarily good modern stories illustrate this truth. Both are mystical treatises of a very profound kind disguised as novels. In *Jurgen: A*

Comedy of Justice by James B. Cabell, one of the most excellent of modern books, the radiant light of the eternal, in the form of a world-deep ironic humor, shines gloriously from every page. We learn profound truths in a delightful and happy way. In *A Voyage to Arcturus* by David Lindsay, one of the most pessimistic but most remarkable of modern books, the light of the eternal is reduced to an unthinkably tiny spark hidden behind a heavy brutal mask. Unless his reader is both sturdy and humorous, Lindsay reduces him to a state of spiritual terror and despair. Both authors are religiously evolving men, but Cabell's humor takes him farther and makes him the surer signpost. This is not to deny in any way the moving quality and honesty and insight of Lindsay's story. His vision is true and valuable, but a strain of humor would have shone through his story like a joyful light. If you come across these two books you will find it an interesting experiment to read them together. Both are very well worth reading. You will treasure *Jurgen* for the rest of your life, and feel obscurely uneasy whenever you remember Lindsay's story.

A vein of humor would have saved the Vatican Council from its grave enunciation of an absurdity, and saved the day for Döllinger. A large infusion of humor—that is, of the eternal perspective—is now needed in the Roman Catholic hierarchy if it is ever to straighten out its dogmatic system. As it is, one can only accept it by laughing at it. How Rabelais would have loved the spectacle of the Vatican Council! It would have drawn many a deep chuckle from him. He would certainly have taken his giants along to attend the Council and delighted us with many an extra chapter to his great book. Could he have resisted getting Pantagruel and Panurge and Friar John to take along Pius IX, with his Central Commission of docile cardinals, to visit the Oracle of the Holy Bottle and be advised (and good advice it would have been) by the High Priestess Bacbec? "All things tend to their end"—even the results in dogma of a college of humorless cardinals, not to mention the life-illusion of a humorless pope!

Humor persuades us to take our life and our illusions lightly. It also persuades us to treat them with whimsical respect. The life-illusion is a reflection of the eternal image of the self. Humor treats eternity with respect, but not excessive respect. Eternity without humor is the dull, heavy, inward-turned, grave eternity of men like Calvin. Eternity with humor is the infinitely light, free, outward-turned, unserious eternity of men like Rabelais. Humor blows up the pretentious balloon of the Spirit of Gravity until it bursts into laughter. The power of humor is shown by the fact that it is now the only thing left that can change Roman Catholic dogma, and yet treat it with respect. No other power in heaven or earth, it seems, can have any effect. Theological differences that men after the Middle Ages tried to solve by years of bloodshed and torture, and that reduced Europe to a shambles, could have been resolved in a few hours if a sense of humor had been allowed some say in the proceedings.

Well! I must have enough humor to bring this long rigmarole to an end with the admission that chatterboxes rarely solve difficult problems. But sometimes it is better to laugh away a difficulty than gravely perpetuate it. Here ends the Postscript.

P.S.

I spend tomorrow in the forest with the police. I always enjoy these days even though I suppose I may one day have to shoot a man. I have thought about this and think it is a necessity.

The Beale Farm
18 March 1954

My dear Pat,

Thanks for your very good letter. This is an answer in a great hurry—contrary to all my life principles, I seem always to be in a hurry these days.

Here are a few brief remarks on your letter. D'Arcy strikes me as a bloody humbug and a man who has never suffered. I know this is probably unjust and untrue, but he strikes me that way. That is not to deny that he has in many ways a fine mind and wide-ranging intelligence. I have read only one of his works, which was *The Mind and Heart of Love*. There is much that is excellent in it, and yet it left me feeling alienated. But I must admit most Roman Catholic thinkers affect me that way. More to the point: the passage you quote regarding hell is abominable, tenth-rate thinking; it is complacent, and reveals an invincible incapacity to pay attention to or to understand the spiritual and intellectual objections to the notion of hell. The tradition of his Church teaches eternal damnation for many, and that is enough for him. He has to produce some kind of defense, however feeble and cowardly and *self-deceiving*, for this unholy dogma.

I liked your quotation from Brother Joachim very much indeed. I quote back to you one of his sentences: "Sorrow is a consideration of Time, but Joy is the *condition of Eternity*."

How fit an *eternal* hell into this framework, which I believe to be the true one?

No Pat, I am not impressed by these lofty stoical spirits who contemplated so easily the damnation of others; they lack the most elementary sense of spiritual decency. These words of D'Arcy are stupid and wicked and confound one by their sheer lack of understanding. D'Arcy has *more than a streak* of the old inquisitorial attitude. Thank heaven we live in the twentieth century, bad though it may be.

Now for the Church's teaching on the possibility of salvation outside the Church. I accept on the authority of your quotations that she does now teach such a bare possibility. She has probably come thus far only under extreme pressure *from outside*. You will think me stubborn and ungracious to write in this way. Yet do try for a moment to see this thing from an outsider's point of view. If I am outside the Church and wish to enter it and ask for instruction, I will be presented with the Tridentine Profession of Faith—be told to read it, study it, think about it, and decide whether or not I can honestly agree with each of its articles. Now I have always understood that this creed is binding *in every word* upon every member of the Roman Church. It is regarded as infallible and irreformable. This creed contains this article: "This true Catholic Faith, *outside which no one can be in a state of salvation."*

To all honest thinking this is a blank contradiction of the words you quote from the Encyclical of Pius IX. But the Tridentine Profession of Faith is the higher and binding and infallible authority. I have explained to you that I cannot accept the explanation of the invisible Church, etc. as honest. This article was certainly not originally understood in that way. The explanation given can only strike an outsider as a dishonest attempt to take away from the words their plain meaning.

However, if such be the meaning of the words, why not alter them to make it plain? Are they plain as they stand? Remember, many men have left the Church, and many men have found themselves unable to enter the Church, because they cannot accept the words I have emphasized as they stand. If they have a hidden, saner, kinder meaning, would it not be honest to make it clear?

Now Pat, to make this thing quite clear between us I suggest you ask some of your priests the following questions:

1. Is the Tridentine Profession of Faith—or, if you like, the Creed of Pius IV—an infallible guide to the true basis and teaching of the Roman Catholic church today?

2. Is it or is it not true that converts to Roman Catholicism have to express full consent to all the articles of this creed?

3. If it is not true, then what formal creed are they expected to confess?

4. If it is true, then can any plain and simple man outside the Church expect to find the meaning in the article "outside which *no* one can be in a state of

salvation" as applying to some invisible Church, when all the other articles apply very practically and obviously to a visible Church?

5. If your authority grants all these points, then ask whether it would not perhaps be wiser and more honest to alter the words of the creed so that they express their esoteric meaning?

6. If he agrees that it would be more honest, then ask him, as an honest man seeking to bring about the conversion of as many people as possible to his Church (and also, we hope, as a plain man devoted to the plain utterance of the plain truth), to start to bring pressure to bear within the hierarchy of the Church for the alteration of these plain words, with their unholy ambiguous meaning, to another equally plain uncontradictory meaning.

7. If he is unprepared to start such an agitation, ask "why not?" Is he by any chance afraid?

You say you have asked priests, read authoritative books, etc. Have you ever studied, article by article, the Creed of Pius IV? It is your official creed as a Roman Catholic. Is the appeal to the existence of an invisible Church the best explanation you can find for these evil words? You say you are everywhere told the same thing. Does this "everywhere" include this article from the supreme expression of your Church's teaching? Why do you need to ask a priest for its meaning if the meaning is plain (as it indeed is)? Here are the words again: "outside which no one can be in a state of salvation." It is true that they do not state that the "one" is damned; no, he is simply not in "a state of salvation." Do you look for another meaning because you don't care for the expressed meaning? Is this honest?

Would you be prepared to leave the Church unless the words were altered to express clearly the hidden meaning we are assured they have? If not, why not? Is it or is it not important that an official Creed of a great religion be expressed in absolutely unambiguous terms?

In your quotation from the Encyclical of Pius IX the learned pope deigns to assert, in flagrant contradiction to the article of the Creed of his Church, that those who labor under "invincible ignorance" of the Church can be saved. It is kind of him. But note well, even he only allows it for those who are what he calls "invincibly ignorant." But can a man be "invincibly ignorant" of God's truth if, as the good pope says, he also is capable of "carefully observing the natural law and its commandments written by God in the hearts of all men." Are all men who honestly, after years of effort and study, deny the Church "invincibly ignorant" people? Simply because they prefer words to mean what they say?

Would you honestly accept such reasoning and duplicity in any other matter, where your religious emotions are not involved? Members of a golf club would be rather surprised to be told that certain of their rules only applied to an invisible golf club!

Well Pat, this is not very pleasant. But in this unpleasantness lies the difference between us. It is just this (it seems to me) ready acceptance of dishonest or ambiguous or hazy or plainly contradictory propositions among Roman Catholics that makes it impossible to fruitfully discuss religious questions with them.

But of course more plainly, and more honestly, the difference between us simply boils down to this: you (at present) believe in the Roman Catholic church. I (at present) do not. And naturally with that fundamental difference we are bound to view the utterances of the Church in very different lights. I look out of my window now. I see a shepherd herding his sheep. I honestly do not believe the pope knows any more about the conditions under which a man attains his immortal destiny than that shepherd. Comparing the utterances of some of the popes with the utterances of many simple men, I am inclined to think that, in general, they—the popes—have known less. This is not just a perverse attitude. Jesus said "it is easier for a camel to enter the eye of a needle than for a rich man to enter heaven." He also said, "Blessed are the poor in spirit, for theirs is the Kingdom of Heaven." Jesus wasn't just referring to men rich in money. He was referring to men rich in knowledge, in wisdom, in leisure, in tradition, in power, in position, in self-righteousness. Few men have been richer in all these riches than the popes. Jesus stressed always that the wisdom of God is not as the wisdom of this world. The riches of God are not the riches of this world. There have been great and good popes, but in all probability (I believe) they would have been greater men had they not been popes. All high position in this world weakens a man in spiritual discernment. From the Christian standpoint the Kingdom of God and the Kingdom of this World are incompatible. And the popes have been among the great ones of this world. They shall have their reward! I have been very slowly—a little each day—reading the Sermon on the Mount and trying to penetrate into its meanings. I honestly cannot see very much connection between this fiery world-denouncing Jesus of the synoptic Gospels and the doctrines of Roman Catholicism. I do not understand the words of Jesus. I suspect I am too contaminated by this world, or too much in love with it; and Christianity has always looked on this worldly love with suspicion. The words of Jesus are a splendid folly in relation to this world, and are perhaps a splendid wisdom in relation to an other world than this; but whatever they are, the popes have not helped me to understand them. They talk another language, and I suspect it may well be the same language the High Priests of Israel of old spoke. Jesus on many occasions expressed His intense dislike of it.

I suspect Roman Catholics of being Roman Catholics rather than Christians. Their first loyalty is to their splendid and ancient and "rich" Church. The voice of Jesus is but a still small voice indeed in their schools and churches.

They have persecuted always any who tried to speak to them in the same spirit that Jesus would have done. The New Testament is a terrible book, and it contains little comfort for Roman Catholicism, with its traditions and pomps and ceremonies and comforts and stupidities and riches and culture. Do these not by and large "protect" one from the terror of the New Testament? The Roman Church is the shield the Western world has made to protect itself from the words of Jesus, just as His contemporaries for the most part hid themselves behind their Church.

Does a Christian need a Church in this world? What would you think of a contemporary disciple of Jesus who followed Him by listening to the interpretations given to His teachings by the priests of Judaism? Would you not expect him to go out into the market place and listen to the words of Jesus from His own mouth? Which has the first claim on a Roman Catholic, the Tridentine Profession of Faith or the Sermon on the Mount? It is but evasion or spiritual insensibility to pretend that both make the same impression or demands. I have spent most of my thinking life trying to decide just what Christianity is, and do not yet know; and think now that I never will. But if to be a Christian is to be a man who strives to bring himself to the limit under the influence of the words of Jesus as given in the New Testament, then I say that Roman Catholicism only provides a blasphemous caricature. This expresses no judgement upon which is the better. It is simply a statement that they are different, and that, if Jesus was God, then the difference is blasphemous. I do not feel sure that we can dispense with Jesus and accept the Roman Church instead. Are things as simple as you make them? If you believe the words of Jesus to be the words of God do you not read the words of the Church that would "interpret" them with fear and trembling? The words of the Church are plausible? Yes they are—now turn to your New Testament and seek the plausible!

Nietzsche was nearer in spirit to Jesus than any orthodox Christian I know. And remoter too! And that is as it should be. Such men only appear on the earth once in a thousand years, but, by God!, they are not the stuffed-up jackasses their "followers" turn them into.

Nine tenths, or perhaps ninety-nine hundredths, of the structure of my consciousness is the tawdry result of the labors of these sawdust-filled followers—ancient and modern. It is hard to conceive of anything more sickeningly mediocre than most of our human reasonings and utterances as coming from these followers and interpreters.

It is necessary to wash the mind, wash the brain, wash the heart, wash the spirit, and forget; wash all that we have allowed ourselves to become with the water of forgetting to become clean. Then look again, listen again—until you vomit. At this point we fall on our knees to vomit, not to pray; but the vomit is a cleaner prayer than all our "prayers." Can one covered in filth help you to wash yourself clean? Perhaps only death can clean us, and in that lies the meaning and value of death.

This probably strikes you as flying off at a tangent from the round of our discussions. Is it? Should we not speak until we are clean? And when will we be clean? Perhaps we should leave it at that.

P.S.

I've been for a walk with Mary since I wrote this, and feel rather different now. Much of this letter is unjust to the whole truth. I don't know what to say. Perhaps it is better to say nothing—except Yes and No, as Jesus advocated. He said that all other words were "from evil." I have enjoyed your letters and don't feel as antagonistic to your thought and your Church as my answers may lead you to think, but it does take some swallowing—the idea that one must be either "invincibly ignorant" or a Roman Catholic to be saved!

I send this for what it may be worth, but don't take it too seriously. I feel confused just now.

Let us leave "hell" out of our future letters. What do we know? Why do we always tend to stress our disagreements?

The Beale Farm
1 April 1954

My dear Pat,

Thank you for your last letter. I am very grateful for it. I had made up my mind that I should not write you any more long letters. Yet now I feel increasingly that I have in my letters placed myself in a false position. I think the trouble is that I have over-emphasized facts and thoughts in a way that does not truly represent my whole thought. I have been trying during these last days to sort out what we have said to each other and to arrive if possible at a deeper understanding of our differences. I would like in this letter to go over some of the ground again, because I feel now that many of my earlier letters have been unfair both to you and to the Church—certainly unfair in the sense that I see now that I have hammered away at certain unpleasant aspects of Church doctrine and history while not fully admitting that these particular aspects by no means represent the whole picture. I have always (until I led myself astray in my letters to you) held that any religion has the right to be judged by the finest flowerings of its spirit and is not to be harshly criticized for its failings and stupidities, which really only represent the "human, all-too human" element in it. Yet I must admit that my discussion of Roman Catholicism in these letters has certainly failed in this respect. Of course in one sense I can justify myself in that I was trying to express to you the things about the Church that disturb me, and necessarily dwelt on the failures, etc. However all that may be, and whether I am right or wrong in the criticisms I have made, I would like clearly and honestly to say that I now realize that from a higher religious point of view I have been less than just. I have pressed many matters that, if they had been put to me by another, I would have rejected as essentially irrelevant. The plain truth here is that, with the exception of the belief in eternal hell, I have in general felt extremely friendly to and sympathetic with Roman Catholic Christianity. With reference to hell I would like to say here that I have just been reading St. Athanasius's work *Of the Incarnation of the Word of God* and was interested to note that he repeatedly seems to imply that a lost soul is simply "lost"—that is, drops out of existence into some extremely rudimentary state of being that is almost non-being. Of course such a state could not be painful, in fact could not really be considered as even conscious. It simply would represent a lost possibility of salvation, and in that sense is infinitely tragic; but the horror and utter evil of eternal conscious suffering is not present. Now about this I would like to say that I can and have always accepted it as a possibility, but a possibility that I hope and pray the power of God's love will overcome. And following from this arises the question: how far was St. Athanasius reflecting the accepted Christian belief of his age in this, and how far may such an interpretation be considered orthodox today? If this was the understanding of the doctrine of hell accepted in the time of Athanasius, how and why did it later become debased into a belief in unending extreme conscious suffering? I would be grateful if you could get the opinion of one of your priests on this point. Let me say simply that I can accept the possibility of the truth of St. Athanasius' view. It seems to me it completely safeguards the belief in man's freedom—that he is free to reject God and to return to virtual non-being—and at the same time does not make a mockery of the power of the love of God. What do you think of this? Here I have felt we may be able to agree?

What I would like to know is, if, as a Roman Catholic, I said I understood the doctrine of eternal hell in this sense, would it be accepted and permitted by the Church today? I admit frankly that I do not know the answer to this, but the case of Athanasius makes me hope it would be accepted. If the doctrine is open to this interpretation, I withdraw my objections to it, but still utterly renounce any interpretation that involves unending conscious suffering as abominable and a mockery of God.

If you could accept this interpretation and assure me it is not heretical, then I would say that I have nothing but respect for Roman Catholic doctrine as a whole and for those who believe in it. Also I would say that, freely and imaginatively accepted and considered *as a symbol*, I believe it represents a possibility of the truth of things—and a noble and sublime possibility. But I cannot myself accept it as the *only* possibility. I do not say this in any spirit of pride. It is simply that I cannot honestly do so. I just do not believe it is the only possibility. I do not dispute that I may come to such a belief; with a growth of understanding and God's help I may do so. But I have not yet reached that stage and so cannot yet believe it is entirely right that I should reach it. But I have no feeling of superiority over any man who has come to accept it as the only possible truth. At present I just don't know.

The sections of Athanasius's *Of the Incarnation of the Word of God* that I have in mind are: section 4 of Chapter I (page 29 and 30 in my edition, Centenary Press), in which, discussing the divine necessity for the Incarnation, he uses the words (referring to men): "as they had at the beginning come into being out of non-existence, so were they now on the way to returning, through corruption, to non-existence again. The presence and love of the Word had called them into being; inevitably therefore, when they lost the Knowledge of God, they lost existence with it. For it is God alone that exists, evil is non-being..., the negation and antithesis of good, which is being." Again, in section 6, chapter 2, he says: "it was monstrous that beings which once had shared the nature of the Word should perish and turn back again into non-existence through corruption." Now if hell can be considered as this "turning back again into non-existence," I do not think I can dispute its possibility. I was pleased to find Athanasius equating the antithesis Good/Evil with Being/Non-Being. This has always been my thought, and it does seem to me quite clear that from this basic insight it is not possible to derive a doctrine of a hell endured eternally by conscious beings. The whole point here is surely that as long as a creature remains partly (however little) in being he retains within himself the possibility of salvation since "God alone exists." I don't want to labor this approach but would like to know your attitude to it, and also whether you can get an authoritative opinion, that of the Church.

One thing more. I do not see how this interpretation, if accepted, can be in harmony with the doctrine of God creating man in his own image. The doctrine of the Divine Image in man is to my mind the most fundamental of all. I have gone into this in earlier letters so won't go over it again except to say that, with this doctrine held clearly and firmly in mind, I can only accept Athanasius's idea of hell as such a remote and abstract possibility that it hardly needs to be considered. But, as bowing to the mystery of freedom, it has to be admitted.

You can justly point out that I say I don't "know," as though that precludes me from believing. You would say that a man should, in Kierkegaard's words, "make the leap of faith" and "choose to believe" what he can never, in this world, know. "Faith is the substance of things hoped for." All the great saints of all the great religions have stressed the necessity for faith and said that a man's faith reveals him for what he essentially is. I accept this. But the problem presents itself to me in this way: What should I choose to believe? The answer is (I think), that which is the highest. What is the highest? It is that man should seek and accept the Truth: the Will of God. How am I to know the Truth? I can only know it by revelation. That is, only God can reveal His truth to me. Has He yet revealed it to me? I think He has not. I think a revelation from God concerning Himself would be unmistakable and beyond possibility of honest evasion. What then is my position? It is that God has not revealed the Truth to me, and in accepting that fact I accept His Will. He may never reveal Himself. If it be His Will I cannot force it. I can only wait and hope. In this sense I, with every other man, am completely dependent on the Will of God. We are all, with Simone Weil, "waiting on God." So what then is my faith? Simply that I accept the Will of God as being Good. That is, I believe God *through reason* reveals to each man as much as he is capable of bearing, and that it is *a sin against the Holy Ghost* to dishonestly pretend to, or claim, or force upon oneself, a knowledge of God that has not yet been revealed. That is, *I have faith in Reason*. I believe Reason is the Presence of the Holy Spirit in man and that he disregards it at his peril. Reason is that in man which responds to Divine Revelation. Reason is the faculty in man that protects him from the power of false gods or false notions of God, if he will but use it bravely and *have faith* in it. I don't at all mean that Christian Faith is unreasonable. I believe that a man who believes it, persuaded by his own reason, has a far stronger faith than one who believes it superstitiously or blindly or thoughtlessly because it is vaguely desirable. The great Christian thinkers have acknowledged this by always appealing to reason. Roman Catholicism has never derided reason even though (I think) it has often been, in practice, unreasonable—as has for that matter everyone else. Although I have read with pleasure and respect the works of Kierkegaard and Nietzsche, they have failed to touch me in the depths because they are both fundamentally unreasonable. They were both of course reacting against the shallow "reason" of their time, but the only true way to do that would be to produce diviner, deeper reasoning, and in this they both failed. I don't reproach them for this: being the men they were in their time and circumstances they could do no other. They were both great men and tragic men. They both suffered greatly for the Truth. But they were impatient of waiting on God. Nietzsche particularly, in some ways the profoundest man of the modern age, failed to wait on God and alas! overturned his reason and wrecked his magnificent mind in the process. Oh! I cannot bear the unthinking, uncomprehending attitude of so many men of our time to Nietzsche. Roman Catholic thinkers, D'Arcy and Copleston, have been kinder and more understanding than any others, and for this they have earned my respect and gratitude, and helped me to feel more kindly in my turn to them. But in general the modern pygmy-man hasn't the spiritual or intellectual guts to love Nietzsche, to love him for his greatness of soul, even in his errors. In the early centuries of our era men asked each other "what think you of Christ?" And from the answer they received they could plumb the deeps of man's soul. And in our age that remains true. And of Nietzsche too it is true. Ask any man who has read Nietzsche what he thinks of him, and how revealing the answer: revealing in several cases of an unbelievable paltriness of spirit in modern man. Roman Catholics (I am thinking now of D'Arcy and Copleston, but their Church deserves the credit too) are among the very few modern thinkers, sadly, who have not revealed their inadequacy, their littleness and meanness of heart, in their words on Nietzsche. How easy, and how paltry and detestable, to mock at a magnificent mind that has striven to the point of wrecking itself. The whole sorrow of our human state is in this hardly endurable spectacle of nobility and greatness in ruin, reduction to spiritual idiocy and blathering. And all they can do is mock! Woe to them, bloody hypocrites. The Scribes and Pharisees too mocked, mocked at Jesus on the Cross. My spirit stinks in itself with the smell of the paltriness of the age I have been born into! Mock at Jesus, mock at Nietzsche, and read the *Daily Mirror* in between times! Let us spew spew spew vomit out the stench of our time.

But Roman Catholicism has revealed an inner greatness in its attitude to this man, and for that I feel more "at home" in it, and more love of it, than I could ever do for these paltry modern pygmy-hearts!

Here in the figure of Nietzsche I can perhaps indicate a meaning. Nietzsche suffered terribly, and in the agony of his spirit overset his mind in seeking the unknown God, Who yet would not reveal Himself to him. This martyrdom, this spiritual and intellectual crucifixion of perhaps the noblest man of modern times, is a partial revelation of the Will of God—for those who have ears to hear, let them hear; and eyes to see, let them see. His last message to his friend— blotched, pitiable, inarticulate words uttered before the final falling away into the abyss of madness of this noble mind, this ruined temple of the Image of God—was signed "The Crucified One." And in this "Crucified One" the modern age finds its judgement, as another Crucified One hung in judgement over the ancient world. "And at the ninth hour Jesus cried with a loud voice saying, 'My God, My God why hast thou forsaken Me?'"

I have spoken of revelation, and waiting on God. For me the whole spectacle of the world and its history is a revelation, chaotic and difficult to understand. So far God has willed to reveal Himself in this (to me) chaotic and bewildering and yet wonderful way. But I cannot go beyond His revelation and pretend to a present knowledge of things not yet revealed. Revealed theologies seem to me only to reflect the deepest and dearest hopes of men. That is, they reveal the nature of man. But do they reveal the Will of God? I cannot yet feel that they do. They reveal a possible will of God, a will of God conceived of as in harmony with all our deepest human wishes and strivings. But the certain Will of God in all things, in the last things, in the Kingdom of God, has not yet been revealed. If His Will in this sense had been revealed the matter would be beyond argument, in the way that the existence of the world as it now is is beyond argument for all rational men. When God reveals Himself all argument ceases, except possibly among men who have lost their reason. I feel I am failing to make myself clear. Let me say: the Will of God is revealed in action in its own "itness." Men will not be able to argue about the nature and presence of the Kingdom of God when it comes. In this sense the Will of God is conceived as identical with its explicit action. And it is conceivable, in humility and honesty of spirit, that the Kingdom of God never will be revealed to men. We may hope for its revelation to us, but cannot demand it. "What is man that he should live out the lifetime of his God?" asked Herman Melville, one of the deepest of all religious spirits among men.

I don't know whether I have made this clear. I feel I have not. I am not clear myself about it. It seems to me a question of resignation to the fact that we do not yet know the Will of God in its completeness, and a recognition of the futility and presumption of either pretending we do, or of trying to mold it to our own all-too-human desires. We can in honesty wait and hope and pray, and again wait. However sublime or noble our desires seem to us, they may be worthless to God. Let us accept this in faith, believing that God's Will, whatever it may be, is better than our will. In a sense I would say that all human theologies and religions and notions about God are foolish presumption. Why can we not wait? Wait in stillness of spirit for what may be our obliteration.

The Singing Apes of Egypt, singing hymns of adoration and praise to the Rising Sun, singing glory to the Resurrected God, singing at the Creation of the World; the Morning Stars singing together in the Dawn of the World before the Ancient of Days; the far-singing of the Birds of Rhiannon over the Sea: these singing Apes and Stars and Birds that sing among the Branches of Man's Spirit—what do they foretell? Let us listen to the singing.

I don't know whether this letter will bring us closer to an understanding; I have certainly enjoyed yours, and they have made me re-think many of my ideas. I admit I was unjust to D'Arcy, but I like Copleston better. Don't worry about answering this until you have the time and inclination—you must be very busy now. I have been reading some of St. Bernard of Clairvaux's letters. Very good. Try to find *Jurgen*—by James B. Cabell—you will enjoy it.

With much love,
Gerard

LETTERS TO MARY

*That supreme kind of True Knowledge
which derives from man's openness to the lasting mystery*[1]

KARL RAHNER

---

[1]. Epigraph chosen by Mary Casey for her 1973 Journal

Epigraph

'There is no way for the Greek but the discovery of intellect by which he knows both thought—the thinking power in itself—and the thoughts which are truth.'

Very gently Origen answered: 'Christ in God is present, not only with those who cleave to Him, but also everywhere with those who know Him not.'

'How do you know him?' Plotinus asked with equal softness and looking at the man with love.

'Friends know not by obscure hints or by mere knowledge of sounds and words, symbols and types, but by a real awareness through which they attain to the nature of the intelligible world, and to the beauty of truth.'

'For this I came to you, for in this intuition of friendship the centre of both circles meet, meet in the centre of the One. From this time it is given us to know one another in the fullness of being in which each man is most alone. For intellectual perception is simultaneous with existence. But since for man, who is not born divine, this real awareness you speak of is, as it might be said, the unconscious consciousness of soul and that by which he lives; and because you and I are forced by consciousness energising to speak to others of that which is the first of things, and in the way of understanding this our human minds are apart, so we two go apart.'

'But this,' and in the intensity of thought movement ceased and they stood still on the shore of the sounding sea as though their bodies were invisible pure spirit, 'is essential for men who come after us, whether it is given them to see it or not, that for every mind, whatever its own endeavour, Truth is One.'

'The Unison is,' Origen said after a silence in the sound of the waves, 'but now the moment has passed will you tell me how you see the difference in what we teach—for this is our destiny—of God?'

'I say,' Plotinus answered, looking away from his companion to the night horizon of the sea, 'nothing is present without the Good.'

They spoke no more after that but continued together in an equal communion of silence neither would experience again. For once they knew peace.[1]

---

1. Mary Casey, *The Kingfisher's Wing*, (Rigby & Lewis, 1987), pp 138-39.

So, after receiving the piece of bread, he immediately went out. And it was night.

JOHN 13:30

The Beale
8 September 1969

My darling Mary,

 I have happy quiet days here, short walks and reading and watching the creatures. There are about sixty rock doves sleeping on the roof, but most of them go off to the corn during the day. The rock martins are usually resting on their ledge as I am having tea in the afternoons. The grass round the house is very dry, all pale gold, so that the Briera trees we have planted are a great joy to see, their leafage so fresh and green in contrast. The weather looks uncertain, may be breaking. The Lord of the Dark Cloud gathers his hosts each afternoon and sends spatters of rain with warning growls. The wind too rises wuthering and moaning in the still rooms.

 I had a walk by the stream this morning. I sat on St. John's tree on the way back watching Bonny and Jenny grazing under the Hammerhead's nest. They go in there these days to find a bite of green. Bonny lifted her head and looked at me for a long time, walked a few paces towards me, then looked again, considering whether she would come and greet me.

 In the mornings I read first Heraclitus in the *Cosmic Fragments*, then Plotinus, then a very good commentary I have from the Advaita point of view on the *Brahma Sutras*. My interest in all three deepens as I compare passages and discover how much common ground they share and how they throw light on each other. I wish I had the scholarly equipment and training to take on an exhaustive study of this field of thought—here lie the solutions in depth of the deepest inter-traditional problems. That would be a task worth, as Mackenna would say, a life. I am sure the right minds are already engaged here in both East and West—the results fateful for the whole future of our civilization, if time enough remains. It seems to me certain now that the way lies through extreme catastrophe and suffering for all men—and the issue?:

 "Sing the song of woe, the song of woe, but may the good prevail."

 When I move under the power of the tremendous prophetic mind of Aeschylus each afternoon (and no doubt the Lord of the Dark Cloud muttering threateningly from the black sky helps along my mood) I see nothing but the dark...

 But last night as I bathed a toad croaked, and this morning another emerged from my boot, and as the sky darkens at this moment I hear three cocks crowing and a hen is clucking to her chicks under the window. I'm writing in Lucy's room. And these little things too are not without meaning for restoring a balance.

> Lots of love to you and Lucy,
> Gerard

P.S.

I am puzzled by the planet in the west near Jupiter. I think now it is Saturn, not Mercury? I'll write next from Nairobi.

Tuesday, 9 a.m.

Darling Mary,

A rainstorm came on yesterday before I set off to post this, so I put it off until today. I noticed on the pad that I could write six sheets of this paper for half an ounce, so thought I'd add a little more this morning.

One thing in my mind is that I meant to order a copy of a book on pre-Socratic Greek philosophy advertised on one of the books we got from Heffers in the summer. I cannot remember the name of it, but I do remember that Kirk, the man who edited the *Cosmic Fragments*, was either the editor of this new work or one of a group of editors. I was rather disappointed in Burnet's *Early Greek Philosophy* because he didn't give the Greek text of the fragments. This work is I think probably what I hoped Burnet's work was. I wonder whether you could order it for me? It is advertised either on the wrapper of A.H. Armstrong's *History* or possibly on the book by Merlan on Neo-Platonism. If it arrives before you come out you can bring it for me—otherwise it can wait at Mappowder until we get back there next spring.

I find my mind centering more and more on this period of Greek thought. I have a notion only an environment of a supreme order in thought could have produced Heraclitus, and I would like this work as a kind of marginal comment on him. I find that at the intellectual level he has become absolutely central for me, and I tend to work at other philosophers in the light of his fragments. As with Homer, this interest and sense of his significance for me goes right back to my boyhood. As with so many other precious hints and clues, it was old god-uncle J.C.P. who first pointed me in this direction. I remember so vividly my excitement when I first read J.C.P.'s brief account of Heraclitus in *A Philosophy of Solitude*, and how the most powerful and secret urge in my desire later to learn Greek was to read the living words of Homer and Heraclitus as they themselves had uttered them.

Well! I'll stop here and leave the rest of the page to finish at Timau, as I feel sure there will be a letter from you.

At Timau

Two very precious letters from you. I'm so glad Will got away well and arrived safely. Yes, he must be much stronger after his time in Mappowder.

I liked very much your words about Berdyaev, and think your criticism fair up to a point; but I don't think that, taking his work as a whole, he dismisses "intellect" as we understand it—though that may be the word his translator uses for διάνοιᾱ. His whole position really rests on νόησις as, in his particular case, crystallized round the great central Christian symbols. I think somewhere, perhaps in his autobiography, he disclaims being a metaphysical philosopher in the universal sense and says he stands in the world first and last as a Christian thinker. Granted this, I think he has thought more deeply, honestly, and movingly about our ultimate religious problems than most other Christians, and certainly more so than any of our "ecclesiastical" Christians that I have read. I always feel reading him that I'm in touch with a great and compassionate man who in his inner struggles has never let himself be easily deceived by words. I think I remember how in his *Freedom and the Spirit* he spoke in highest praise of Plotinus, but went on to say something to the effect that the kind of impact made on him by the tragic element in life, as revealed in Dostoievsky, or Aeschylus, or the Gospels, was such as to leave a question mark against all purely intellectual formulations of ultimate truth. And I think I share this reaction of his. I have always at the back of my mind a suspicion that such forms of thought are only ultimately satisfactory to those of us whom Fate or Chance or Destiny has protected from the most terrible stresses men may be called upon to face.

In the secret recesses of my mind, when I read in so many philosophers that the wise man always remains essentially "unmoved"—ἀπάθεια—there rises the image of Jesus in Gethsemane; and I must confess that to me Jesus in His agony and distress—no ἀπάθεια here—reveals Himself as essentially greater, not less, than any of the philosophers. No, I think here I am on the side of the great poets: no ἀπάθεια in Homer or Aeschylus or Shakespeare or the great artists; no ἀπάθεια in Dostoievsky or Van Gogh or Blake or the great saints; no ἀπάθεια in St. Paul or St. Francis, in Dietrich Bonhoeffer, Helmuth von Moltke, Pavel Florensky, or the great religious spirits; no ἀπάθεια in the Psalms or Jeremiah or Kierkegaard. Or, to put it more generally, I'm on the side of "ordinary" men in this, and I think in this lies the strength of the Bible: it reveals the deepest response of men just as men, not as in any way exceptional men, to certain terrible ambiguities at the roots of things. This doesn't mean one won't use one's intellectual (and all other) powers to the limit, but it does mean some of us are left with a certain sense of ultimate unresolved ambiguities in existence that can never be resolved at the level of intellect, even of transcendent intellect; and it is at this ultimate level that the symbol of the cross stands as our final faith and hope. Here I stand with Berdyaev unreservedly on the side of Christianity. But my sense of the immense power and insight of traditional metaphysics, and its wondrous value for us all, remains unshaken except at this ultimate religious level.

Lots of noise and many interruptions here, in the Timau Store, so all this is probably rather confused. Two more letters from you just arrived. But I have an idea, darling Mary, you're with me in this.

P.S.

Your letter of 5 September here now. About those books from Pates Manor, perhaps you could send one copy of Guénon's *Crisis of the Modern World* to Nigel as from me. I meant it for him. Guénon's thought is so opposed to Nigel's in fundamentals that I think if he reads him it could be a valuable corrective. This is Guénon's great value for our time—as a corrective. Even if a somewhat intolerant and polemical one, he is no more so than most of the people he is reacting against. The other copy, and the copies of the essay, can remain at home.

Thank you for replying to Peter, you said just the right thing. No word here yet from Christopher.

I'll write again from Nairobi on Thursday or Friday.

I haven't heard a yellow whiskered Bulbul in the forest since I got back.

Lots of love always,
Gerard

The Beale
9-10 September 1969

My darling Mary,

I have had four letters from you, all coming together. I scribbled off some words at the end of the letter I had taken to Timau to send off to you—rather confused and incoherent I think, as I was in the shop and several interruptions and a few telephone calls intervened. I'm starting this here and will finish it and post it in Nairobi.

I'm so pleased Faber and Faber are going to read your *Kingfisher's Wing*. It is a very fine and exciting and thought-provoking work, and I feel it is our duty to try to make it accessible to anyone who is able to respond to it. The real obstacle from the point of view of publishers is that they may be afraid of losing money on it. It won't, I am sure, make a best seller.

No, I won't want those extra copies of *Studies in Comparative Religion* here, or Guénon's book. The Guénon is a new translation; as they went to the trouble of a new translation I thought it clear it was felt Osborne's was inadequate in some way... and I remain interested enough in Guénon to like to get as clear as possible in my mind what he is trying to say. The other copy is for Nigel, it may perhaps stimulate him to be more radically aware of some possible objections to some of his ideas.

I'm glad you've heard from Peter—I'll send him a line too to reassure him about the fare. I do pray Christopher will get permission to come away for a time. His country won't achieve any good result from attempting to force the issue on young people like Christopher. If the survival of the U.S. was at stake one might feel some sympathy, but it is hard to think their situation is so desperate.

My dearworthy, darling Mary, how you put your finger on a *crucial* point in your words on Berdyaev. Just here lies the source of all my own most exhausting inner wrestlings. I think though he is not easy to know in depth; he is never a systematic thinker and it is rather from the totality of his thought, insofar as he has been able to express it, that one is left with a sense that here is a man who does in fact leave us questioning some of the basic presuppositions of traditionalist metaphysics. I was myself disappointed too in his *Truth and Revelation*—the note of exhaustion and near despair (and a certain incoherence) was apparent. Like many men possessed by deep intuitions that they try to share with others he has probably tried to say too much at too great length. I think he does in fact very well understand the strength and value of much in the great metaphysical traditions, but, inwardly shattered as he was by irreducibly terrible experiences in his life, he remained haunted by a sense of a certain final ambiguity and inadequacy in these traditions that could only be resolved by the Cross—not the cross as a symbol in traditional metaphysics (which remained for him shadowed by the same ambiguities), but the Cross as revealed in the Christian Gospels. I think he would say that for men caught up in certain frightful situations—situations that men do in fact find themselves in and that are always recurring and are as it were always potentially there—the cross as a metaphysical symbol (as revealed for instance in a masterly way by Guénon in his *Symbolism of the Cross*) would prove a woefully inadequate support. He would not accept that the Cross of Christ is nothing more than a particular example of a universal cross, which is the way that traditional metaphysics sees it; he saw it as something irreducibly more that cannot be rationalized into an empty universal. It is something that cannot be understood, but only accepted in faith. There is in fact a radical incapacity in man to understand the ultimate mysteries, and his cherished understandings are in fact only misunderstandings. He would say the death of Christ reveals to us our inability to understand, an offense indeed to all of us who insist on understanding. In the case of Berdyaev this devaluation of the intellect before the ultimate divine mysteries (for he does not in fact devalue it at any lower level) springs from an unfathomable depth and anguish of spirit, an anguish born in sufferings of experience too deep for tears. No man who has not in his own flesh and nerves and life passed through such sufferings can lightly dismiss his protest. I don't think it is a question here of philosophical incapacity or a personal weakness needing religious support (in him as an individual) but rather that he saw all men, when tested *in extremis*, as equally weak and in need. To him philosophical invulnerability was just a childish self-deception... it was just a question of any particular man being lucky enough in his life to escape the intensity of stress that would reveal to him his particular breaking point. He would say that strengths, all realizations in depth of great human potentialities, however lofty, are always in fact privileged, protected, won at the expense and sacrificial sufferings of others; and that the great schools and masters of philosophy have never sufficiently realized or acknowledged this fact, or its implications for the ultimate value of their achievement. These questions put by Berdyaev to traditional metaphysics seem to me fair questions; they do not I think rise from lack of understanding. Perhaps he has understood too much... have they received equally fair answers? As far as ἀπάθεια goes, he would see nothing admirable in it, even if achieved. Here I think he is certainly right.

Darling Mary, I hardly know why I take this up at such length. I'm very well aware of how much can be said, with a certain persuasive evasiveness, on the other side. I am myself I think much nearer the metaphysical position than Berdyaev, but the honesty and relevance and testing quality of his position is clear to me. I cannot dismiss him as lightly as Plotinus (or so it seems at least to me) dismissed those who brought up the sufferings of Priam when he was speaking of ἀπάθεια. This insistence on a kind of personal impassability and invulnerability as a personal achievement on the part of Plotinus seems to me not to bear examination, and is in fact a weakness springing from a kind of blindness in certain directions. The question is not whether ἀπάθεια is attainable: the Stoics and Spartans and many forms of Eastern and Christian asceticism bear witness that it is, at a certain level, attainable. The question is whether, when attained, it is either admirable or right; whether too it is as courageous as it pretends to be. Is there not hidden in it a shrinking from the sufferings of real existence? or a demonic hardening of the heart and spirit? Why it may surely be (and here Jesus would be with me) that the spontaneous tears of a little girl over a broken doll are more acceptable to God than any form of Stoic ἀπάθεια, however heroic: a Stoic cannot or would not cry over a doll; a small girl may for all her tears be stoical.

> no tears for Priam—
> why even Achilles wept...
> sightlesse he drownes
> againe he strides the blast
> in teares teares teares...

It seems to me that the coming into the world and the death of Jesus have indeed left these questions indelibly marked against these notions of solitary self-sufficiency in any man or group of men. It was for this reason I said in my essay 'True Listening' that all traditional forms lie equally under the judgement and mercy of Christ. And I believe those words, "judgement" and "mercy," correspond to eternal, inescapable realities in the divine nature. I do not believe that at any level of spiritual or metaphysical realization they become irrelevant. Whatever the relationship is or was of Jesus to God, His death certainly revealed the inevitability of judgement and the necessity we all as men stand under to hope for mercy. Can we escape the fact that He was rejected and despised and tortured to a shameful death by the representatives of our lofty traditions, that in fact in history as we know it these representatives have never hesitated to use such weapons against those who disturb their equanimity—their ἀπάθεια? Of course, if frightful forms of suffering are so easily transcended in ἀπάθεια, then the infliction of such suffering becomes a trifling matter; it may be so, but the divine judgement stands over it, and it is at least possible that in the light of that judgement it will not appear trifling.

I know the kind of replies made to objections of this kind. I can only say that for me they always savor of self-deception and "artful dodging." The wise man, the philosopher, stands before us as humanly speaking great—to be revered—but he too stands under divine judgement; and it does remain that he sometimes speaks as though he does not. For the claim to invulnerability rests in the last analysis on the claim to no longer fear God, to be able to stand above and not be under the judgement—old-fashioned religious language perhaps, but with a meaning we dare not disdain.

Well! I must stop going on, as they say, in this vein. I had the impulse to tear up all this, but let it stand; it serves at least as an indication of the kind of value I believe Berdyaev to have: like Guénon and Kierkegaard, in their different ways, he has the value of a corrective, and perhaps for some of us a very necessary corrective.

It has just struck me that I've been writing all this before my woodcut portrait of old Jacob Boehme, who was a great influence on Berdyaev and so is perhaps defending his disciple through me! Anyway, bless them both! They remain loved and precious and gratefully accepted influences in my life.

Now to bed, and I wish my darling Mary was beside me. Tomorrow shearing starts below.

Wednesday

Down to the shearing this morning. The sheep look very thin as their wool comes off. I am going to bring the ewes and lambs up here and sell them to the Government, they are dying so fast now below. I went down to the cottage and into the Spring Place. Your gourd is tall and strong and has put out fifteen leaves! Brock and Snow greeted me quite cheerfully. I went on down to Will's house to visit his men and dog. They were all pleased and enquired at length about Will. All is very, very dry and rather bleak down there.

I've written to Peter and to Christopher and find myself praying the Draft Board won't be too fierce with him. We are cutting grass here now to re-thatch the cottage. The porches back and front are built but not yet thatched.

My mind today has gone on revolving round Berdyaev, and also Boehme, who is the source of so many of Berdyaev's distinctive insights. It is some time since I read Berdyaev's major works—*Freedom and the Spirit* is probably the weightiest of them—but I do recall that he continually refers back to Boehme and Plotinus as two major influences on him. I just glanced into the index of one of his books and found him referring in both cases to these two men with their names coupled: their prodigious gifts, their immense range of spiritual experience—expressions of this kind. Yet it remains clear that he is in some degree reacting against the influence of Plotinus; there is a certain uneasy tension in his attitude, and this tension seems to rise partly from his apocalyptic expectations that the creativities hidden in the divine dark—Boehme's *Ungrund*—are inaccessible to pure intellectuality, and even that a danger exists that such intellectuality can prove a lure preventing the realization of these hidden possibilities. The necessity, from a certain point of view, of the acceptance of limit is stressed. This is interesting in that here Berdyaev reveals the instinctive spiritual distrust of the Western mind, in almost all its manifestations, of *the unlimited*. Rist, in his studies of Plotinus, makes the point that what distinguishes Plotinus from all Platonism before and after him, is that he passed on to the unlimited, the formless; and again it is just this element in Plotinus that has lead to the suspicion of Eastern influence in his thought. The moment Christian mystics have in a similar way attempted to pass on to the unlimited they have been declared heretical. There has always been in the West a profound misgiving in the face of this possibility, and a sense—clearly here arising from the unfathomable influences of the great central Christian symbols—that this adventure is indeed open to man in his final irreducible freedom, but that it is not the will of God for man, *or not at least for Christian man*. There is the sense that the final image God wills, at least for Christian man, requires for its realization the free acceptance of the limited, the free rejection of the unlimited. I was fumbling in this direction when I said in one of our walks that you portrayed Plotinus in your book as what the Hindus would call a *jivanmukti*, one who has realized the unlimited ground of his own existence. I went on to say that such men do not occur within the Christian tradition; that in some sense the hidden dynamic spiritual forces working in the tradition inhibit this development; that in a sense, although it was a possibility, *it should not happen*. I think, Mary, that we are on unfathomably mysterious ground here: the implication seems to be that God wills different spiritual destinies for men in different spiritual traditions, or rather that the Divine Universal Man realizes His final destiny through a divinely willed differentiation at lower levels. Of course this fact is in a certain limited sense understood and accepted in the traditional doctrines, but have we realized all its possible implications? However all this may be, I cannot believe—there is no reason to believe—that Western man, more particularly Christian man, is intellectually or spiritually incapable of realizing the possibility of the unlimited; rather he deliberately rejects it insofar as he remains under the influence and guidance of the sacred symbols of his own tradition; and here we must remember that, traditionally speaking, the sacred symbols in any particular tradition express the divine will for that particular tradition and for the human beings living under their protection.

Here is a passage typical of many others I have just found in Berdyaev's *Freedom and the Spirit*. You will notice how conscious he is of this problem and how worried by it: "While the consciousness of man as such is capable of attaining the infinitude of the divine and of the cosmic, Christian man protects himself against these unlimited forces as well as against nature by jealously guarding the isolation of his consciousness. In the ancient and Eastern worlds man was more open to these influences, and to the inner life of nature and to the mysteries of the universe, than in the Christian world where he wins freedom for his spirit and realizes his divine destiny *by setting limits to his consciousness*. But if it be necessary for him to protect his spirit from these infinities, he does at the same time run the risk of increasing his isolation and separation from the divine world."

Here one senses the terrible tensions pervading his mind and the anguish of spirit rising from these tensions. There is certainly no lack of understanding of the issues involved, rather an extraordinarily clear consciousness of them, together with an equally clear certainty of what is demanded of him as a Christian.

I have often been struck by the prevalence in our tradition of symbols of darkness, darkness impenetrable to intellect; and in this ultimate darkness the only light for us is Christ. Abraham fell into a horror of great darkness, and the Semitic tradition was initiated. Think of all those moments of supreme revelation. God speaks out of the midst of fire and thick cloud and darkness: "Cloud and darkness are about Him, a fire goeth before Him, wrath and judgement are about Him"; "the day of the Lord, a day of darkness and gloom"; "He maketh the day dark with night"... Then Christ comes into the world, "the Light of the World"; but at his death "darkness fell over the earth." The religious consciousness of Christians is saturated with and centered upon these awesome symbolic utterances, and innumerable others like them. God mediates His Presence through darkness, suffering, and death. On the other hand, in the ancient and Eastern traditions, this stress is muted. Rather the divine is immediately intuited as "bright," "deathless," "untouched by sorrow," "unpierced by evil." Spirit is as it were absolutely present to man. *Satchitananda*: Being Consciousness Bliss Infinite Eternal. It would seem that the central revelatory utterances spring from an immediate vision of the divine glory untouched by dereliction, sorrow, affliction: these are transcended as illusions. But the Christian cannot escape the terrible power of his central symbols, cannot see the suffering of Christ and the world as illusion. Revelations so radically different in emphasis cannot but lead to a tremendous difference in spiritual experience and orientation. The Christian sees ἀπάθεια as stony-heartedness. "I wept not, so of stone grew I within." The sage sees it as a kind of divine common sense that it seems absurd and sentimental to quibble over.

Men of our time, who have in some degree come under the influence of both sets of symbols, may experience states of painful conflict. They recognize the legitimacy of the alien symbols, but cannot accept them for themselves. At the same time they cannot escape them. How to bring into being a creative rather than a destructive tension between them? In the past each tradition remained more or less enclosed within its own spiritual world. Today we live among traditions inwardly in crisis while outwardly overflowing into conflict. All we can do is to strive to make a response to the situation both honest and creative. Painful problems arise in the depths of men's souls. Earlier in this letter I spoke of the cross, as a purely metaphysical symbol, as "empty" to the Christian. To others it may indeed overflow with all divine plenitudes of meaning; but to the Christian, without Jesus of Nazareth it remains empty. It may even constitute for the Christian a disintegrating, alien symbol. The Cross, a purely metaphysical symbol, unburdened by the sorrows and accretions of history? Yes, but that burden is an illusion and concern with it but sentimentality! Withdraw—seek a quiet place and meditate in peace. So be it; but what am I to withdraw from? From an illusion? Why withdraw? The Cross, unburdened by the Body of Christ, and, in Christ, by all men? Perhaps that Body is not an illusion; is it not rather an offense; a terrifying, overwhelming, unmeetable demand? Are you not perhaps punishing this offense by pretending it doesn't exist? The wrath and judgement of God an illusion? Are you quite sure?

This kind of conflict in states of anguished inner darkness scarcely imaginable to those to whom it is meaningless you symbolized when, in *The Kingfisher's Wing*, you brought Plotinus and Origen together. A moment of utter testing for both men. Berdyaev chose the path Origen followed, but I am sure that, no more than Origen, was he unaware of all that was involved and all that he was turning away from... *sunt lacrimae rerum*.

Well, I've used up my quota of paper and must stop and take Moss and Bess up Windy Hill. Slate is in the garden, as Bess is in heat. Golden evening sunlight flooding into Lucy's room! Tomorrow I'm off to Nairobi, back on Friday. Darling Mary, I hope all these words aren't too many and too confusing and obscure. I think when all is said and done that I'm probably on the side of Origen—but not without saying of Plotinus, "Blessings on his head!"

With my love always, and to Lucy and Will if he is back with you,

Gerard

The Beale
17 September 1969

My darling Mary,

Three letters from you all arrived together. How I rejoice to see them. I suppose Gilfrid is in England now and has seen Will. I read years ago somewhere a story about a fierce old lion that lost one of his paws in a trap and led everyone a fine dance afterwards... Yes, I think the planets are Mars, Mercury, and Jupiter, but Mercury has set now. I haven't tracked down Saturn, but will look out for him in the eastern sky this evening.

I noticed Michael was very quiet the evening I visited them at Kisima, he hardly greeted me and looked very pale. It is really a good thing they have to go away to school I think.

Oh I wish I could touch you now... I read in a book on Hatha Yoga that some perfected yogis claim to be able to leave their earthly body and move out in their astral body to touch distant objects, for instance the moon. Well, they could perhaps have saved the astronauts a lot of trouble, but I'd like a share of this power just now, to touch your hand across the curve of the world. Your words on Greek Tragedy touch a quick issue in my mind at present. The gigantic shade of Aeschylus seems ever beside me these days, forcing me to ever deeper transvaluations. What strikes me especially in reading him is the sense of enormous intellectual power held in a kind of brooding reserve behind his tremendous imagistic utterances. There is left a haunting sense of the inadequacy of the purely philosophical mind in penetrating into the deeper recesses of the tragic vision. And, too, the sense of the tragic as penetrating all existence—one is not reading just a story of a certain time and place, one is being initiated into a dimension of suffering underlying all time and place, a suffering irredeemable by mind, by adjustments of philosophical attitude or increase of insight; in fact the deeper the insight the deeper the suffering. It was surely the break into this dimension of consciousness that prepared the European mind for the advent of Christianity, which carried this sense of the tragic into the depths of men's consciousness even of the divine? This too seems to me to throw light on the question of "limit." Tragedy, suffering, springs ultimately from limit. The unlimited does not know tragedy, and in moving on to the unlimited the spirit of man leaves suffering behind, *but does not redeem it*. This is the solution to the problem of suffering and evil, in the ancient metaphysical traditions. From this point of view it *is* possible to see suffering and evil as illusory—and to seek refuge from it in ἀπάθεια. But the suffering remained very real for the multitudes of men, of all creatures, who either could not or would not realize the unlimited. The question Christianity, in its profoundest depths, puts to the Classical traditions is this: is it not in truth the destiny of most men to remain within limits, and suffer? The problem *for these men* is to redeem the suffering inherent in their condition. They cannot move out of their condition into the unlimited *and remain men*. God certainly wills for most men to remain within limits: in Christ we receive the divinely willed redemption for men *as men*. Jesus urged men to accept the limits ("you cannot add a hair to your heads or a cubit to your stature") and trust in God's promises through Him for redemption. This means that in the Christian tradition man as man is understood as a limited being. He comes up against the divinely willed limit at every level of his existence. The limit is God's will. The limit is—limit on ultimate freedom. The limit is acceptance of suffering. The limit is unknowing in the face of death, of ultimate spiritual destiny. The limit is one's ultimate self as creature. It is also the ultimate self, the ultimate spiritual reality, *of all those we love*. Love demands the preservation of the limit. We cannot in love will the dissolution of those we love. We in love will the acceptance and preservation of the limit, and in faith believe God in Christ will keep His promises and redeem us into an eternal destiny that preserves us and those we love as real spiritual beings—limited as over against God, but integrated into His Will for us. Jesus said to us: with God all things are possible, and this is His Will for you as men, accept it. All this is shadowed gloriously forth for us in the Lord's Prayer. So the Christian message and hope for all men *as men*. Here the Cross—Christ on the Cross—is understood as the symbol of the acceptance of our limits, with all the suffering implicit in this acceptance; there—in the Classical metaphysical traditions—the Cross stands in the profoundest sense empty, the symbol of the realization of the unlimited. Man is free to choose, to will, his ultimate destiny "under" God in love—the Cross of Christ; or, "in" God in absolute identity—the metaphysical Cross. Insofar as man loves *the other*, he will choose Christ. Insofar as his "love" is desire for the absolute identity, he will choose another way. These ultimate acts of choice are made in depths of the Spirit inaccessible to rationalization or judgement by other men.

Once the choice is made to remain in oneself as man there is no escape from suffering or (and this is more terrible) from evil, for the irruptions of the forces of the unlimited will be experienced within the limits as evil, as the dark illimitable ultimate forces seeking to dissolve all *spiritual life as love*. The tragic vision of the Christian pierces into the recesses of the divine nature, and finds there too conflict and suffering—the unlimited utter ungrounded transcendent experienced as Wrath, Fire, and Darkness, what Boehme spoke of as the Agony of the Unmanifested Godhead—and sees too Christ on the Cross as Symbol of this Utter Incomprehensible, this Wrath not so much *of* God as *in* God. Yet from this very Divine Agony is uttered forth the promise of redemption. This Wrath is experienced by the spirit insofar as it chooses to remain other, to remain separate from the undifferentiated; it is the dissolving radiation of the absolute ground as over against all that would remain separate. But for the spirit seeking identity and ultimate dissolution it, the ground, is experienced as eternal peace, stillness, rest—and the rest is silence. The Classical traditions seek to return to this ultimate *Ungrund*; the Christian seeks to grow in it and from it. Boehme saw the Christian God Himself as growing from it and therefore in some sense experiencing all the anguish and wrath of His eternal divine becoming in Himself. He symbolized the Trinity as the Three-headed Lily growing from the *Ungrund*. And the spiritual life of man as the growing of the Lily in him. When your grandfather, on that occasion J.C.P. writes of, rubbed his hands together and exclaimed "Glory be to the Father and the Son and the Holy Ghost!" he was rejoicing in this growing of the Lily, this Christian acceptance of creatureliness with all its joys and sorrows...

My darling, darling Mary, what am I trying to say? This at least: I had traveled a long, long way on the path to the ultimate dissolutions before I met you. After I met you I found I was seeking love and a peace beyond all understanding, not a peace rising from a way of knowledge that leads beyond all distinctions. To move beyond all distinctions into the unlimited would be to lose you, and this I found I *would not do*. But an ocean liner underway can only slow down and change direction slowly; anything else invites disaster—yet change course I have. For many years it must have seemed to you that you were living with a ghost. If so, you were not far wrong. It is a ghostly business, keeping tryst with what is, humanly speaking, an ultimate emptiness, even though it be in itself a divine fullness. And one cannot go on a great journey and just will oneself back at the beginning unchanged. No, one has to work one's way back and can never again be as though one had never been away. One had been seeking to dissolve limits, now one is seeking to preserve them. Only in long striving and inner anguish are limits partially dissolved restored to their inherent reality under God; but the secret will of the spirit is now to save into an eternal life, beyond the circles of this world, our loving relationships—and what is the Resurrection of the Dead but the symbol of this achieved, the restoration by God of the limits dissolved by death, those limits that constitute the very reality of those we have learnt to love?

I do not know whether there is an inherent and utter apartness between the two ways. From within the limits of the finite there seems to be. Yet it may be only in seeming. Origen taught the ἀποκατάστασις, the final restoration of all beings in God to their inherent, divinely-willed natures; and those beings who will and realize the unlimited return to the same Divine Real that wills this restoration. Here too then "he who loses his life shall save it." It is certain too that each way has been trodden by many of the noblest and most kingly among men. Each man follows "his own way"—yet that way is chosen for him. And each one of us remains caught in the suffering and ambiguity of the finite, whether we accept our condition or seek to transcend it; and, in this world at least, the rest is unknowing and silence.

The evening sunlight is pouring—a divine and ineffable benediction—into Lucy's room. Perhaps, in the words of Ramana Maharshi, the supreme contemplative of our time, "it is better to be silent."

Moss and Bess are reminding me of their walk with short impatient barks. I stay out with them until the stars come out, those ancient and remote yet familiar and friendly constellations that shine down on us, on our births and livings and dyings, with a hint, it always seems to me at least, of ultimate reassurance.

And at their coming out each evening I salute them for your dear sake, my dear dear Mary.

Gerard

8 p.m. Home again.

Just came in down over the hill in faint moonlight. The Southern Cross setting over the shoulder of the North Facing Form; that Other, "There." Fire again on the slopes of Lengishu. Jupiter setting, Mars at the zenith. No planet rising in the east? Scorpio sloping under Mars to the west. A gentle wind blowing down from the peaks, the glaciers ghostly. Nightjars on the hill and hyrax along the forest edge and in the valley, and yes! the word came to me, on the hill: the two Crosses are—One.

The Beale
20 September 1969

My darling Mary,

I am just now thinking of you bending down in love over that small bronze-colored snake and touching it; and, as you try to escape symbols, take this as a symbol. The way beyond the symbol to pure consciousness, to the naked unimplicated subject, to pure absolute abstraction, is the way of the East. It remains that the moment this subject seeks to leave its absolute abstraction (granted for the moment such an aim is attainable) and to enter into relationship again, to communicate, it involves itself in symbols. In this return it will find the great traditional symbols as the only even remotely adequate symbols it has in its attempt to pass on its experience, or knowledge if you like. Such symbols are crystallizations from the deeper reaches of the consciousness of many generations of men on the earth in their approach to ultimate realities. There are stages in the movement of the spirit when it does find itself seeking to divest itself of the symbols, to cut away everything, to lay aside everything, and advance stark naked. Probably the supreme manifestation of this way followed to the end in utter integrity of spirit in our time is to be found in Ramana Maharshi, whose ashram in Tiruvannamalai I have long thought of visiting as an act of simple and grateful devotion to a supreme contemplative who is "all the time in the most perfect way helping men." At a critical moment of his life, in which he echoed the words of Jesus to *his* mother, "woman what hast thou to do with me?" he added the words, "it is better to remain silent." At a later stage in his life he made the return and re-entered into face-to-face communication with anyone who approached him.

Just as you tend to live and think and have your being under the protective and creative radiation of the spirit of another great contemplative, so do I tend to accept myself as under a similar grace and influence from Ramana Maharshi. In my copy of an account of the life of Ramana I find I wrote in under Radhakrishnan's introduction the note: "The *Enneads* are the supreme Western example of *vichara*. They supply the doctrinal basis, articulated in terms of Western thought, for the understanding of Sri Ramana Maharshi." *Vichara* is a Sanskrit word meaning "discrimination." Used in traditional Advaitic Hinduism it implies "discrimination in relation to the Supreme Self;

self-enquiry leading to knowledge of the Supreme Self." In my case, my reading of the *Enneads* is from this point of view.

It seems that at this time you are moving to the realization of the naked utter Spirit whereas I am trying incoherently and confusedly to "return," to enter into communion again; and I find that only certain traditional symbols reflect my experience. I am compelled to use these, or else give up the attempt to communicate, and "remain silent." Perhaps I have not yet reached the stage where I can return and should remain silent. Yet in relation to you a strong inner compulsion seems to force some utterance. And so I find myself writing these letters—contradictory, muddled perhaps, you must forgive that. You too touch the slow-worm, and attempt to communicate. Much that I try to say must seem to you very much at variance with my adherence to contemplation, yet contemplation—θεωρία—is a seeing; and certain kinds of seeing remain almost impossibly difficult to clothe in words, certainly impossible without the use of traditional symbols. You must not feel too impatient with my attempt (after all, the *Enneads* were also an "attempt")—and in fairness, be it said, an attempt not by any means devoid of confusions, contradictions, and obscurities. I am one born into the Christian tradition. I stand in the Christian tradition. I naturally use Christian symbols, symbols expressing universal truths that transcend Christianity. Yet the deepest insights, the deepest realizations of truth in the Christian tradition do pose problems for the other traditions, just as the others do for Christian vision. I do not pretend to have solved these problems, but I am in a very intense degree aware of them and I have no desire to explain them away, or pretend they don't exist. I prefer, if nothing else seems open, to leave them as utter, seemingly irreducible contradictions in my thought, trusting in divine grace for final resolution.

What seems to have forced the issue is your reference to Berdyaev. Perhaps—for who can limit the action of Providence?—this too is under Providence. However that may be, I find myself forced to respond to your words in depth. When you say "Berdyaev" in this context you say "the Christian Vision." The reason I take Berdyaev with utter seriousness is that he, more than any man of our time known to me, takes the Christian Vision seriously. He is not an ecclesiastic, not essentially a philosopher: he is a man who sees the Christian Vision, and takes it seriously. He has a profound, subtle, by no means naive, and intensely critical mind. Intellectually he is well equipped to face the philosophers on their own ground. Intellectually also he is immensely indebted to them and gratefully acknowledges this, but it remains that he has seen the Christian Vision and takes it seriously.

In Berdyaev this Christian Vision is not rationalized away into philosophy as it is with so many thoughtful Christians, not dogmatized away into superstition as with many theologians, not naively accepted into a credulous mind as with so many "simple" Christians. No, he has seen θεωρία, the Christian Vision; and awkwardly and stubbornly and intractably takes it seriously... such a man is not to be taken lightly.

Yes, but the confusions, the muddles, the contradictions? They are the confusions and contradictions—fairer to say, problems—of the New Testament itself, and of a man who takes it seriously. The New Testament is irrational, apocalyptic, eschatological, prophetic, subversive, other-worldly... without these elements it is reduced to naive moralistic fabling.

Words like "irrational," "apocalyptic," and "prophetic" are hardly to be applied in any sense seriously to the Classical philosophical and metaphysical traditions; in fact these traditions repudiate such categories. They cannot accept them and retain their own integrity. This is the problem, the abyss hard and bitter as death to cross, from either side.

The philosophical approach is to take the New Testament for the most part as naive fabling and read its own meanings into it.

The Christian approach is to take the New Testament seriously; but the man who takes it seriously as "revelation" is not very likely to utter words entirely acceptable to philosophers. He has "seen" a vision—irrational, apocalyptic, in a glass darkly—that does not fit into the categories of philosophy. Heraclitus says: "The sun will not overstep his measures; otherwise the Erinyes, helpers of justice, will find him out."

But this is not possible: the pure intellect in principle sees clearly into the ultimate nature of things; there is nothing hidden, apocalyptic.

We have a foreshadowing of this conflict in the ancient world. Heraclitus was obscure, enigmatic, self-contradictory, irrational, by some called ἀνόητος: senseless, a fool. Plato and Aristotle, and most of their followers, adopted superior airs: there was, it is true, something disturbing about the man, but one shouldn't take him too seriously—he had not been to the Academy or learnt the law of contradiction. There was too a certain tinge of religious fanaticism in him: "fire will advance and convict and judge all things"—even, it seems, the philosophers. He thinks we are all asleep, even the philosophers; he sees only knotted contrarieties, paradoxical tensions giving rise to insoluble antinomies in existence; but our whole hope lies in resolving these tensions, unknotting these knots. He sets at nought the elaborations of ordered reason flowing from ὄν, being; an ultimate irrational will break in from τὸ μὴ ὄν, non-being; there are disruptive hidden eschatological forces threatening history; the eternal, the ultimate divine, cannot be contained by or explicated by or reached by our notions of rationality; let us quickly hurry back to our intellectual vision of Truth, Goodness, Beauty, which is, it seems, inaccessible to this man... something like this seems to have been the impact of Heraclitus on "the philosophers." Meanwhile, Aeschylus was revealing in great poetry the tragic vision as piercing unfathomably deep into the spiritual world, no less a prophetic preparation for the coming Christian Vision than the prophetic voices of Israel. "His Ways are not our ways."

Apocalyptic vision senses something hidden, disruptive, something that will effect utter transvaluations, at once working in history and transcending history. This "hidden" is coming. It is in the dark, inaccessible to reason. It is a force, a spiritual dimension of eternity realizing itself in time; it redeems time, and the sufferings of time, not by emptying time of ultimate meaning (as in the traditional metaphysical philosophies), not by escaping from time, but by incarnating itself *in* time. The apocalyptic vision is always waiting for this divine redeeming incarnated real to enter into its final transvaluing manifestation. This divine real, this Christ, is both utterly present though "hidden," and "coming" in an approaching "end." It is not eternity transcending time but eternity dynamically invading, redeeming, and fulfilling time. All this is "dark" to the pure metaphysical intellect, for which there are no such "hidden" possibilities—for which all lies open to pure transcendent intellect. The difference in vision comes out particularly clearly in the attitude to death. In traditional philosophies there is, as it were, a kind of metaphysical transparency about death: it is the falling away of the body, separation from time, escape into the eternal—the being realizing an inherent eternity after being lost in illusions. But for the Christian death is darkness, unknowing. It is a personal apocalypse concealed in an utter difference, or a possible spiritual obliteration in judgement. It hides a mystery inaccessible to, impenetrable by, intellect. "Nature is wont to hide herself." And "the invisible attunement is superior to the visible."

All this implies that the eternal is not accessible to an immediate, essentially timeless, metaphysical intuition; the eternal is mediated to man through time, through an apocalyptic divine force disruptively invading and obliterating his human, all-too-human notions, subjecting him to punishment and judgement—yet to a punishment and judgement utterly conditioned by divine mercy.

But this is all dreaming you say, a kind of spiritual romanticism! How or why should the eternal concern itself? Punish, judge, redeem, show mercy? These are childish, anthropomorphic fantasies. What meaning can we attach to the eternal moving, invading, involving itself in time, in suffering—in evil, contaminating itself in shame and sin? The eternal is in its essential being timeless, unchanging, unmoving, untouched by sorrow, unpierced by evil—our salvation is to reach it, not to wait for it to redeem us.

All that you say is true, yet it remains an incomprehensible truth too that this other childish fantasy is truth also.

But this is utter contradiction—the absurd.

So be it.

In such irreducible oppositions of insight lies the conflict. "They cannot apprehend how, being at variance, it yet agrees with itself—here lies an attunement of opposite tensions, as in the bow or the lyre.... Wholes and not wholes... the concordant is discordant."

But one must confess in the empirical, historical world a discordance of opposite tensions rather than an attunement. The terrible conflicts of history arise from discordances between the intellect and the irrational, between necessity and freedom, between good and evil; and in all these conflicts it is the will, at once both many and one, at once both manifest and hidden, at once both reasonable and irrational, at once both good and evil, that is involved and divided in its unfathomably mysterious depths. You cannot track it down—so deep is its cause—by irreducible ambiguities. It is the will that hides the ultimate secrets and denies their revelation to intellect. Intellect too lies at the mercy of will, at the service of will. Berdyaev's paradoxical utterances on the relationship between intellect and will are by no means the product of confused thinking. Plotinus says somewhere that "the soul can through intellect see the Good *if it wills to do so.*" In those last simple words lies all the mystery. And the will, in all the manifestations of its ultimate irrational freedoms, remains still the "Will of God." What is will—in ultimate, utter seeing?: the realization of irrational freedom in movement. The order of intellect, necessity, good, beauty, spiritual fulfilment, is "being"—but "being" lies ambiguously rooted in τὸ μὴ ὄν: the infinitely mysterious ultimate *Ungrund* inaccessible to light, to intellect; the ground of the ultimate divine willing; an utter irrational unconditioned freedom. The rational is always a mode of being; the irrational of τὸ μὴ ὄν. This is why evil can never be rationalized away. Yet too it is from the hidden creativities in the divine dark that the creative redeeming movements hidden in apocalypse emerge from τὸ μὴ ὄν into being. These multitudinous irrational dark creative movements and conflicts in the *Ungrund* (which constitute the Agony of the Unmanifested Godhead) flow out eternally—disrupting, invading the realms of being; bringing into being an endless procession of new worlds and hitherto unrealized modes of being; bringing destruction, and suffering, and evil; bringing death and all our woe-bringing too secret, hidden in sources of utter dark; bringing all redemptive restorations and reconciliations—blow from the dark, blow blow blow blow wind blow wind blow...

Something like this then is the ultimate seeing, the complex, irrational, barely communicable vision of Berdyaev and Boehme and of all Christians who haven't rationalized away the influences flowing to them from the central Christian symbols. A vision not easy to accommodate to the categories of rational philosophies flowing from a central dependence on pure intellect. It is true that the utter source of seeing here lies in the will, in the divine incomprehensible Will that comes to man wrapped up in thick darkness—fire and wrath are about Him! Symbolized as personal, as possessed of will and knowledge, but flowing from an utter beyond personal. How deny a vision so honest?

Over against this Christian Vision stands unperturbed, ancient, the θεωρία flowing from the ultimate uncreated Light, the θεωρία of Goodness, Truth, Beauty: Eternal, Still, Self-creating, Self-contained, unpierced by any evil, unshadowed by any dark, unmoved by any Agony. The One Unutterable Perfect—Knowing Itself as *Satchitananda*: Being-Consciousness-Bliss—redeeming All by Its utter transcendent Itness, which yet pervades All.

> The Bright, The Utter, The Still
> This we adore! This we worship!
> O Bright! O Utter! O Still!
> Thee we adore! Thee we worship!
> O Bright beyond Bright beyond Bright
> O Utter beyond Utter beyond Utter
> O Still beyond Still beyond Still
> Thee we adore! Thee we worship!
> O Bright-Beyond Utter-Beyond Still!

How deny a vision so resplendent? In what sense—if any—such seemingly ultimate oppositions are reconcilable I don't know. Yet in truth there are, too, apocalyptic elements in the Eastern traditions. We are, they say, approaching the end of our own world-age; we are in a very real sense suffering the invasion of dark disintegrating forces. They speak of the "black fire" of Brahman advancing on the world, heralding a final dissolution. But the end of a world is a beginning too—Ξυνὸν ἀρχὴ καὶ πέρας said Heraclitus—and too the Bright, the Utter, the Still remains unmoved. Here are doctrines closely parallel to apocalyptic Christianity. But for the moment, leaving aside this traditional corrective doctrine in the Eastern metaphysical traditions, if we consider pure Platonism or Vedanta (which seem as it were untroubled by apocalyptic insights, unconcerned with or unseeing the irrational, inflowing, creative, apocalyptic freedom advancing as an obliterating destructive force on our particular world), we ask, what is this?: unconscious, utter absorption in the eternal? Plotinus particularly put great stress on the "unconsciousness" of the One. Here the rest is silence: "it is better to remain silent." Yet at the level of multiplicity, of differentiation, it does not seem beyond thought to see such a metaphysical doctrine as an inner truth to be transcended ultimately in an outer apocalyptic that remains hidden in the inner truth, so that the spirit centered on this truth remains unconscious of it—abstracted into the unconsciousness of the One. There seems no inherent impossibility in this.

Moving then to the consideration of the Christian Vision or the Hindu eschatological doctrines, again it seems theoretically possible, at least in a parallel fashion, to see here the apocalyptic vision as an inner truth transcended ultimately in an outer, unchanging, pure, metaphysical reality that remains hidden in the inner truth, so that the spirit centered here remains unconscious of this utter unchanging. In the one case the metaphysical is seen as disrupted into history by apocalypse. In the other, apocalypse is seen as in very truth ultimately transcended in an utter unchanging. In the one case the transcendence of Intellect is inverted by apocalypse into transcendence of the Will. In the other, Will is seen as inverted into Intellect in the Utter Unchanging. And these ultimate possibilities merge into one absolute Real that cannot be apprehended as changing or unchanging, as many or as One— an utter Ineffable!

Here each Tradition seems to relegate to the "unconscious" certain aspects of ultimate truth—those aspects not accessible to it.

My darling, I left off here and went for a walk with Moss and Bess round Windy Hill. Came back in windy moonlight and lay under our bush there. Suddenly terrors ran shouting through my soul. I felt too as did old Jacob Boehme—I write now before his portrait—that we all in this world are lodging in a melancholy inn. I came back trembling—some kind of reaction— for I have been writing this letter under extreme spiritual pressure. I thought of your reassuring story in today's letter, how Eric counselled you, *when shut in a dark shed by the door suddenly slamming in the wind,* never to be afraid. Well! This story was for me at a moment of terror oddly and wonderfully reassuring. Strange how words said long ago by a boy now dead, killed in war, to another child should move up out of memory in your mind to bring courage to another—long afterwards—one unknown to him and a stranger! Anyway here I am back safe and ready to have my bath and then to bed. I don't know whether all this I've written will make much sense to you, but it's the kind of thing that goes through my head! It seems to me now to oversimplify and need so much qualification that the wisdom of Sri Ramana's words comes to me with double force: "'Tis better to be silent!" So I'll try to keep off this particular ground in writing again. But the inner command was to speak!

How I *rejoice* to see your letters! Don't worry too much about *The Presocratic Philosophers.* If it is at all heavy or bulky leave it at home in Mappowder. I have so many books here, and it will be something to look forward to there. I feel more at home among the pre-Socratics than the later Greeks.

Yes! You are probably right in your reaction to *Truth and Revelation*. I reply out of a long saturation in Berdyaev's major works. He is a difficult thinker to grasp in depth and he does at times seem to lose himself in paradox. However bless him! When he wrote that book you read he was an old soldier who had been sorely wounded in his time, and well!, such old warriors always arouse a certain affection and admiration and leave behind them in their passing a sense of greatness. It can in truth be said of him, he suffered much. *This I know*. I understand his reference to the icons.

I like to think you have had Gilfrid to stay. I hope in our cottage. We hardly ever see him here, so it is an occasion to accept gratefully. I do hope and pray Will grows stronger each day.

Well my dear, that small snake you met produced some reactions too many miles away over the curve of the earth! I have too before me, beside Boehme's portrait, Dürer's portrait of his father. What a formidable and noble countenance, with just a hint of courageous apprehension about the eyes! Yes! We are all wrapped up in unfathomable mysteries!

> Love to you always,
> Gerard

Next day, Sunday

P.S.
I am putting in a Song of Praise, one for you, one for Lucy.

The Beale
21 September 1969

My darling Mary,

I want to share with you some thoughts about my reaction to Plotinus. I've been reading him rather intensively, and he poses some problems for me. I had been trying to sort it out a little in my head and then the thought came to me to think on paper for a while and see if I can arrive at some clarity.

First of all I want to say that I very well understand that any great mind that is grappling in depth with complex, and often obscure, problems will, at the level of articulate utterance, involve himself in ambiguities and contradictions; and even, at times, in defending what may seem to others indefensible positions. I would recognize this as inevitable. Consistency and clarity are *always* (I think) bought at the price of a certain oversimplification and superficiality. One probably wouldn't be very interested in Plotinus if he didn't, as does Whitehead or my friend Berdyaev, seem so constantly and radically to contradict himself. I have come to think that if this contradictory tension isn't evidenced in a man's expression of his deepest thought, it is because he is either evading the deeper issues or relatively unconscious of them.

However there exists in Plotinus, as it seems to me, a certain contradiction that is not perhaps quite acceptable as flowing only and altogether from the stubborn, irreducible contrarieties at the roots of things. This contradiction in *him* (not only in his expressed thought) reveals itself most clearly whenever his thought approaches ethical problems. I see clearly of course that he had the mind of a supreme metaphysician, and that all his real intellectual passion was devoted to metaphysical speculation—so that he is almost inevitably impatient of ethical problems (as he is of social or political problems). Nevertheless he does not just leave aside ethics; he seems rather to advance an ethical theory that stands in rooted contradiction to his metaphysical vision. It is as though he had (possibly in his youth) crystallized, in his ethical attitudes, around Stoicism, and had from then on accepted these doctrines without ever becoming fully conscious that his fundamental metaphysical insights stood in opposition to his ethics. Had he become conscious of this he would have seen his ethical attitudes as untenable. This is understandable in him as a man of his time—very much, I would say, a citizen of the late Roman Empire, when

Stoicism seemed to offer to so many thoughtful men a strengthening factor in their struggle to preserve their world from dissolution. And Stoicism was far more a product of the Roman mind than the Greek, and as such was alien to the ineradicable Greek temper of the mind of Plotinus at its deeper levels. Yes, this is understandable (even to be expected), yet one is left in the position that, in the light of Plotinus's own metaphysical doctrines, his ethical attitudes are to be, I would say, quite decisively rejected. The fundamental contradiction is clear, and not to be verbalized away. Can a spirit centered on Truth, Goodness, and Beauty—at their supreme level and in their inherent eternal living reality—remain unmoved in face of the invading malignant forces in the world that seek to obscure, and even to destroy, their temporal forms and images? A man may be helpless but he cannot, as man, remain unmoved without, in simple ineluctable truth, becoming an accomplice. The disciplined striving to develop Stoic attitudes cannot but involve hardening of the heart; it *is* hardening of the heart consciously and deliberately cultivated for what is, in the last inescapable analysis, a self-regarding purpose. Stoicism produced great men—who would wish to deny it?—but not one man of supreme stature; and it certainly didn't leave us with the last word in ethics—that was left to men of an incalculably finer spiritual fibre.

Plotinus speaks of the "passion for the Good"; but one must, it seems, prudently (what the motive other than prudence?) avoid what is, in simple *intellectual* honesty, the inevitable corollary: the equally passionate rejection of evil. He does not see, or does not admit, that this prudent avoidance inescapably involves cooling and weakening of the passion for the Good. These tragic dilemmas and tensions are rootedly part of the spiritual life, and striving to escape into Stoic ἀπάθεια is a human, all-too-human evasion. The philosopher seeks to realize the truth from behind a self-protective barrier; takes care in common prudence that he shall not suffer for the truth, even in the depths of his spirit. He seeks an anaesthetic: ἀπάθεια. We are all involved in these shrinkings and fearful withdrawings, but Plotinus's metaphysical doctrines in truth demand their overcoming, demand that we see them for what they are—simple weaknesses—and not dress them up as something admirable and call it ἀπάθεια.

One must in honesty admit that one senses very little in Plotinus himself of these shrinkings; he was patently a brave and honest and compassionate and concerned man. He wasn't, I would wager (and I honor him for it), very good at practicing what he preached in this direction. His was too princely a heart to confine itself within ἀπάθεια. He may have liked, as a human foible, to pretend he was a Stoic, but he was not a Stoic at heart. His marvelously clear metaphysical insight into the structure of eternal reality as Goodness, Truth, and Beauty did not spring from a heart or mind "cabin'd and confin'd" in Stoic attitudes. I find this distressing—this Stoic influence, albeit at a very superficial level—in Plotinus because, in his simple honest humanity, *he was too good for it*. And I have an idea this Stoicism of his has perhaps done more to alienate many from him than his metaphysical audacity has.

There is another aspect of his thought that may partly explain why he never, it seems, grew fully conscious in himself of this contradiction. And this, significantly, is again an aspect with ethical implications. He sees evil—not here as a metaphysical source in non-being but rather, in its practical revelation of itself in character—as nothing more than "a failure to be reasonable"; but surely most of us would think of a failure to be reasonable as rising more often from ignorance, confusion, weakness, and stupidity. This is not *in itself* the evil—the positive, malignant, often fully conscious willing of the dark, destructive forces in life that most of us think of as evil: the evil that deliberately rejects the good and seeks to destroy it. It seems ludicrous to refer to the German concentration camps and all their practices as a simple failure to be reasonable. Equally, the words seem quite meaningless if used in connection with the Crucifixion, or indeed in multitudes of instances it is only too easy to think of. It is as though a certain dimension of human experience just did not consciously exist for Plotinus. But it is this very dimension, in its own terrible itness—an itness that cannot be talked or attitudinized away—that lies all round and agonizingly pervades Greek Tragedy and the Passion and Death of Christ; and these stories are symbols, revelations, of this spiritual dimension as inherent in all our existence. These are not just special cases; they are rather manifestations of forces always and everywhere just below the surface. One uses the word "spiritual" here in that they flow from perverse forms of consciousness, not from natural unconscious forces.

The thought comes to me that for Plotinus, as for Whitehead, the spiritual life is a life of spiritual adventure, of movement into novelty. For some men this form of spiritual life is inherently legitimate and to be honored, just as a life of physical adventure is for men of another temperament. But for men of a certain spiritual cast it is a matter of wrestling with utter truth, of wrestling with the dreadful ambiguities—right to their source in the divine ground of all things. Men such as Jeremiah, St. Paul, Boehme, Dostoievsky, Aeschylus, El-Hallaj. All that they have is demanded of such men in a way, it seems to me, more absolute and unconditional and all-obliterating than the demands made on themselves by the adventurers. The adventurers go out and seek... on the others, the dreadful conflict bursts—and there is no escaping.

In myself, as an individual temperament, I am among the adventurers. I say this without reservation, and I can never (I hope) fail in gratitude for all I have received from the adventurers, among whom number all the famous names in the great Classical philosophies and metaphysical traditions. Before the wrestlers I can only halt in astonished humility, and salute a greatness that transcends anything in myself, or, I suspect, in any of the adventurers. A carpenter, a weaver, a shoemaker—I hasten back to the philosophers secretly chastened, humiliated, and questioning myself...

Well! Such thoughts and obstinate questionings go chasing through my head as a result of reading Plotinus and Aeschylus together. Leaving out of account monstrously wicked men like Nero or Caligula, it is hard to imagine two men of more opposed temperaments. For years I shrank from Greek Tragedy; I had, as they say, a hunch that it would set itself before me as a radical questioning and challenge. I tend too, I think, to read philosophy and explore metaphysical doctrines as a protection against darkness. To face men who move out into darkness is a test I am hardly prepared to meet... all that remains is, like a good philosopher, to talk: λάλος γε ἄνθρωπος ἐστι καί, ὡς ἔοικε, φιλόσοφος...

Nevertheless I have happy walks, not unduly burdened by the spirit of Aeschylus, and fairly well propped up by the spirit of Plotinus; and, all in all, well content with the pleasure there is in life itself. I rejoice to see the winter suns redly shining in the shadows of the forest and the snowy solitary bird on his high branch facing the morning. I am not one who is in truth much given to exploring the dark; one rather who rejoices, in his mild unheroic way, in the light; and it is with relief that I return to Heraclitus (dry light), and Herodotus (dry stick), and Hesiod (dryer still), and that supreme poet Homer (bright light of a sun that sees all and shines on all, the just and the unjust: light seekers and dark explorers, the puzzled and the wise...).

> With my love always,
> under the sign of the four H's,
> Gerard

The Beale
24 September 1969

My darling Mary

News to rejoice at in this letter—that you hope to fly October 14th. Valentine has been in my mind. I think so much all the time of the great courage she will need from now on.

I have some quiet happy moments each day in the morning at about ten o'clock, sitting at the base of St. John's tree. Almost always a pair of dusky flycatchers are not far away. There is an old olive stump across the stream and shooting from the top of it a small *menjere* tree, light green leaves trembling all the time in the bright sunlight; and just beside this seedling on the stump is one of the favorite perches for the dusky flycatcher. There are also two wintersuns glowing in the grass near the base of the stump. I wish I had Will's gift and could send you a sketch of it in color. This morning I saw also a white paradise flycatcher and a red-winged laurie at the same time in the branches above the olive stump. I get visits on the verandah from a robin and Herr Reichenow the cisticola as well as the regular sunbirds and rock martins. Many toads, large and small (too many), come into the dressing room, bathroom, and garage each evening. I don't see them in the morning and haven't had one in my boot again.

I often remember our walks to Ball Hill and would like it to be nearer. If we could roll Mappowder and Beale into one it would be perfect!

"Saying or writing anything one believes one has thought immediately makes it in some way unreal... what is real is the living or process which continues." Yes, I agree. All this reflects the, in some sense, unreal character of time and process. Yet, too, the underlying real leaves some trace always of itself—all our thinking and attempted expression of thought would be unintelligible without this. I rejoice that so many great poets and prophets and philosophers and artists of all kinds (and, too, multitudes of more humble people) haven't felt themselves too inhibited by this Heraclitean insight. And, my dearworthy, darling Mary, I especially rejoice that it didn't inhibit the writing of your splendid stories, which are so much more than just stories. And most precious of all your study of Plotinus. It is to me that you caught, in the flash of light from a kingfisher's wing, the essence of that great man, unclouded by the finally irrelevant influences that partially obscured his own expression of them. I seem to have written so much about him in my recent letters that is not altogether sympathetic, but that after all is a tribute to the enormous weight of sheer intellectual impact he makes. I have been trying to reduce to a very brief expression my final reaction to his formidable, continuing presence in my intellectual life. Something like this: I revere him as a great contemplative who in some degree darkened the brightness of his vision in his extremely rationalistic expression of it. The Stoic element in his ethical doctrine is unacceptable to me. On their ethical principles, every tear—of joy or sorrow—shed since the beginning of the world is an offense. I cannot accept the monstrous inhumanity of such a notion. I am sure that, in practice, most Stoics found it hard to live up to this doctrine. In Plotinus's case I am sure it was utterly alien to the nature of the man.

The other element in the expression of his vision I find not altogether congenial is his, to me, excessive rationalism. His towering greatness of spirit flows from his θεωρία. His rationalism, διάνοιᾱ, cannot carry the weight of splendor flowing from his νόησις. This is why later rationalists (instance Bertrand Russell), however impressed they may be, finally reject his philosophy. This excessive exercise of the faculty of διάνοιᾱ, discursive reasoning, in Plotinus puzzled me at first. I now have this idea about it. He was a man of tremendous *mental* vitality. His mind was intensely and naturally alive, active. He could not as it were succeed in altogether assimilating this mental energy into his purely intellectual contemplation. It overflowed and was *used up* in διάνοιᾱ, but at the price of partly dimming his expression of his θεωρία, which was his essential self. Again, we rejoice that he didn't allow this difficulty, which I am sure he was aware of, to inhibit him in making the attempt to express something of his vision.

Having brought up the subject of rationalism, I feel I should say something of my own reaction to and evaluation of it. I think the particular problems that have always engaged me are not accessible to a rationalist approach. At most it has here a certain negative value. It helps to detect and get rid of rubbish—it has little of positive value to contribute. For the most part Western philosophy has tended to be excessively rationalistic. It has approached problems that are only to be considered in the light of νόησις, in the spirit of διάνοιᾱ. Its results are deadening and barren. As this rationalistic spirit became stronger in Western philosophy it gradually revealed its emptiness, so that in recent centuries we have seen it busily and self-importantly seeking, in every way possible, to empty the great spiritual traditions of man of all significant meaning, finally holding up its hands in horror when it finds itself face to face with a vacuum, and then prophetically exhorting us to resort to despair as a palliative: a "rock" that in due time turned into a morass. I have grown to understand why the Churches have always been so wary of this so-called philosophy. It would be ludicrous to translate it, in this instance, into its Greek meaning. This philosophy, under many disguises of approach, is always inviting the Christian vision to surrender its own distinctive insights, to surrender its vision to the dissolving influences of rationalism. For these reasons I feel alienated from it and hostile to it. If one has to be a rationalist in order to be a philosopher, then I am content not to be a philosopher. I prefer the company of the great poets and prophets: their vision of things pierces unfathomably deeper into the mysteries of existence. The reason I have been and am so strongly attracted to Heraclitus is that he was a seer and an apocalyptic prophet rather than a philosopher. Every rationalist since, who is aware of his existence, has either ridiculed him, or tried to explain him away; that is, to rationalize him away. Well! In this case they face one who dived deeper... one not accessible to their rationalistic explanations. He had had glimpses of apocalypse and became, as well he might, dark obscure riddling incoherent. Like Moses he stuttered, though not, like Zacharias after his vision in the temple, unable to speak. Heraclitus was no more able to unsee the vision he had seen than any of the great prophets, or poets, or scientists, or philosophers, or contemplative sages could unsee theirs. The demand of the rationalists is that we should all unsee our visions and see only their meagre and starveling substitutes. But visions once seen, that flame up out of the abysses, are not so easily unseen again—and certainly not at the behest of a rationalist.

And now to leave so barren a subject as the barrenness of rationalism. My own perplexities of spirit have always been at bottom Christian perplexities, and as such not easily accessible to philosophical resolution, even when the aid offered is from truly great philosophy. The Christian vision is involved in enigmas dark to intellect, even at its highest. Here the pride of the intellectual man—not of pure intellect as such—grows impatient that a vision rises in the world which asserts depths in existence not open to the penetration of intellect. But the seer cannot unsee his vision, and goes on uttering things mirthless, unadorned, unperfumed, alien to all facile resolutions of the enigma of the world. By some, wise in their own conceit, he is dubbed ἀνόητος—a fool—but the great multitudes of men and women on the earth, their vision not clouded with vanity, know that such men do not speak in utter vain, and listen with an awed respect: the great religious traditions rising out of these dark and questioning revelations will never cease uttering their word before the world's end.

All this I accept, and in the depths of my spirit always have accepted. This is the primordial utterance of the world out of its own uttermost depths, and from depths deeper still. It utters itself out of the eternal unchanging *Ungrund*, the dark; and how shall one escape that which never changes? Here is the root of all darkened, anxious self-questioning. Perplexities enough—

but, too, outflowing perplexities through all the levels of existence, from the deepest and most solitary to the most superficial and social.

In my own case some unalterable awareness of these utter impenetrables and darknesses crystallized in me when a child in connection with the subject of 'South Wales Echo'. Since then all answers offered me by philosophy, ecclesiastical religion, science, and rationalism have been measured against this dark center, measured in secret knowing not open to facile deception—and all found wanting, except the Christian Vision. But that certainly too issues in new perplexities in relation to the world and how this vision is to utter itself in truth in the world. The Churches can only offer a pale semblance attenuated by rationalism, darkened by superstition, distorted by fanaticism. How could they offer more? They are only ourselves writ large.

Here are my perplexities, and not mine alone; they are the rooted perplexities of man as such once he has reached, had revealed to him, a certain level of self-awareness. I try in this letter to bring them into the light a little, only a little—how uproot into the light of time an eternally-rooted darkness? I try to, shall I say rather, let a little light into them perhaps, to help towards understanding some of the harsher words I may have written in earlier letters. I try always in civilized sanity to remain in the easy light of everyday seeming certitudes, which are ultimately the reassuring certitudes of light and reason. Aye!—even of bright shining intellect in its transcendent center. But always beyond and beyond and beyond again is the invading dark, a dark not utterly empty it seems, but full of questions, demands, unutterable threatenings. All this; yet here, very here, lies the hint and hope of all possible reconciliations, but reconciliations on God's terms, not ours.

God's terms? What God? An Utter Transcendent lying infinitely out and beyond all knowing by us except on Its own terms. And His Ways are not our ways, and His terms are not the kind of terms thought acceptable and sensible by rationalists. And here too the darkness darkens; we do not know the terms, yet the demand is made that we meet them. How pass on, how move from here? Yes, we see that light shining, the Plotinian Intellect in all its full-dazzling splendor. Think not we do not see it. Yes, we see it shining out against the utter beyondness and darkness of the *Ungrund*. Yes, we see it. Yet our very seeing of it is—darkness. And here the darkness is final, impenetrable by any Light on our terms. This is the darkness that fell and falls on the earth at the death of Christ. Think not I speak here of One who died two thousand years ago. He died then, but in utter untellable truth He dies now and always in time. So here we return to the metaphysical wisdom: yes, He dies in Time, this must be; turn then from this dark to the Eternal Light beyond Time. Leave Time in its darkness, turn with us to That Shining we know beyond all the circles and reaches of Time. Oh my dear dear one say not these words...

He is *in* Time, moving ever more deeply into Time. He is utterly in Time, redeeming Time, dying in Time, yes, but dying too into Time—we cannot move out of Time without leaving Him in His Darkness... in His Darkness, which holds in its utter heart the promise of a Light more dazzling, more dazzling beyond utter untellable, than the Light you bid us seek. We do not know, my dear dear one, how this Utter Light will be born—it is in very truth born now in Christ—yet again not born and waiting to be born in this Darkness we are in. So we wait, wait on in this Darkness... This seems the one thing demanded of us: that we wait on in this Darkness... we would ask you to wait with us in this Darkness... but there is no need—for in utter truth your light out beyond Time is but part of this darkness... and it may be—may surely be—His Will that you wait there while we wait here... we are all waiting, even though we know it not... there is no escape from the waiting... Time is the waiting—not this time or that time—not time in this world or in that world... Time is the waiting my dearest one—and deceive not yourself—your being is in time—that is His Will—Time is the waiting, Time is His Dying, Time is His Darkness, and your timeless state out there is but a mode of His Time. It is in His Time we will be born anew—not in your timeless—your timeless too is but a mode of birth into His Time—but we must wait—all of us—this is all that is demanded of us... this very waiting is the prayerful asking demanded of us... and from this asking we shall receive what He wills for us... go, my dear, and wait out there as it is your wish... and as the waiting grows dark in emptiness, then know that we too are sharing your darkness and emptiness and waiting... yet be comforted, for you must know this great emptiness in His Fullness is being born for us... utter glory...

Something like this was the wordless word of Origen to Plotinus in their last meeting... something like this Gerard tries to say to Mary at this time...

You say, "I do not choose to be alone, but I am." You are my dearest of dear friends, not alone unless you choose to be. The last, and perhaps *only* word of Jesus (rather, all He said implied this) to us was that what we ask for we receive. You are not alone unless you choose to be. I love you, and not I only; and love demands not understanding but acceptance. Who would love or be loved if understanding were the condition? No, the demand is... ultimate acceptance out beyond the circles of this world, or any possible world—acceptance of the unknowing as well as the knowing—acceptance that for each and every one of us in His Will is our end and our peace—acceptance too that in His Will all we can rightly ask for is granted. Acceptance too of all the perplexities and difficulties and sorrows and failures—often petty failures, all the more difficult of acceptance in their pettiness—acceptance within this world. You are not alone unless you choose to be. How could you be alone when there are those that love you? In this world or beyond this world?

Your work on Plotinus rose out of a great and splendid vision of the world and God. For this very reason I have tried to utter in reply a word not unworthy of that vision. If my own vision seems a darker one, that too is part of the acceptable whole fulfilled in His Will. And in His Will is our peace.

Now Moss and Bess demand their walk, evening is darkening. I wait until this time and stay out on Windy Hill until full dark. I'll finish off this letter tomorrow.

8 p.m.

No, not tomorrow. Here I am back after the walk, out not, as I said, to full dark, but to bright moonlight and a strong wind coming down from the mountain. Something remains to say, something that would escape all saying. Yes, I think you in your story symbolized us, us two, when you saw as in a vision Plotinus and Origen standing on the shore of the infinite sea at night so long ago, each leaving with the other a sense of a question unanswerable; and now, in very very utter now, so long afterward repeating the same unanswerable questions... the waiting is not ended nor will be ended until the end of the world. Yes, Christ on the Cross until the end of the world was a word uttered by Origen in his time... and repeated by Pascal long afterward in his time. He dies now, very now, in you in me in all men; dies on and on, always dying not out of time but back into time and the suffering of time... dying back into time to the redeeming and dying of time itself in an unutterable mystery of consummation. "I will be with you always even to the end of the world."

In that last silence between Origen and Plotinus as they gazed at that remote sea horizon, in that indrawn silence full of all utter questionings, did that wind blowing from the illimitable sea to the land in their faces, or blowing from that very land trodden in earlier time by Jesus out over the sea, or perhaps gustily veering, who knows?—did that wind that had received into its breath the very breath and vibration of His Words, did that same wind carrying its untellable burden of mystery, did it breathe into the souls of those two men some hint of a final meaning utterable by no human lips? There we leave them. There too we leave Mary and Gerard. There we leave all men.

But faintly in the night wind blowing round our home tonight, blowing under the ancient constellations that shone down on Him, blowing over the same ancient earth trodden by Him, blowing, and in its blowing this night receiving into its breath the dying breath of who knows how many men, receiving too the first cry of who knows how many new lives to be lived out on the earth, in its blowing, faintly infinitely indrawn what is it? A fancy, a memory, a dying trace of an ancient hope? A hope unquenched in the hearts and last darkening conscious moments of so great a number of men on the earth before us, a faintest of all faint echoes, seems to come to me, immeasurably remote, yet nearer, oh, immeasurably nearer than the beating of my own heart—a still voice, and barely caught words: "I will be with you always, even to the end of the world."

So long, my dear dear one, so long as even the faintest trace of a memoried whisper of these words remains in the hearts of men, so long as even the faintest of faint traces of these words remains to burden the night winds, so long the Christian hope and the Christian vision lives on, and all other hopes and visions seem dark and empty before it.

Gerard

The Beale
26 September 1969

My darling Mary,

Your letter of the 18th has just come. It is hard to think that Will is not fitter to travel now than when he came to England. Oh, I do feel bad about those tickles; one would need to be a real Stoic to put up with them for so long a period—it must be four years since they started. And too it is distressing to have confirmed one's fears for Valentine.

I think in this letter you do perhaps come a little nearer to seeing just where the difference lies, shall we say, between Plotinus and Origen? I agree philosophy likes to think that the great spiritual traditions are *ancillae*. By philosophy here I mean Western rationalistic philosophy. I do not in fact feel any of the sense of conflict we have been writing to each other about in my approaches to the Eastern metaphysical doctrines. I think my difficulty, in the last analysis, arises from what appears to me an over-valuation of the efficacy of reason in the approach to ultimate problems. I understand very well the necessary transcendence of the pure intellect. That is not the difficulty. It is stressed, if anything, even more emphatically in the East, and I have never found it objectionable there. Intellect remains the principle of mind—accepted; but here the question arises as to how far it is realized in its pure integrity in the mind of any particular man. One suspects it is in practice always in some degree broken, darkened, distorted by the limitations *of all kinds*—not only intellectual—of the man. There is too the fact that most Western philosophers (and I do not think Plotinus is free of this) speak freely of νόησις when in fact they are using and in the realm of διάνοιᾱ, which is inherently broken and in part darkened. This is, I agree, recognized by Plotinus; yet he continues to use it (one might almost say) interminably, and this is a characteristic he shares with all Western philosophers. It seems to me a way of using up an overflow of mental energy, but it remains that not all of us are equally impressed with the results. So, getting down to rock bottom, I would say that I do not accept discursive verbal logical constructions, διάνοιᾱ—as an adequate instrument to penetrate τὰ βάθη τοῦ θεοῦ; and this is the instrument predominantly used in Western philosophy. I agree that Plotinus has his θεωρία, but I think his intensive, almost obsessional, use of διάνοιᾱ distorts and darkens his θεωρία in its expression. Yet from outside one can only approach his θεωρία through his διάνοιᾱ; and, approached in that way, his θεωρία itself seems to some of us not full. He saw life, world, universe, and God steadily, with a splendid concentration of intellectual vision; *but he did not see it whole.* You say there is no conflict, and quote St. Paul; but I can only reply that if you do not see or sense any conflict in the depths between the ultimate visions of these two men then you are not truly seeing them as they are. I do not believe St. Paul could or would have accepted Plotinian philosophy as in any real sense a parallel or a substitute for his "faith" in Christ. And I do not think Plotinus would have accepted St. Paul's faith either as a religious version of his own vision. There is a conflict, a rooted conflict. That there is an ultimate resolution we do not doubt, but we do not accept that the nature of that ultimate resolution is as it were automatically to be accepted as laid down by the philosopher in view of his assumed superior intellectuality. We continue to say bluntly (and as it may seem to the philosophers, stupidly) that there are depths in existence not entirely accessible to the intellect *of the philosopher*. We do not say these depths may not be accessible to absolute divine intellect. No, we are not here dealing with anything so exalted; we are dealing with intellect as mediated through an individual man. The intellect in this case seems to us necessarily limited by the human limitations of the man. It is, we think, not so unlimited that all other visions of the structure of the world have to be abandoned if a certain philosopher cannot accept them as readily intelligible within his system. I would say, in spite of Dean Inge, that there are vital elements in New Testament Christianity—St. Paul's Christianity, and even more so in the Synoptic Gospels—that cannot be assimilated into Plotinus's θεωρία without robbing them of all their real significance. Apocalyptic vision is not explicable in terms of the *Enneads*. It is open to say then that "apocalyptic vision is nonsense." Perhaps it is, but we cannot see why we should accept that it is nonsense, on authority—the authority of rationalistic philosophies that remain to us manifestly inadequate. I do not think this conflict can be expressed in terms of "religion" versus "philosophy." It is a conflict between ultimate world visions, and we remain unmoved if our ultimate vision remains inexplicable to philosophy. We cannot unsee what we see. We too abide by our θεωρία.

This tension does not exist in anything like the same acute degree in the East, where such rationalism as exists remains more or less in subordination to the total tradition. It is a part, and recognized as a valuable part, of the whole tradition. It does not, as it does in the West, seek to usurp all the functions of the whole tradition and ultimately to displace that tradition or reduce it to an *ancilla*.

Religion is not, or should not be, an *ancilla* of rationalism. Philosophy is not, or should not be, an *ancilla* of religion or of anything else. It has its legitimate function. Both are elements—as are science, art, ethics, politics, law, crafts, and innumerable other activities—included in the totality of the tradition. None of these separate elements can assume a dominant position without damaging the whole. They all act, or should act, as correctives, balances, supports to each other. In the West, for a long time now, it seems a fact of history that both rationalistic philosophy and science, which are in intimate relationship, have been tending to usurp the function of other elements in the whole tradition. In the Middle Ages religion had a similar tendency. This is part of the flow and conflict of history within the Christian tradition. It is not a question of my wishing religion to dominate philosophy or science; but I do not wish religion, in its legitimate field, to be dominated by philosophy or science either.

The *whole tradition*, in its balanced integrity, is the authentic vehicle of the spiritual realizations possible to the members of any particular civilization. Rationalistic philosophy cannot on its own usurp the function of the whole tradition. The function of rationalism within a tradition is to explore the processes of reasoning to their legitimate limits, and then to bring this necessary influence to play its part in every sphere. It cannot go beyond this in seeking, as it does, to make infallible pronouncements on ultimate problems that involve the supreme metaphysical order of the infinite. It cannot do this because it always stands rooted in the final contradiction (of which it cannot rid itself) that its reasoning processes, in the case of each individual philosopher, spring from an intellectuality conditioned in finitude; and, try howsoever it may, it cannot transcend this limitation into infallible metaphysical knowledge of infinitude. It receives this knowledge, insofar as it is able in any particular individual to receive it, from the central revelatory symbols of the tradition, which are transcendent in origin and do not have their source in finite reasoning processes. Yet it is these central traditional symbols that Western rationalistic philosophy tends to ignore, or explain away. I have never identified the capacity for metaphysical realization with the capacity for discursive reasoning. In fact I see such reasoning, uncontrolled and unpervaded by the central symbols, as completely ineffective. Of course rationalism does not see itself as uncontrolled. Nor does present-day science, nor did the religious cult in the Middle Ages. It is extremely difficult for any legitimate activity vigorously pursuing its own ends to know just at what point it is passing into ineffective encroachment, and it is just here that the corrective force of other elements in the tradition should come into play. Naturally and inevitably, differences of evaluation and emphasis will arise to be worked out among all the living stresses of history, and this process is always continuing. I think it not unfair for me to claim that I have always in the past been just as quick to defend the rights of reason as I now am to defend the even more central and precious rights of revelation. In spite of anything I may have written in these letters, my ultimate position is metaphysical. But my metaphysical vision legitimately and inevitably includes the insights and values of the religious tradition I am living in. And I cannot but discount the claim of rationalism to attenuate the significance of these insights, which flow from the influence of the central sacred symbols. A tradition, at its heart, is concerned with the sacred, and the realization of the sacred, and finds this knowledge mediated to it through forms of revelation crystallized into sacred symbols. It does not and cannot receive this transcendent influence and grace from the extremely limited operations of human reason.

To put the problem no higher—Christian civilization would not exist without the New Testament. And the New Testament is not explicable within the intellectual terms of Platonism. Platonism can only pretend to explain it by devaluing it. Porphyry said of Origen that he would have been a philosopher had he not been a Christian and "moved by strange fables." Porphyry was right, his vision was clear, he saw the conflict. What he did not see was that the "strange fables" he so contemptuously dismissed had in them the power to bring into the world a new and powerful civilization on the ruins of a civilization his Platonism was powerless to save. He was right too in seeing that, within the terms of his Platonism, the New Testament could only be dismissed as strange fables. But he could not see, or explain, the strange power of these strange fables. For rationalism the sacred, mediating itself through revelation in forms accessible to all men insofar as they will to receive them, seems not to exist. For them the sacred mediates itself through the reasonings of philosophers, who are always disputing among themselves. In the churches too this approach arises where rationalistic theologians have never allowed revelation to stand on its own ground, but must needs interpret it.

I have said that I think Plotinus to be a seer of extraordinary and unique value to the West, more especially in helping us to understand the East. I still think so, and I think the time of his greatest influence is still to come. And it will be a beneficial influence. But I think too that if he is to exert that influence his θεωρία will have to be interpreted in the light of the central traditional symbols of the West—only so can it exert its full power, West or East. The more rationalistic element in his expressed doctrines will be of relatively little value. Plotinus was essentially a great contemplative visionary, as you portrayed him in your study. His attempt to "rationalize" his vision was unsuccessful, as the true rationalists have always seen. His vision was a divine grace explicable only within terms of the sacred; it did not flow from his immensely active rationalizing mentality. He himself recognized this, as you did in your story. But the danger remains that the very splendor of his vision, insofar as it is thought to be the result of his διάνοια, may become a dissolving influence as against the even deeper and more splendid vision hidden in the sacred Christian symbols.

Darling Mary, I am aware of a confused and contradictory character in the expression of my evaluation of this great man. It at least partly flows from the fact that there are as it were three Plotinuses, of varying value, inextricably involved with each other in his expression of himself in the *Enneads*. There is the Stoic, and this influence is very pervasive—but not, I think, essential to the man. There is the rationalist, overflowing and most of the time dominant. This element is certainly part of the man, an expression at least in part of his intense mental vitality. And this element is a disintegrating influence once it flows as it were outside himself into the world—instance Porphyry (whom I have been reading up), who seems to have been a complete rationalist with no inner vision of a sacred order transcending his own reason. Then, thirdly, there is the great contemplative seer (unhappily at times, to outer approach) almost submerged under the Stoic and rationalist. It is in this complex nature of the man that the extreme difficulty of evaluating his influence arises. Which Plotinus will exert the most influence in an age rationalistic to a degree Plotinus himself would have surely recognized as disintegrating and dangerous to the vision of the sacred? This is why, from my point of view, to meet this danger I would insist that his θεωρία be related to the Christian symbols.

His influence could lose nothing of its truth, and would be enormously strengthened in this way. And this influence will be strengthening and illuminating in our contact with Eastern tradition. Yet too it will be as it were controlled in the necessity that exists of preserving in depth all the power of the Christian vision, which at the profoundest level transcends even Plotinus's θεωρία.

This is the level where world vision darkens into utter apocalypse. Insofar as Plotinus remained untroubled by intimations of ultimate apocalypse transcending his own vision, he has nothing to say at this depth. What is this ultimate apocalypse that is so disturbingly and darkly uttered from the deeper levels of Christian vision? It is the Will of God as in ultimate judgement *and fulfilment* of even the most sublime human vision. Looked at from the point of view of the *Enneads*, it might try to utter some such intimation as this: Plotinus says *rightly* that the soul, through Intellect, can see the Good, if it wills to do so. Now this is true, although the enormous difficulty here, *from the Plotinian point of view*, of the Intellect's dependence on the Will is not resolved in the *Enneads*; nevertheless the statement is true. The Christian vision says that this is true, but not as it were immediately true, for the Good reveals itself through final apocalypse. Apocalypse intervenes. The soul will see the Good through Intellect transcended in apocalypse, if it wills to do so. And the Good *wills* apocalypse. It remains hidden as it were until it *wills* to reveal Itself.

I think it is this "hiddenness" of the Good that Plotinus tried to rationalize away as unconsciousness. However that may be, the ultimate emphasis here is on the Will, the Will of God and the will of the soul. The Intellect should be seen as ultimately dependent on the Will of God, on grace; and the Intellect itself is not able, in ultimate Truth, to realize itself without the consent of the Divine Will. All the mystery of the Will, the hiddenness and inexplicability of the Ultimate Divine, intervenes between us and the Good, until the Good reveals itself in apocalypse. This utter ultimate apocalypse is bound up with the divine meaning of history as process, not as mere image of the eternal; and history involves the spiritual destiny of every soul. It is something incomprehensibly and unutterably more than a "flight of the alone to the Alone": it is the movement of the many to the One-in-All through Christ "on the Cross." And this movement we all share in, we cannot escape it; we cannot see the Good face to face in Utter Glory until this movement is consummated. And "how" and "when" it will be consummated we do not and cannot know through Intellect. Here we are utterly dependent on the Divine Will. We are "waiting" for the "Coming" in apocalypse of Christ. Apocalypse is the mystery and meaning of history. And Platonism seems never to have become fully conscious of this mystery. This mystery is in its utter depths at one with the mystery of "person": God as "person"—man as "person," confronting God. There is a depth of mystery, of hiddenness, of ultimate meaning in each man, each soul, which again Platonism never became fully aware of. And this meaning too is revealed in ultimate apocalypse.

Platonism, as does Vedanta, tends to obliterate the person, both human and divine, in an absolute undifferentiated Absolute. For Christian vision person has meaning, ultimate divine meaning, that will be revealed in apocalypse. And each person bears hidden within itself such ultimate meaning and fulfilment. This is why the Christian vision remains questioning before the possibility of attempting personal dissolution in the unlimited. It does not deny the infinitude of the Divine as ultimate ground, as *Ungrund*; it does not deny that the Beatific Vision in some sense shares in this infinitude; but it does question whether the realization of this infinitude in contemplation involves the dissolution of personality. Certainly the vision of Jesus (and this is decisive for the Christian vision) seemed to see man as person, every man as person, fulfilled in the "Kingdom of God," while remaining a "real" within his divinely willed limits.

Again, the mystery of history, of time, and the mystery of each person, faces personal apocalypse in death. Death is not, to Christian vision, metaphysically transparent to eternity. It involves the Will of God for each person, and the hidden will of each person for himself and before God. And Will is always, until final apocalypse, "dark"—in its utter depth and root—to Intellect. Here in very truth Will conditions Intellect. The soul *cannot* see the Good until it wills to do so. It is dark in that it is rooted in the ultimate *Ungrund*, which is the ground of utter unconditioned freedom. Freedom here *is* the unconditioned, which, under the Divine Will, learns to enter into and accept conditions (that is, limits) and to realize, out of its dark, unconditioned, pure freedom, a freedom penetrated by light and Intellect (that is, Divine grace), and, in this new freedom, to become a true person, a true image of God.

To Christian vision, the longing to return to the unconditioned *Ungrund* is longing to return to our pure potentiality before birth. It makes birth meaningless, as it is in pure Platonism. "It were better never to have been born": here, as you say in your letter, Christianity reveals itself as Eternal Hope. It transcends the despair hidden in Vedanta and Platonism. But insofar as it leaves to and sees in each soul an ultimate freedom, it leaves open—indeed it cannot deny—the possibility of return to *Ungrund*; but it sees this, from its point of view, as a return to non-being, to dissolution, to "eternal death."

These ultimate possibilities of being and spiritual destiny for man *as man*, *as person*, lie implicit for Christian vision in apocalypse. Insofar as they rest in a divine Will issuing from *Ungrund* (which is an ultimate "irrational"; or, rather "transcends" the rational) such a vision *cannot be rationalized*. Rationalism as such, which remains unaware of *Ungrund* and apocalypse, cannot approach it or apprehend it. For Christian vision there *are* mysteries—divine mysteries—that transcend the rational.

For all these reasons Christian vision sees the depths of existence and God—τὰ βάθη τοῦ θεοῦ—as mystery, as hidden, as dark. It welcomes the Intellect with its shining, but sees, beyond that shining, dark. And it looks to the revelation of the divine meanings hidden in that ultimate dark to the "end of the world": a divine Act issuing from the Will of God.

Well darling Mary, I must stop. I think I partly write these letters to feel in touch with you. Perhaps too for both of us, we who live so intensely in our inner visions, it is no bad thing sometimes to try to express something of those visions in words. And all differences of insight and emphasis are ultimately transcended in our common desire and pursuit of the whole. At different times too one finds oneself at different points on the circumference of the circle whose center is everywhere and whose circumference is nowhere! That is a fine contradiction, but as an irrationalist I don't feel too worried. I think too that I write not so much in reply to your present letters as in an attempt to get some problems clear that seemed to present themselves to me in my encounter with Plotinus, and to share my attempt with you.

I hope it doesn't all sound too hopelessly obscure to make anything at all out of it. But we are here attempting, however ineffectually, to rummage among the roots and foundations of the worlds and whatever brought the worlds into being!

Lots of love,
Gerard

The Beale
29 September 1969

My darling Mary,

I have had a happy weekend. I spent much time in the forest with the cattle. They graze in there most of the time now, it is so dry outside. Quiet, sunny, and still in there. I spent Friday evening with Rose and Francis. Foolishly, I'd forgotten Francis's birthday, and they took it as a birthday visit! Rose showed me a film of her visit to Arizona and Alaska. Arizona rather like Kenya, and Alaska reminding me of pictures I have seen of the Himalayas. Rose told me Sam Small died suddenly last week reading on his verandah! His man found him. He'd had no warning.

Each afternoon now there are great build-ups of dark clouds and much lightning in the nights. Green skies to the north and east at evening, all heralding the coming of the rains. I think of Will coming on Thursday. He is going straight to Ngare Ndare. I told Rose I would visit him from Friday on, as they will all be at the Show over the weekend.

And then, not too long after that, you will be coming! I have been thinking of you so much and longing to see you again. But I mustn't be selfish, and I remember that in this case Gerard's gain is Lucy's loss. I have written to Wilkinson and the Norfolk Hotel, assuming you arrive on the morning of the 15th; but if for any reason you'd like to stay longer don't worry. I have to see Wilkinson anyway, and collect Teresa for her holiday here.

I feel my letters must be so confused, and fear you may misunderstand them. My head seems to seethe with such a medley of notions these days. I only get a few of them on paper to share with you. But it does give me a sense of being in touch with you to write.

I have been thinking again about Stoic ethics and trying to get clear with myself why, as doctrine, it strikes me as unacceptable. Their doctrine—the four absolute ethical predispositions, which they think are attainable—is unattainable, for it requires absolute knowledge, absolute mastery of desire, absolute justice, absolute control over pain. They saw these requirements as interdependent, and in some sense possible of achievement. So they sought to place themselves beyond the ambiguities. Insofar as they sought to make these ideals effective in their ethical striving, they inevitably tried to "harden" their hearts and turn to the world a face somewhat cold and repellent, or so it seems to me. I agree that in Marcus Aurelius and Epictetus there remain warm and loveable qualities of heart, but these shine through *in spite of* their doctrine. The root of the difficulty perhaps lies in their tendency to centralize ethics. In fact their ethical doctrines lie in strained opposition to their ultimate religious and metaphysical insights. They certainly had eschatological insight with their doctrine of ἐκπύρωσις, in which they are at one with New Testament apocalypse and show close affinities with Eastern cyclic cosmologies. In this direction they are one of the most interesting and arresting of philosophical schools. What they seem to have missed in their understanding of eschatology—and this is explained by their tendency to center in ethical striving—is the implicit insight that it is the very impossibility, in finitude, of resolving the tensed ambiguities into "relative" absolutes that makes inevitable the resolution in ἐκπύρωσις. This oncoming, obliterating divine fire, the ἀείζωον πῦρ of Heraclitus, is their vision of the threefold fire of apocalypse, the threefold fire—at once baptismal, pentecostal and apocalyptic—of the New Testament. They did not see that in their ethical striving they were seeking to cool down, to freeze into rigidity, this divine fire. I don't think the question of merit comes up in my comparing the tears of the child over a broken doll with ἀπάθεια. It is rather that, to Christian vision, the tears of the child are more consonant with the divine nature than ἀπάθεια, which seeks to maintain an attitude of indifference. The fiery inflow into the world of the divine cannot in its loving creativity be indifferent to all that is broken and helpless, rather it seeks to restore the divine image to all things, even the broken doll; and in a sense it grieves even as does the little girl until the final restoration of all things is brought about in the "Kingdom of God." The little girl, in her grief, hopes for restoration; her very tears are a prayer for restoration. The Stoic's ἀπάθεια rather seems to congeal in despair; it cannot believe restoration possible and tries to harden itself into indifference. Humanly speaking (or perhaps I should say, rather, philosophically speaking) I do not think that any other response than ἀπάθεια was possible to the frightful disfigurements of the divine image in the world, before the breaking into history of the Christian vision. The little girl is not better, has no more merit, than the Stoic. But she remains a symbol that tears are not in vain, that God does not deny our living humanity, our frailty, our warmth of heart, which partakes of the fiery nature of His own creativity—does not demand that we crush our hearts in impossible standards of virtue and duty. Something like this I tried to indicate in speaking of the child in tears.

But this valuation of ἀπάθεια is derived from Christian vision. In the New Testament a Word is uttered from "before the foundation of the world." A Word that sounds on "until the end of the world." A Word that remains after "heaven and earth are passed away." A Word that promises restoration in

God of all things "acceptable," all that is true, and good, and beautiful, all that is consonant with the divine creativity. All this is, I would agree, in a certain timeless sense implicit in the vision of Plotinus. Yet in Christian vision this divine promise is mediated through history, and obliteration in judgement of evil "at the end." We cannot realize it until the end; we wait for the end. This prophetic note does not sound in Plotinus, for history seems to have been for him in some sense unreal. Yet history is for Christian vision a real incarnation of the divine, not just a falling away from the divine. For this reason Christian vision remains to me something decisively and overwhelmingly more than any philosophy. It is a divine promise, not a construction of human reason open to all the assaults and attenuations of other human reasonings. The historical Word is acceptable as an echo and affirmation of the same Word uttered in the depths of our souls—if we choose to hear it.

A little Chinese poem I came across a few days ago and like very much:

> The owl calls—I hear
> the owl's "I" is its calling
> my "me" is my hearing
> What is that which is both—
> calling and hearing?
>
> (Shen Hui)

The question arises: In what sense can apocalyptic vision be contained in pure metaphysical vision? It can only be hidden—locked up in its secret power—in the instant; even as, in the physical structure of nature, immense destructive and creative powers are locked up in the atom. Here we think of the instantaneous character of total metaphysical realization as we learn of it from the East. For total realization must include what I have called apocalypse. It is an apocalyptic experience. And this realization, as experienced in the East, issues in a state (*Satchitananda*—Being-Consciousness-Bliss) absolutely unqualified. And it arises in a traditional doctrine that contains apocalyptic doctrines, which means that the possibility of apocalypse is ever present to the sage in his approach to realization. But what interests me just now is that the absolute state of unconditioned being is experienced as "consciousness." Plotinus—and it is his rationalism that leads him to this position—sees the unconditioned as "unconsciousness." I keep coming back to this, as I am convinced it is of crucial importance in evaluating his doctrine. However, leaving his rationalism aside and seeing this doctrine of his in the light of the totality of the traditional doctrines of both East and West (which both contain metaphysical and apocalyptic elements that support each other), it seems to me that this unconsciousness that Plotinus attributes to the One is really a projection into his total vision of a blind spot in his own consciousness, where his awareness of apocalypse should be situated. Of course the Eastern sage may be equally unaware, at the level of his individual consciousness, of apocalypse; but he *knows it exists* because he accepts the support of his tradition in its totality.

Whether East or West, the traditional doctrines see the approach to full spiritual realization as conditioned by a mental consciousness utterly saturated by the power of the doctrines and sacred symbols. Only in a consciousness so conditioned can realization be effectively sought, apart from very rare outflows of divine grace, which are always accepted as possible. In the Christian tradition the emphasis seems to lie in waiting, a hopeful inner waiting that suffers the stresses of history without seeking to escape them, a waiting sustained by its apocalyptic vision. In the East the emphasis seems to lie more in escaping, that is, emptying the mind of process and waiting in a kind of still emptiness. The Christian waits in *hope*. The sage waits in *stillness*. Each shares the other's perspective, but the traditional emphasis is different. The Christian waits for the coming of the "Kingdom of God." The sage Ramana Maharshi, a God-realized man as this is understood in Hinduism, said to one who approached him for guidance, "All that is required is to be still," and then added teasingly, "and what can be easier than that?"

However, he didn't always simplify to that extent, and wrote a small number of poems in Tamil that leave us with a fuller picture of his own way. These are of great value and interest in that they show "the way" as practiced by a Hindu Vedantin. A way of knowledge is not, or at least was not in the case of Ramana Maharshi, always a process of absolute abstraction from the world of appearance.

Here is a translation of one of his poems that I have just received:

> This is certain
> Worship, praise and meditation
> Being work of body, mind, and speech,
> Are steps of orderly ascent...
>
> Fire, air, water, earth,
> Sun, moon, and living beings,
> Worship of these
> As forms of His
> Is perfect worship of the Lord.

> Better than songs of praise
> Is repetition of His Name;
> Better low-voiced than loud;
> But best of all
> Is Stillness in the mind...

Well, I left this to go for my evening walk. Coming back and seeing that last line—"Is Stillness in the mind"—brought me to the realization how unstill my mind has been in these last weeks!

Coming down off Windy Hill each evening in the dark I meet Bonny and Jenny. They graze and spend the night there at the bottom of the hill near Punda and Cherry. Bonny comes to greet me each time. I saw a large owl too tonight, swooping and circling over the hillside. Slate comes for the walks again now.

Now for my supper and bath.

Lots of Love,
Gerard

P.S.
Toad in my boot again this morning!

The Beale
1 October 1969

My darling Mary,

Here are letters from you and from Will, and Christopher Grey, and my mother. I thought I'd start this letter (another exercise in what J.C.P. called "dithyrambic analysis") and leave it unfinished until after I have seen Will. I will go down tomorrow to meet him when he arrives with Gilfrid and spend some of the day with him. I think Gilfrid will be flying straight on to

Rumuruti Farm, and Rose at the Show. I feel really distressed at this damned tickling he has, it really does seem the last straw on top of everything else.

I felt, my dear dear Mary, so happy thinking of you coming after having your letter last evening, as I came down in the last light over Windy Hill with Arcturus bright in the north-west and the tree frogs filling the air with their liquid notes. There had been a ruddy smoky sunset—distant grass fires. Jupiter and Mercury have set now. I see Saturn rising in the east about eight o'clock. Mars very dominant above Scorpio, still high but sloping to the west. Bonny seems to look forward to my coming, sometimes greets me with a very faint whinny, and usually comes up to me for her nose to be stroked.

I had a letter from Christopher. The Draft Board, he says, "turned down flat" his application. He has gone back to the "Ashram." I must ask him to tell me more about this—how and when and by whom it was started. Somehow I always feel a little sceptical of ashrams outside India. Perhaps this is unfair; after all, we accept Christian missions anywhere in the world as quite properly Christian. One may have this feeling because one knows that Hinduism is not a genuinely proselytizing religion, like Buddhism or Islam or Christianity. However that may be, I hope very much Christopher is under a sane and balanced spiritual influence there.

We seem to "get" (as they say) Guénon differently. I don't think he would "hold up his hands" at the notion of "changing human consciousness through the powers of mind." In fact, I think he would say that is essentially just what traditional metaphysical doctrines seek to do. It is hard to conceive of any purely present-day mode of thought or "consciousness" achieving anything remotely comparable in this direction to the possibilities inherent in the different forms of Hindu Yoga. And he was nothing if not friendly to Hinduism in all its manifestations. I agree though that he would note the contradiction implicit in the idea that "absolute scepticism" can change anything in any acceptable creative way—all such scepticism can help to bring about is a radical disintegration of any structure of consciousness it comes into contact with. Guénon was right to react against absolute scepticism. I think many of his pronouncements are of dubious value, and he opens himself wide to a very wide range of fair criticism. But I think too his fundamental insights and deeper criticisms of modernism were very close to the mark. They have never, as far as I know, been met by any "modernist." They have only been ignored. A civilization wobbling at the edge of Armageddon cannot afford to feel too superior to Guénon. A civilization that is generously providing for possible "changes of consciousness" in the form of the manufacture of "nerve" gases designed to send people insane (enough to infect the whole world is the boast) or invites animals to share in abominable changes of consciousness in the form of widespread indefensible vivisection—a civilization that threatens at any moment to obliterate all life on the planet and so be done altogether with consciousness and its problems—is hardly in a strong position to ignore one who suggests it might apply some of its "absolute scepticism" to an examination of itself and its values. I do not think Guénon was a medievalist in the sense some Roman Catholic thinkers are, but even if he were? well, even that might be preferable to the alternative modern civilization is busily preparing for the world. It is true, as Berdyaev saw (but he saw it with all its implications), that we have no choice. We *have* to go forward; but we can't all pretend we think the prospect is fine when we know it isn't. Guénon's was one of the first voices lifted—over forty years ago now—calling for a radical self-examination on the part of Western civilization of its basic presuppositions, from the point of view of traditional metaphysics. If he saw in traditional metaphysics, and in their vehicles in history—the great religions—repositories of immensely valuable insight into the meaning of the world... well, he has yet to be proved wrong. Instead he has been ignored. Modern man has, in Aeschylus' words, "put on the yoke of necessity," and "the case now standeth where it doth—it moveth to fulfilment at its destined end." But it remains that Guénon was right to speak as and when he did, however open to criticism many of his relatively superficial comments may have been.

I think it is an immense burden and painful destiny for a man to have some share, as both Berdyaev and Guénon did, of prophetic consciousness. And if at times they spoke harshly or confusedly, they did so less than the prophets of old—and facing a more urgently dreadful situation. The prophetic consciousness sees meaning in history. It sees history as the unfolding of human freedom, even though it knows the use man almost always makes of his freedom is to "don the yoke of necessity"—and sacrifice Iphigenia. It is difficult for the purely contemplative mind, absorbed in its "adventure of ideas," in its "advance into novelty," to enter sympathetically into the prophetic consciousness. But perhaps it should be prepared to make the effort at times; it may be that extremely unpleasant variations on the theme of novelty are being prepared for it outside the circles of its own consciousness. Insofar as history seems unreal to the contemplative consciousness it may "escape" into the timeless—but *is* history so "unreal"? The prophetic consciousness senses in history "real" issues that cannot be evaded.

All this, I know, brings up difficult issues. Men are as they are, or so they think. The structures of consciousness are not easy to change. If a man has no share in prophetic consciousness he cannot pretend he has—this is true. Yet it is true too that the will, all too easily ignored in idealistic rationalism, plays an immense part in determining the structures of consciousness. We are as we are—very often because we choose to be as we are. The will is the movement in choice of our primordial freedom, but it does not necessarily choose to see the whole truth about itself or the world. That might be, almost certainly would be, very painful—so we choose the pleasing partial truth. In this field of human striving, then, lie opportunities for changing and enlarging human consciousness. The man can always strive to see more of the Truth that transcends himself. Essentially, the traditional spiritual disciplines ask no more than this. It is absurd, pathetically absurd, for modern man to claim he is the champion devoted to enlarging human consciousness as over against traditional wisdom. Traditional wisdom is the crystallized experience of the past in trying to achieve just this. It has to be interpreted sympathetically, and honestly, and intelligently, with a proper sense of all that is involved. Traditional wisdom, if it does nothing else, opens up to man a perspective into the past inner consciousness and striving of innumerable generations of men so that, insofar as man today ignores it, he is limiting his consciousness—not enlarging it. Scepticism (especially of the kind called "absolute") as to the value of the past and the precious deposits of wisdom held in tradition can do nothing but deprive modern man of insights and correctives he desperately needs. I know you accept all this, but why tease Guénon for saying the same thing—that "absolute" scepticism is a thing of no value, a disintegrating force hostile to all genuine creativity and value? When reduced to essentials, what he tried to say was no more than this.

What seems to offend the specifically modern mind in tradition, when one has taken off all the wrappings, is the insistence of all genuine tradition that the only changes of consciousness of value are changes in the direction of greater truthfulness, and that always man stands in the presence of God, Who "judges" the changes. But modern man has no taste for the presence of God, and he does not care for some of the changes He is interested in, or being "judged." It is comfortable no doubt for a vivisector to reflect that there is no God. But granted the one condition that man never forget he stands in the presence of God, then tradition has no objection to any conceivable, or at present inconceivable, change or new orientation or radical development of consciousness. This one condition, the sense of the presence of God, is seen as what it is—the Truth—and also as the ever necessary inner corrective and control to inhibit the growth of demonic perversions and iniquities. In reference to our present age and its pursuit of scientific knowledge, it does not seem unfair or obscurantist to say bluntly that "iniquities abound." Science remains what it is, a legitimate activity of the human mind. But it is iniquity, monstrous iniquity, for governments to devote vast resources and the gifts of scientists over years to the producing and perfecting of means of hideous destruction for the whole human race—nay! of all life (we are assured) on this planet. To be able to destroy it all once is not enough; no, we must be able to destroy it all ten times over. But here a difficulty arises. We would prefer not to destroy ourselves at the same time, so "more merciful" techniques are developed. We develop nerve gases that can send whole "hostile" populations insane—then find we've made so much of it that we don't know what to do with it, and set about polluting the oceans. This is but one extreme example of an all-pervading "modern" tendency. There are no limits. "God is dead" becomes the cry. Who is to judge? The very notion of judgement is childish fancy! We are absolute sceptics! But a still very small voice comes in: "it may be, there remains the remote possibility, that God is not dead"—if a phrase so utterly absurd as "God is dead" (the "new theology," we are told, centers on this illuminating dictum) has any meaning at all. Rank piffle is elevated to the status of theological statement. Unmitigated evil is condoned as scientific necessity. This is not fancy (Gerard or Nigel or young Christopher on his hobby horse); this is the world we live in, our modern civilization (as it confesses itself)—loud and blatant and unseeing of its insanity. If some few voices are lifted in protest, an indication that something hideous and indefensible is invading the world, is it surprising that they perhaps sound at times inarticulate and confused? The modern mentality knows well how to make any protest that puts a question mark against its pretensions sound a trifle absurd and foolishly alarmist. This is what Guénon saw coming before most of us. If he glanced back at times to the Middle Ages why ridicule him? Even Nigel, hardly a traditionalist, said he'd be glad to get us back to the Middle Ages, seeing it as a comforting but hopeless fancy!

Here, in the younger generation, lies any hope we have of survival. Many of them are cut off from any living contact with genuine tradition, thanks to the kindness of their modernistic progenitors; but more and more of them are (as Nigel tells me) ever increasingly turning their instilled scepticism not against the ancient derided traditions, but against "modernism" and all it means. They know, and cannot be undeceived, that something has gone wrong, utterly wrong. They are young and do not know where to turn or what remedy to hope for, but they know, know to the roots of their awareness of the world, that modernism is rotten, a hollow and unlovely sham. Some try to re-establish contact with any traditional form that seems available. Insofar as they identify Christianity with the civilization they abhor, they seek other traditional forms, but their instinct is right: they seek tradition, increasingly disenchanted with any Siren song they hear from modernism. They want, like Odysseus, to get back to their "dear native land," the land, the only land in which any hope remains—tradition. And all this the prophetic vision sees as "real." A huge and terrible conflict in which the spiritual destinies of millions of men are in the balance, in which the very survival of our civilization—possibly of man himself—is at stake. A painful and costly and real *jihad*. The modern world in *crisis*—that is, facing judgement. The purely contemplative vision, let us admit it, tends to see in it a vast shadow-play that it cannot get to grips with. Insofar as my own spiritual temperament tends to the purely contemplative, I admit this reaction. But something in me admits too that there are prophetic visions that transcend my contemplation, and demand my allegiance.

For this reason men like Berdyaev and Guénon will always find in me a fierce champion. I'm not much of a fighter out in the terrible battlefield, but I'm not going to start playing the modernistic game. Any influence, however small, I have, especially with young people, will be exerted to help men return, however falteringly and doubtingly, to traditional influences: *any* traditional influences in this context being preferable to none.

And what does all this mean, this turning to tradition for help, in the depths? A turning to God, yes, but more than that: a turning to God through the mediation of the dead, the innumerable dead who have lived and suffered and died on this earth, the dead who are involved in us and in our destiny and in God's will for all men. We are keeping faith with the dead and the mystery of the dead—what is tradition in depth but keeping faith with the dead, and, through the dead, with God? To whom should we turn for help in a conflict so terrible but to the dead, who yet are not dead, hidden in Christ in God beyond the reach of all "modernisms"?

And hoping too to keep faith with the unborn, the unborn multitudes fated to be born to who knows what terrible destiny if we fail.

This is the prophetic word coming to us today. And who, having even partly understood this word, can remain unmoved by it?

We know what will be will be.

We know too what will be will be at least partly decided by our choices.

The freedom of the spirit is a real thing, and a terrible thing.

But darling Mary, I feel all this is so open to misunderstanding. Perhaps I am just trying to get something clear in my own mind and pounce on these names—Berdyaev, Guénon—as an opportunity to share my thoughts with you. I have written fierce words in judgement against what I call modernism. But what is this modernism? It is unthinking, unconcerned failure to keep faith with the past. Failure to lovingly try to understand and forgive and accept the past. But this failure is in every one of us. We are all involved. Modernism is a failure in me, not just in other men. Tradition is keeping faith with the past. Receiving from the past its word to the present. But again this is something we share with all other men in some degree. This conflict then between tradition and modernism is in every man. And always has been so. But in our time, the dreadful stresses under which men live, the ever-increasing pace of living and thinking, the endlessly multifarious demands made on men at the centers of our civilization—all these forces weaken tradition, strengthen modernism at a time when more than ever we need tradition. If we cannot keep faith with the past we cannot keep faith with the future. It is tradition that releases us into a "real" future, a spiritually valid future. Modernism is essentially absorption in the present. It looks no more to the future than to the past. It is unaware of the mystery of history and time. Or, becoming partially aware, it recoils from the sense of numinous dread that haunts the mystery of history, and returns fearfully, but too with a sense of being comforted, to the concerns of the present. In all this, modernism is weakness—human, all-too-human weakness. How can we, any one of us, view modernism in our time? For every age has its own "modernism," its own absorption in its own present. How can we introduce any notion of "judgement" in relation to this? It is a thing we all share, and the more ease and leisure we have as individuals the more responsible we are for our failure. And yet, though we cannot judge, judge we must—not other men or individuals, but the whole movement of our civilization, for which we are all collectively responsible. We *have* to try to see it for what it is—weakness and failure—and try, each one of us in our degree, to overcome it.

I must stop now and leave the rest of the page for news of Will. I hope these letters don't tease you or overtire you. They are, as you say in this last letter, an attempt (necessary at times) at recollection; a new attempt to win understanding, in however small a degree. It would be idle for me to pretend that the prophetic voices of our time leave me undisturbed. There is a tremendous, almost overwhelming, need for contemplation in our time. Only in contemplation can we keep faith with the past. Only through contemplation can we keep our traditions strong and living for the future. All this is true. All this is certain. But too we must learn to listen to the voices of prophecy, voices coming from men who face, as it seems to me, a harder destiny than ours. And, too, learn never to fail in compassion for all men in our time caught up in such a truly terrible dilemma. If we fail in these things, we fail in our contemplation; for what is true contemplation but prayerful vision for all men, and a prayerful sharing in the destiny of all men? And true contemplative vision in any man or woman is something won for and shared in by all other men and women, shared in that it becomes in a real sense part of the Kingdom of God to which all are invited.

And now another page. I went out to the Rhino Dam for my walk. Watched two hawks circling and wheeling. Watched another smoky red sun go down and a sunset as splendid as any Aurora Borealis. Looked an instant into utter glory. Back to our bush on Windy Hill until dark, and fading fire all along the west. Arcturus again, and Bonny waiting at the bottom of the hill. I looked for glow-worms where we have sometimes seen them, near the nettle patch, and so home. But it comes to me that something remains to be said:

that it is clear our civilization, in all its vast structures, is being sustained by all-pervading traditional forces (in spite of all appearance), else it could not survive another day. Another thing to be said in simple honesty: I have come in these days to total acceptance of the Christian vision. I have come to see how trivial, pedantic, insincere, and *wilfully* uncomprehending I have been before this supreme spiritual tradition vouchsafed to men. I have come to this vision in reverent acceptance of all truly traditional forces—wherever they may be, under whatever name they go. All I have said of modernism and rationalism applies to myself. All sense of judgement I have of modern civilization is tempered by a sense of the terrible dilemmas that civilization faces. I see I have spent years of my life inwardly battling over words. What matters what we call, each one of us, our striving for and relationship to the Truth, as long as it *be* Truth insofar as we can see it and approach it? Another thing to say: I have received in your dear companionship and friendship a grace and support I can in no way deserve, ever since you ran out to meet me that evening in the Shootash garden. A grace that shames me with a sense of how meagre has been my response and a wonder that so many do so much better than I have ever done without such a grace. I feel, I know myself to be under divine judgement. Not in the sense that God advances on me like the Cerne Giant with a club and threatens, no, in the sense (and this is what divine judgement always means) that God in His pure Presence reveals to us just what we really are; and this is judgement painful indeed, but not in any sense of punishment. One just sees oneself *in His Presence*.

A last page and I *must* leave some of this one for tomorrow. You should hear the night wind moaning and then again booming round the house. I write again in front of dear old Jacob Boehme with his Three-headed Lily thrusting down through dark clouds above his head. *This* old Jacob was a wrestler—just as was that other one of old under the stars. I remember our hours here years ago in the evenings when we studied Latin by ethylene lamplight until nine o'clock or later each evening and then had our bath, carried in in empty cans from a blaze outside to George's tin bath, and how Jess would come to the bathside and invite a game... these nights. Bess is naughty, and when Bonny and Jenny come back to be near the house each night about midnight, she challenges them just as fiercely as I do modernism; and each night I feel indignant, but am always too lazy to do anything about it!

And now to tonight's bath and I finish this in the morning.

9 p.m.

Just looked out: Scorpio setting, Saturn rising, wind blowing. Bess barking. Goodnight, Gerard.

9.30 a.m. 2 October

Here I am on Will's verandah waiting for him to come. Mwirichia has the house looking very spick-and-span. Rukaria polishing up the Land Rover ready for Will, but I will take along our Peugeot in case Will finds it easier to get into. I think I will close this letter now as I've used up the number of sheets allowed for two stamps, and write another airmail after Will has arrived. About these longer letters—I am sure there is a lot in them that won't perhaps bear close examination, but I'm talking more to myself than anyone else. I've been a great modernist and rationalist in my time! And I'm saying to myself: a lot of my own past (and present) attitudes don't seem any longer to hold living water.

Lots of Love darling Mary. We watch the sky over Simangwa for Gilfrid's plane now.

Gerard

Spring Cottage
20 February 1971

My darling Mary,

Here I am back at the cottage. I could see you sitting in the airport bus last night and watched the great plane climb up and disappear among the northern constellations. I think of you now with Lucy and pray all was well with you during your long flight through the night. I think of adding a few lines to this letter each day until the end of the postal strike is in sight and I can send it with some hope of delivery.

The hadadas have just flown over with a great clamor. The cottage is very empty without you. The next two months stretch ahead like a desert. I feel like running away and coming to you sooner! I'll go down to see Will now and add a few words when I get back. I am writing sitting in your chair in your room. I have such a vivid waking vision of you as I saw you sitting under your fig tree in the Spring Place on Thursday afternoon when I brought you Will's letter and the cutting describing the Canadian wedding. Broch and Slate are looking expectantly at me through the window.

Evening

I found Will cheerful and reassuring, reading *The Western Gazette* on his verandah. He told me many amusing stories, and we had a drink together (his hot rum and lemon). Rose is bringing down the boys for a picnic tomorrow and he asked me to go along, but I think I will go for a ride on Jenny instead. I've just had my bath and looked out—Simangwa very dark against the zodiacal light. And now to sleep, very tired, the cicadas filling the air with their sound.

I have just read your beautiful poem 'Odyssey.'

Sunday afternoon, 21st

I went off for a good ride on Jenny this morning, to a duet of neighs from Jack and Jill. Jenny was fine, keeping up a brisk walk out past the dam, round the back of Lion Hill, and back through the Dip Paddock. I saw most of the cattle still looking surprisingly well.

I read your dear poems this afternoon, each one a precious time shared with you. I will read them again, one each evening before going to sleep. 'Narina's Trogon'[1] is perfect. I have read it over and over, my heart falling still before its beauty. It is "brilliant and perfect," this marvelous birdsong. Now along the river with Broch and Slate.

Evening

Sitting on the rocks as the evening darkened I heard the Windy Hill nightjar calling. Now to sleep; too tired to read. It seems a long time to April 23rd. If I can sort things out I may come on April 2nd instead!

---

1. Gerard is referring to Mary's poem 'Phoenix', published in *The Clear Shadow*. The Narina's Trogon is a vividly colored African bird. In view of this glowing reference, and others to follow, the poem is reproduced in its entirety at the close of this letter.

Monday

Just in from our after lunch walk. A wagtail was hopping over your place on the roots of the fig tree. I walked slowly, looking long into the treetops hoping to glimpse you in a Trogon—a prayer not granted, but did see a flash of red translucent wings at the place we saw them together on our last walk that way. I have a quite extraordinary sense of Mary not far away. One of your poems I like best is 'Cuckoo'—for Lucy! I rejoice to think that now, for Lucy, her beloved bird has flown home again.

I plan to ride Jill this afternoon and visit Kibrono at Boma-Ine, then in to see Will on the way back. I am reading again *Ennead* III. 8, 'Of Nature, Contemplation, and the One.' I think this is my favorite among the *Enneads* I have been able to read in the original...

'Narina's Trogon' haunts me. I wonder... shall I ever be granted this vision?

Like Plotinus you are a seer rather than a philosopher—I rejoice in his defense of the divinity of the sun as against the rationalists.

Tuesday morning

Darling Mary, I am writing now sitting in your chair with my newly made cup of coffee beside me. I have these sheets in my Faber & Faber *Blake* lying on your little table beside your tattered Liddell and Scott dictionary, and each day I will add a little to the letter as I wait for the coffee to cool! Then after the coffee I will read a little in your copy of Taylor's commentary on the *Timaeus*, which I see here close at hand. I may even feel inspired occasionally to comment on this extraordinarily massive commentary that is so many times longer than its subject! I saw Kibrono last evening; he had been across to Sirakoi and met quite a big herd of elephants, with many cows and calves, below Kongoni Ridge not far from the Duggle-Bear's Drift. We are going to move most of the cattle in there, so the hungry elephants will have to move on I fear, but perhaps they will not mind the cattle all round them.

When Tony and Rose were here they both asked me, as though it was of some importance to them, when I planned to leave. It occurred to me later that perhaps they are worried about Will when they visit England in May. So I may decide to stay on here until they get back, but I'll (as my father liked to say) "give it due thought and consideration" before deciding. If I do stay longer for this reason it will mean I shall probably come towards the end of May instead of April. I will have to find out Rose's dates first. At the moment I feel rather rebellious. Your white cock has just crowed.

Night Horizons

Afternoon

Back from midday walk. I found Marangu under the laragai trees below St. Paul's Spring hollowing out a beebox from a laragai trunk. I asked him not to set it up near the path. He replied, "no bee from one of my boxes has ever stung you or Memsahib!" I told him about the bee that stung you on the path into the Tortoise Grove—he said that was one of Mukendia's bees!

Evening

Back from a good ride on Jenny. I called in to see Will on the way back and found Delia, David, William and the tutor there. David told me it is possible to phone England without any great difficulty if one chooses a good time, when the business men are off. I think I'll suggest to Will that we ring you up from his house on Sunday evening!

I saw two great flocks of Kavirondo Cranes flying across the face of Swan's Hill over the plough land—a great clamor—as I rode round Eland Hill this evening.

Wednesday morning

Back from a ride on Jill. We set off about seven and followed a lion track along the road from just below the maize fields here almost to *Euskopos*. Taking Kibrono's hint of yesterday I rode on down below Kongoni Ridge, then back across to Ngara Gorge. There just below Ngara I met a herd of thirty elephants, of all sizes—big bulls, tiny calves. They were on the far side of the gorge from me, on the Lion Hill side. All quietly feeding. I watched them for nearly half an hour. They were not much more than a hundred yards away, in full view. They paid no attention to us. Jill watched them intently for a few minutes, then fell to grazing. Among and around the elephants were quite a number of giraffe, zebra, and eland. Then a dik-dik emerged only a few yards away and quietly watched us. Broch and Slate went to sleep! How I wished you were there. None of the animals showed any sign of nervousness.

Evening

Just back from Will, very happy after a day at Kisima with Gilfrid, who got back from Abyssinia yesterday. Will told me that a bus packed with passengers coming fast down the Suboiga Hill after dark ran into a herd of buffalo. It badly hurt eight of the buffalo and could not itself go on because a huge bull buffalo was under the front axle. The drivers and passengers were afraid to get out because the hurt animals were all round and some cow buffaloes whose calves were hurt were rampaging round. A friend of Tony's, who had been staying the night at Kisima, found the bus at first light as he was going down to Isiolo. He went back to Kisima and told Tony, who collected Eddie and came down and shot all the hurt animals and got the bus off the dead buffalo and towed it back to Kisima for repair.

Christopher Gibson came in today and had lunch with me. He was fresh from his discussions with Wilkinson. I gather Wilkinson told him, more or less, not to be so touchy. We had a long talk, I spoke very forcibly and frankly about his secretiveness, etc., and he surprised me by saying when I had finished, "I know you're right, because I've been told all this before by my mother and Anna. That was why Anna broke off the engagement. But however hard I try I can't be different!, and now I'm in trouble with Caroline." I responded, "Christopher, this is the first time you've spoken to me like a human being, and the moment you speak like this it seems possible to get going together again!" The result was that he is bringing in Mohammed tomorrow, and we will all three, as Tim says, "come to some agreement." I suggested he should leave the organization of the labor to Mohammed, and leave me to help him out if difficulties arise. I ended up by inviting him to come for a ride with me tomorrow afternoon, and he agreed. I do feel perhaps some more straightforward and happier relationship may result from this present general upset. He was ready to cry at times, and I like him much better like that. He has certainly got over his sulks and that makes everything far easier. Now to bed. Tired.

A splendid view of your grey-headed kingfisher on the garden fence near the lucerne.

Saturday evening

I took Will to the new dam yesterday evening. You can guess his lively interest in everything. He is going off to Rumuruti tomorrow and coming back with Gilfrid on his birthday. I must remember to take his present of parti-colored socks!

I've spent most of today with Christopher. In the morning we went round the ring road and caught about five hundred Nderobo cattle near Muriel's View. We drove some back here (to find out the owners). Lots of elephant about.

Night Horizons

Sunday afternoon

This morning I rang up (following a hint from David) Telephone International and booked a call to you this afternoon at 5:10 p.m. The time was chosen by the operator. I can hardly believe I will hear your voice so soon. I hope you and Lucy will not be out for a walk! I have had a quiet day. The thorn trees are in flower, filling the air with their scent. Distant cocks, near Gilfrid's cottage, crow in the brilliant sunshine. Now I must go up to Mohammed's house to await the call. Back at the cottage: what a disappointment! I could hear the bell ringing in our cottage. But no answer. The operator has found another free time for me tonight.

Monday morning

Another disappointment last night. You were probably in with Lucy, but I thought you would hear Mrs. Allen's loud ringer even so.

Kimutai has gone and I have brought Mugambi Midogo back to help with the outside work, bath, firewood, horses, garden, etc. He doesn't come into the house, which means Kisiom has to do something.

Evening

In from my evening walk. I sit in our old place on the rocks by the two euphorbia trees, and watch the light fade over Simangwa. Each evening I hear the hadadas' clamorous return. Then the last song of the robin followed by the first calls of the nightjar. Then down the path to the stepping-stones to watch in the last reflected light on the pool the three black ducks silently swimming upstream. They are not so nervous now and do not fly away at my approach. Back under brightening Orion to the cottage. I like to see the lamplight shining quietly out. Broch and Slate are very unobtrusive companions.

I had a visit from Mlefu this evening, on a borrowing expedition. I am well into Taylor's commentary now; much of great interest. He is a doughty champion of Plato. I would have liked a commentary from him on the *Phaedo*, the only work of Plato I know fairly well. Perhaps as I grow more fluent at Greek I'll tackle some of the other dialogues, but Plotinus will keep me busy for some time.

Tuesday

Darling Mary, how I miss you. I don't like not being able to write to you and hear from you. I think I'll stop this diary letter today, as you will probably find it confusing. I'll post it as soon as I hear that the strike is over, and then write you air letters. I'll leave space for a word after I've seen Will tomorrow.

Evening

I came in a little earlier this evening—the robin still singing in your Spring Place. The northern constellations faintly shining. How I wish I could touch your hand. I read these lines in a Chinese poem a few days ago:

> One night sleeping alone, I dreamed I was home again
> At her window
> She was combing her hair
> We looked at each other
> We brought no words
> Silently looked at each other
> In tears...

My dear, I don't like at all this long separation. I look at Will's painting of Vera's cottage in Mappowder and long to be walking past it to our cottage. I did so long to hear your voice the other evening.

I think I will go on adding a little to this letter, as it helps me to feel in touch with you. I spend the afternoons in your Spring Place now—not under your gourd, but at the foot of a marera tree a few yards beyond it where I can sit and pretend you are in your place.

I am going out to Sirakoi tomorrow to spend a few nights there. I have asked Christopher along, perhaps we will have a few games of chess. Now to supper and bath. I read one of your poems each evening, and one from a Chinese collection. I find that your poems and these Chinese poems speak to my condition these empty days. I hear growling outside—perhaps Snow has turned up from Sirakoi. After bath: the Pleiades near the crescent moon over the hills. Hyraxes in the Spring Place. Do you remember how one evening, coming down over Windy Hill after dark, we found so many glow-worms shining in the grass?

Night Horizons

Wednesday the 3rd—Will's 83rd birthday

This morning in the Tortoise Grove I had a splendid view of a kingfisher very close to the place you saw one, and also a lone impala grazing just in front of the marera you used to read under when visited by the tortoise Bwana Katendu.

Lions grunting again at night across the river.

Evening

I didn't go to Sirakoi, went to see Will instead. I found Rose and Crystal there. I took Will the socks, he was very pleased with them. I stayed with Will after Rose and Crystal left. We had a happy time looking through some of Will's old African photograph albums, Will telling stories that came to mind as he saw the photographs. He gave me two bedtime books to read by Laura Ingalls Wilder, *Little House in the Big Woods* and *On the Banks of Plum Creek*. He has got them for Rose's children but I am to read them first. Looking through them, I think I will enjoy them.

Gilfrid has given Will as a birthday present an Abyssinian painting he got in Addis Ababa of an elephant being disembowelled by hunters! Will is delighted with it. A very gory picture indeed.

Thursday evening

A great forest fire has started over the shoulder of Mount Kenya above Nanyuki. The sky along the Simangwa hills is dark with smoke. The sun went down very red, like a winter sun. I did not go to Sirakoi, felt somehow rather defeated; but I think I may have a cold hoving. There were six hadadas in the Spring Place today. I've spent most of the day out reading—Homer, Herodotus, Plotinus—then indoors, Taylor. I wish I weren't so slow at reading Greek. I still have to work quite hard at it. I find this in one of your books of Chinese poetry:

> The Milky Way has wheeled across the heavens
> The Northern Dipper slants then stands upright.
> Though the River of Stars can move about like this,
> How can it know the secrets of my heart?

Friday

My father's birthday. There is an excellent review in a *Times Literary Supplement* that arrived a few days ago of a book titled *Ascent to the Absolute*. I have an idea this book would be of great interest, judging by passages quoted by the reviewer. Perhaps you could order it from Heffers? It is by J.N. Findlay and published by Allen & Unwin. Mugambi Midogo is doing very well in the garden and around the cottage. He has it looking very neat already.

Another dark red sun moving down into a smoky sky this evening. The forest fire will burn on for some days, I fear. I sat by the stepping-stones this evening watching the three ducks on the pool in the last glimmer of light:

> Green so green the reeds in the river
> endless my thoughts of that far-off land
> I dared not think of that far-off land
> but then last night I saw it in a dream
> dreaming, it seemed she stood right by my side
> but suddenly I woke in another place
> in another place and in a different country...

Saturday

Just in from Will's. He is doing a fine new chalk picture of a landscape on the Rumuruti: a fiery evening sky behind a hill, with a cheetah hunting an impala in the foreground. I went round with Wamiti this morning. We reckon that about one thousand Nderobo cattle are grazing on to the farm at night from Engelbrecht's! Elephants and zebra everywhere. A great flock of Kavirondo cranes along the furrow of the dam site where we walked our last evening together here. The dam not yet finished. They are having lots of trouble with their machinery.

This evening before I went down to Will I was reading in the Tortoise Grove. I felt a gentle drop of rain! Looked up, sky gray, and saw a splendid double rainbow arched across a black cloud, rain falling along the escarpment. The days since you left have been brilliant and clear, this is the first sign of a change. The great forest fire has burnt right over the shoulder of the mountain to Naru Muru, says Christopher, who came in for lunch.

Night Horizons

Sunday morning

I have had a happy walk through the Tortoise Grove, a robin singing splendidly and gazelle leaping away as I came near; back by the waterfalls. I sat a long time by the stepping-stones, watching the swift-eddying river, and found myself saying over in my mind, the words singing out in my heart, your 'Narina's Trogon.' My dear dear Mary, this poem comes to me a descent of the Paraclete, a jet of perfect birdsong, clear and ringing as the sudden song of the Cape robin in the evening sunlight. It comes with a touch of healing and hope and reassurance. I like to think I will be able to remember and repeat these words in my heart as I am dying, but that would be a thing too great perhaps to hope for.

I would like to copy out a little story from Herodotus that I have always found strangely moving. It may perhaps serve as, in some dumb inarticulate way, a pointer to the meaning of the strain in my thought you find perhaps perplexing and even irritating—the need I stand under to see essential Christian vision as centered round a final apocalypse:

> The next king of Egypt, they said, was Cheops' son Mycerinus. He, being displeased with his father's doings, ruled his people with great clemency, yet calamities befell him... of which the first was the death of his daughter, the only child of his household. Greatly grieving over this misfortune, he desired to give her a burial something more excellent than ordinary; he made therefore a hollow cow's image of gilded wood and placed therein the body of his dead daughter. This cow was not buried in the earth but was to be seen even in my time, in the town of Sais, where it lay in an adorned chamber of the palace; incense of all kinds is offered daily before it, and a lamp burns by it all through every night.... As for the cow, it is covered with a purple robe, and shows only the head and neck, which are encrusted with a very thick layer of gold. Between its horns it bears the golden figure of the sun's orb. It does not stand, but kneels; its stature is that of a live cow of great size. This image is carried out of the chamber once in every year, whenever the Egyptians make lamentation for the god whom I name not in speaking of these matters; it is then that the cow is brought out into the light; for Mycerinus' daughter, they say, entreated him at her death that she might see the sun once a year.

I have booked a call to Lucy's number this evening. I am going to spend the evening and have supper with Will and take the call there so that if we get through Lucy may be able to hear Will's voice!

A strong wind blowing this morning under a clear sky, and the continual crying in the gusts of the Abyssinian scimitar bill, a cry that makes even the sunlight seem empty and lonely. I saw Bess yesterday; her feet seem all right now.

Oh, my dearest dearest Mary, I have just come in from sitting at our place of rocks by the euphorbia trees and watching the sun drop all brilliant and flaming behind Simangwa as a scarlet-chested sunbird scolded me from the euphorbia and in my heart all the time your dear voice saying:

> See my dearest the bird
> vivid and virid-winged
> crimson with quick-shed bright blood
> brilliant and perfect this bird

Darling Mary, this sheaf of poems and very especially this particular poem, is more precious a word to me than anything I have ever found in all the volumes of formal philosophy and theology I have ever ploughed through, and in my foolish masculine head I have been half afraid you were turning into a rationalizing philosopher—such beings as frequent the academies and lyceums of the learned and glance at Parnassus with a certain cool detachment. Of course this foolish fancy of mine was an absurdity, yet it had somehow got itself lodged into my simple skull, and always I have at bottom and in secret been stubbornly and unreservedly on the side of the poets and prophets rather than of the scientists and philosophers and theologians, all of whom, I confess, I approach now with a certain ineradicable scepticism—although when I was younger there was an element of awed reverence in my approach to these great ones of the intellectual world. Your uncle John told me once that I had a "highly developed bump of awe and reverence" (and he was certainly right) for such great ones; "but all the same for that," as he would say, my love and devotion was for the poets and seers and prophets, and I feel in my spiritual bones as it were that they are the ones who see deepest and most honestly and completely—though of course those others would raise their learned eyebrows at this! But however all this may be, and whether or not I am just airing my own prejudices, among these poems there are those that say a "word" to me that I will never forget for its beauty and truth.

Now I must go off to have supper with Will, and I pray hear your voice again before the sun rises once more!

Night Horizons

Monday

I was so happy to hear your voice last night, and know all was well. I had had a feeling you had been swallowed up. The drought is getting very grim now; all over the country things will be desperate if no rain falls before the end of this month. We hear too that cholera has definitely broken out in the N.F.D.

Tuesday evening

A very hot, sultry day with thunder muttering and heavy clouds gathering in the east. It does look as though some change is brewing. If so, only just in time: the older and weaker cattle are starting to die, and so, we hear, are people in the N.F.D. The government is organizing widespread famine relief now. The great fire is under control. About twenty thousand acres of forest land is black and smouldering along the slopes of the mountain. There have been bad fires in other areas also and the air is murky with smoke. It is said that this is the worse drought for over fifty years, and Will says the last one as bad was that in 1919, described by Llewelyn in *Black Laughter*.

I am going out to Sirakoi tomorrow and will stay three nights. Mugambi Midogo will take out Jenny and Jill and help with the cooking out there. Christopher Gibson may turn up.

A little poem I liked from the Chinese anthology—perhaps for its wateriness in this drought:

> south of the Yangtze you can gather the lotus
> the lotus leaves float like little boats
> in among the leaves the fishes play
> east of the leaves
> west of the leaves
> south of the leaves
> north of the leaves
> the fishes play

This evening as I watched the pools among the stepping-stones, a pair of white-browed robins came down to drink in the last light. I thought I recognized their shapes, then one flew to an overhanging branch and broke into brief song. Numbers of small birds come down to the water at that time; I see their movements, but it is too dark to identify them. At such moments much that burdens my mind falls away and all grows still. The ducks too were quietly swimming round the rocks.

Wednesday

Coffee time. I've been out with Wamiti organizing relief for the cows and calves, which are the cattle most hard hit by the drought. We've pulled out about thirty of the weakest and brought them up to the house, where they can be helped more easily. Fortunately we have just finished harvesting the maize so are able to turn them into the field and give them lucerne. But we may have to start buying feed soon. The sky is murky bronze in color this morning. I go out to Sirakoi after tea.

Looking back at my comments on philosophers, scientists, and theologians, what I should rather have said is that I distrust them *as vehicles of ultimate vision*. Of course the great minds among them contribute enormously to all sane thinking, and they are absolutely necessary as correctives, but when they usurp—as they often tend to do—the place of traditional religious doctrines that are centered in the sense of the sacred, then I part company with them. Religious doctrines need to face valid criticism, *as a purifying process*, from philosophy and science; but philosophy or science can never take the place of true religious vision, which flows always from revelation.

Revelation crystallizes in history around traditional religious symbols. False or inadequate theology can weaken and deface the symbols, but cannot destroy their ultimate validity. Philosophy and science can help in the criticism of inadequate theologies, but cannot take the place of the central symbols. My own rather critical response to Greek philosophy and science, which is in general Western philosophy and science, is that it tends either to deny altogether the reality and validity of religious revelation, or to assume within itself the capacity to *judge* revelation—a claim that can only seem fatuous to a genuine religious consciousness. What redeems Plotinus out of the ranks of the purely rationalistic philosophers into the rank of great religious thinker and seer (something far nobler and higher than any rationalism) is his inward response to revelation: he does not allow his rationalism to weaken his revelation, but only to purify it. The same is probably true, but perhaps in lesser degree, of Plato, though I think Taylor brings out in his wide-ranging and excellent commentary how large a part political considerations and scientific cosmology played in Plato's thought. But I think it fair to say that both Plotinus and Plato are in large degree outside the mainstream of Western *philosophical* thought, that their significance has been for Western *religious* vision and their influence assimilated into Christian or near-Christian vision; whereas the mainstream has flowed down from the early Ionian philosophy, through Democritus, Anaxagoras, etc.—men whose "philosophy" was for the most part little more than a rationalized theoretical groundwork for the natural sciences (which were what really interested these thinkers); and it is the natural sciences that have, in the widest sense, been the basic preoccupation of distinctively Western philosophy. It is this philosophy that I distrust, not in itself with its own legitimate interests and methods, but insofar as it seeks to dissolve and replace religious perspectives, perspectives of an incomparably higher and deeper order. It is significant that this kind of natural scientific philosophy finds it easy to ridicule and dissolve popular pseudo-religious superstitions of all kinds. Why? Because such superstitions are not essentially religious at all, even though they may collect round religious symbols. Such superstitions are, rather, childish, immature forms of false natural science. This is why true scientific thinking has such power over them, a power truly devastating. But this scientific perspective is helpless when confronted with genuine religious vision: it can do no more than help get rid of the rubbish that accumulates round religious vision.

Well, I must stop. I was tempted into this perhaps rather elementary digression on some basic problems by the sense that my remarks on philosophers and scientists might give a false impression. I included the theologians because they too often seem to try to rationalize and denature true religious vision by a false pseudo-scientific approach.

A flock of fire finches and sparrows has arrived on the grass just outside your window—I am sitting in your chair. They spend a lot of time round the cottage these days; like all the creatures they are short of food. I see two dark clouds gathering to the north. A lion grunting again last night. I found this amusing line in a Chinese poem: "Try to retire, you're a goat with horns in the hedge."

Friday

I came back from Sirakoi sooner than planned, as it looks as though heavy rain is imminent. Christopher turned up for one night and we had a ride together to Lengishu Beacon and back across Gerenuk Valley, at the lower end. It was a strange evening ride. The sky covered with dark clouds, very still, the grass on the plains ashen. I had two sunrise walks to the top of El Khalil. The dogs are all well there. Koroi as boisterous as ever. He has shown no sign of tick fever yet.

Saturday

Dr. Birkett came in this morning and left me with an evangelical tract that I read and which left me, in spite of all its obvious good intentions, depressed and ruminating. What good is there in this kind of goodness?

Perhaps we suffer from a surfeit of ineffective articulation—*rumpite libros ne corda vestra rumpantur*. But I had a happy time by the Driftwood Falls watching a pair of wagtails! Today the clear, scorching weather has returned; no cloud now in the sky, and a thick haze over the distance. So, the drought continues.

Sunday

Went to collect letters from Will this evening. He told me Nigel was chased by a buffalo yesterday and ran behind a small tree. The buffalo tried to get at him round the tree and Nigel had to hold it by its horns, one each side of the tree trunk. Nigel managed this for some time and then suddenly ran backwards into a small gully. The buffalo followed him and tumbled down into the gully beside him. Nigel just managed to scramble up out of the gully before the buffalo could buffet him, and then got away, as the buffalo couldn't climb up out of the gully to follow him!

The elephants are watering at the pool in our new dam now.

Monday morning

My 53rd birthday. I read in Taylor that a Greek was not considered an old man until he was sixty! It is a beautiful morning and I'm just off to Nanyuki. I hope to get this letter posted today, if the P.O. here has started accepting mail for England. Perhaps too there will soon be a letter from you!

A very great clamor of hadadas flying over your Spring Place this morning—six of them.

My love to Lucy.

Always my love,
Gerard

Phoenix

'life brilliant and perfect'
hear this and believe
known by soul clear as light
as spring water the one note
of bird-throat in canopied night

quick the word pierces clear to the soul
wait now and listen
the soul unseen is near
clear as the vision here

of the silent bird that called
the lovenote into singing
in sunshine no more
but the soul in light shines clear
vision to soul in waiting

see my dearest the bird
vivid and virid-winged
crimson with quick-shed bright blood
the living heart of the rose

brilliant and perfect this bird

MARY CASEY

Afternoon

Springs Cottage
9th August 1971

My darling Mary — Ahmed has to go down to Nairobi tomorrow so I take the opportunity to send off to you a few thoughts more or less in the back of my mind when I wrote this morning about Taylor. But first a prayer to the Son of Chronos of the Crooked Ways before venturing into treacherous (and stormy) waters — the prayer I found Will had jotted in one of his diaries some years ago ———

A tiny green moth has just landed beside here.

   Spare me hatchet
   Spare me blast
   Spare me lightning
     to the last!

your always Gerard

For although Athene sprang fully-armed from the head of Zeus — Zeus remains the Son of Chronos of the Crooked Ways and remains too the progenitor of other offspring than Athene! So the poets — who so often — it is a notion of mine — see more penetratingly than philosophers — or at least than rationalistic philosophers — who claim for the most part that all true philosophy is rationalistic in its basic presuppositions. I see that Whitehead quite explicitly makes this claim — and I think in this he is fairly and squarely and honestly speaking for the mainstream of the European philosophic tradition which flows down to us from the headwaters of this tradition — Plato and Aristotle. Now no one with any sense of the greatness of this tradition challenges it on basic issues without serious trepidation. Hence my preliminary prayer. But there are

Night Horizons

Spring Cottage
9 August 1971

My darling Mary,

Mohammed has to go down to Nairobi tomorrow so I take the opportunity to send off to you a few thoughts more or less in the back of my mind when I wrote this morning about Taylor. But first a prayer to the Son of Cronos of the Crooked Ways before venturing into treacherous and stormy waters—the prayer I found Will had jotted in one of his diaries some years ago—

> Spare me hatchet
> Spare me blast
> Spare me lightning
> To the last!

A tiny green moth has just landed beside here.

For although Athene sprang fully-armed from the head of Zeus, Zeus remains the Son of Cronos of the Crooked Ways, and remains too the progenitor of other offspring than Athene! So the poets often—it is a notion of mine—see more penetratingly than philosophers, or at least than rationalistic philosophers, who claim for the most part that all true philosophy is rationalistic in its basic presuppositions. I see that Whitehead quite explicitly makes this claim, and I think in this he is fairly and squarely and honestly speaking for the mainstream of the European philosophic tradition, which flows down to us from the headwaters of this tradition—Plato and Aristotle. Now no one with any sense of the greatness of this tradition challenges it on basic issues without serious trepidation. Hence my preliminary prayer. But here goes!

Whitehead writes: "that we fail to find in experience any elements intrinsically incapable of exhibition as examples of general theory is the hope of rationalism. This hope is not a metaphysical premise. It is a faith that forms the motive for the pursuit of all sciences alike, including metaphysics." Whitehead here, with his customary acuteness, sees "rationalism" as springing from a faith *beyond itself*. I think his statement of the case is here accurate, except that I would deny, in common I think with all whose deepest orientations of spirit are religious rather than philosophical, that this faith forms the motive of the pursuit of metaphysics in all cases. I do not share this faith; it does not seem to me basic to metaphysics. It is a faith some have, some have not. But of course here the question resolves itself into the definition of metaphysics: to me it is the attempt to enter into and realize as living transforming truth that which transcends—in the sense that it is not immediately accessible—the stubborn givenness of the empirical temporal order. And this attempt has seemed to me more successful when springing from a religiously integrated non-rational basis. So that I would quite seriously claim—this is the religious as over against the rational faith—that in the West the great Christian saints and mystics have penetrated more deeply into the metaphysical order than the philosophers. From this point of view, rationalistic modes of thought can only offer secondary clarifying procedures, immensely valuable, but never quite capable of acting in place of religious revelation, religious vision, religious θεωρία.

Whitehead gives his list of "supreme masters of thought," starting with Plato and ending with Kant; and in this, his chosen tradition of thought, he says rightly: "the final court of appeal is intrinsic reasonableness." The name of a supreme master of thought conspicuous by its absence is Plotinus. Why? Because Plotinus was not a rationalist. For Plotinus the supreme metaphysical reality, the One, transcended Intellect. Armstrong, in a revealing note on one of the key passages in *Ennead* III, 8, writes: "Plotinus is arguing here *against the Platonists*, who accepted the identification of the totality of being with Intellect, and did not see the need for the transcendent One." Plotinus's explicit doctrine on this is that the supreme metaphysical principle, the One, is "beyond Intellect." It is not conditioned by Intellect or subject to its categories. Thus at one stride Plotinus placed himself outside the ranks of the rationalists, and this is the reason why he has been so neglected in the West, *except by religiously oriented thinkers*. For let us be honest and clear here: what Plotinus asserts is that the supreme reality, the most truly real, cannot be penetrated by Intellect, much less by discursive reasoning. Such a position is entirely alien and unacceptable to the rationalist faith as fairly stated by Whitehead in the words I have quoted. This is the reason why Plotinus has always been looked at askance by the rationalistic orthodoxy of Western philosophical thought. His noble θεωρία is a religious not a rationalistic θεωρία. He does—and this is admitted all round—push rationalistic processes of thought as far as possible, but he sees clearly and states clearly that these processes cannot carry him beyond the threshold of the supreme mystery. He reasonably sees that there are limits to reason, even to the highest forms of Intellect. The rationalist has the irrational faith that there are no such limits. In this, Plotinus seems to me more truly rational than the rationalists. He sees that the Supreme Mystery is *unconditioned by Intellect*. Jesus said, as does Homer, that "with God all things are possible," implying "even what may seem to us to be unreasonable"; and in this Plotinus clearly shared the vision of Jesus.

The basic reality the religious man sees and seeks to respond to is God. When the rationalist quibbles "how do you know you are seeing God, how do you know there is any God to see?", the simple-minded religious man remains unmoved by this seemingly so penetrating and portentous question. He simply replies, "open the eyes of your spirit," as he would to a man who always closed his eyes before venturing out into sunlight and staunchly denied the existence of the sun. Or it might be a truer analogy to think of the religious man as one who feels the warmth of the divine presence on closed eyelids, who is allowing himself, like a new puppy, to grow up—as he senses he will one day be able to open his eyes. The rationalist is, it sometimes seems, determined to keep them shut. For to the religious man the "God" of the rationalistic philosophers is little more than the projection of their own manifestly inadequate reasonings, so that it is possible for a man of the highest intellectual calibre, like Pascal, to say, "Not the God of the philosophers, but the God of Isaac." To the religious man God reveals Himself as, by inadequate analogy, the rising sun reveals itself. All the creatures rejoicing in the rising of the sun do not try to understand the warmth they feel and the life-giving power of the sun "in terms of general theory"—certainly not in the sense in which "theory"—a very anemic θεωρία—is understood by rationalistic thinkers. They respond to "revelation."

I suppose all this seems remote from Taylor's reluctance to relate his ethical thought to "metaphysical first principles." Yet surely it is clear that there is in his hesitation the implicit assertion that he does not in fact find himself able to accept the metaphysical first principles of rationalistic thinkers as *genuinely first*. He is in effect criticizing the truth and adequacy of these principles that do not recognize their own limitations in the face of the Divine. What the thoroughgoing rationalist—perhaps, happily, not a very common being—does not sense is that his theories are not only more or less inadequate, but are infinitely inadequate in the most stringent sense of the word "infinitely." The issue is clear, shall we say, in Plotinian terms: the Intellect is conditioned by the One, that is, it is limited, finite; the Divine, the One, is absolutely unconditioned, that is, infinite—and the falling short of the Intellect from the One is *necessarily* an *infinite falling short*. I find all this clearly stated as necessary metaphysical doctrine by Plotinus. He insists on the necessity Intellect is under to cease to be itself, to return backwards from itself, etc. in its approach to the One. It is abundantly clear why the rationalists have edged away, muttering of "atavistic mysticism," as Whitehead does.

Taylor is probably aware that all the strange and terrible ambiguities that underlie ethical striving, that underlie all existence conditioned by the finite, *cannot be rationalized away*; and is well aware, it may be, that the whole urge and motive of rationalistic thinking is to seek to rationalize them away. And here perhaps we come to the truth that rationalism as defined by Whitehead is inherently anti-metaphysical insofar as it refuses to recognize that the supreme metaphysical order remains unconditioned by Intellect—and that the simplest peasant who catches some glimpse of the unconditioned glory of the Divine is more truly metaphysical than his more learned fellow.

I think it fair to say that rationalism is always in fact man-centered and not God-centered. How can it be otherwise when it recognizes no principle as higher than man's intellect—nothing that it cannot in principle penetrate and understand? It is surely significant that the type of "religious" thinking that emanates from rationalism in its more extreme forms calls itself "humanism." Man, insofar as he seeks to limit the Divine to his own capacity for understanding (and this is in effect what rationalism does), seeks, to put it quite bluntly, to condition the Divine; that is, to condition the essentially unconditioned. The deeper urge behind all this is, it may be, that the whole life of the rationalist is an active, never-ceasing reaching out into deeper understanding that can only falter into stillness and ceasing once it starts to realize that it is in fact not deepening its understanding when it seeks to penetrate the divine mysteries, but is revolving endlessly in a self-consuming inner circuit of the finite. To recognize its limitations is death to the inner life of rationalism; and it knows, can know, nothing beyond this life until it accepts this death. Could it die this death, it would be reborn in a new life, breathless and still with adoration before the Divine Truth that transcends all possibility of finite understanding; and as Intellect, the root of understanding, is essentially finite, this human limitation cannot be transcended from inside its own processes. It is here entirely dependent on that which comes to it from outside its own processes, that is on Divine Grace. I do not think it true, as claimed by some (Paul Henry for example), that there is no doctrine in Plotinus comparable to that of the action of Divine Grace as taught in Christian theology. In fact, in an absolute sense, Plotinus sees all as the action of Grace, and this is a supreme metaphysical insight—yes all, even the limitations of rationalists. Time, as Blake said, is the Mercy of Eternity to those not yet born into the eternal. And there remain the necessities of "not yet being born," as of "being born."

Well! I must stop with this page—thank heavens you will perhaps say. These reflections, such as they are, are only meant as brief and inadequate indications on problems and themes at the deepest levels of the life of the spirit. They do not imply any lack of a sense of the true greatness of our

Well! I must stop with this page — thank heavens you will perhaps say — these reflections such as they are are only meant as brief and inadequate indications on problems and themes at the deepest levels of the life of the spirit — they do not imply any lack of a sense of the true greatness of our philosophical tradition as far as it can legitimately go — but they do find in that tradition a certain lack of humility before the ultimate mysteries. I think I have read widely enough and attentively enough in our philosophical writings to know how eloquently and forcibly and to some, convincingly these great thinkers could and would reply to the kind of reaction I represent. And we all recognise there is much on all sides that escapes expression in words. The spirit in man realizes itself in its true wrestlings with the tensions wrought by opposing — or at least differently orientated — perspectives. This is one of the senses in which all is Grace. I have found my recent reading of Whitehead stimulating and exciting — he utters many thought-provoking λoγoι. In large part too I confess he is beyond my understanding — and it may be that in these areas lie the replies to my difficulties and protests against his rationalistic presuppositions. But he seems to me a predominantly scientific thinker seeking to break into a genuinely metaphysical point of view but never quite succeeding — his intense rationalism inhibits this birth. He can only see true metaphysics as what he slightingly calls 'atavistic mysticism' — but the very choice of the word 'atavistic' here indicates notions of 'progress' incompatible with true metaphysics. Enough! enough! Bring the hatchet! as Panurge said to Gerard.

philosophical tradition as far as it can legitimately go—but they do find in that tradition a certain lack of humility before the ultimate mysteries. I think I have read widely enough and attentively enough in our philosophical writings to know how eloquently and forcibly and, to some, convincingly these great thinkers could and would reply to the kind of reaction I represent. And we all recognize there is much on all sides that escapes expression in words. The spirit in man realizes itself in its inner wrestlings with the tensions wrought by opposing—or at least differently orientated—perspectives. This is one of the senses in which All is Grace. I have found my recent reading of Whitehead stimulating and exciting—he utters many thought-provoking "logoi." In large part too I confess he is beyond my understanding, and it may be that in these areas lie the replies to my difficulties and protests against his rationalistic presuppositions. But he seems to me a predominantly scientific thinker seeking to break into a genuinely metaphysical point of view, but never quite succeeding—his intense rationalism inhibits this birth. He can only see true metaphysics as what he slightingly calls "atavistic mysticism"—but the very choice of the word "atavistic" here indicates notions of "progress" incompatible with true metaphysics. Enough! Enough! Bury the hatchet! as Panurge said.

            Love,
            Gerard

[On envelope]: Will has given me a beautiful watercolor done years ago at the Beale. No need perhaps to take the metaphysical "jeu d'esprit" within too seriously. The Son of Cronos of the Crooked Ways always has the last word—and probably takes philosophers no more seriously than anyone else!

Spring Cottage
20 August 1971

My darling Mary,

Your dear letter, so helpful to me in many ways on Whitehead and Collingwood, has come to me today. Your words, on Whitehead more especially, give me much to think of. Certainly the Whitehead of *Adventures of Ideas* is more in my line than the Whitehead of *Process and Reality*, if only because I find the first far more comprehensible. I do think his tendency to develop a private language leads to unnecessary obscurity at times. In this he does not follow his master Plato, who always wrote as simply and clearly as possible in the common language of educated men in his time, without any sacrifice of depth of insight. But I do value Whitehead as a fine and stimulating thinker. I would not wish my remarks on his rationalism to make it seem I undervalue him. In any case, he is in an ancient and honorable company in his rationalism, a company not likely to be perturbed by comments from me! The truth is of course that rationalism is of many kinds and inwardly determining tendencies, and Whitehead's rationalism is certainly not one I feel fiercely hostile to, as I confess I do to some others. I suppose at bottom any way of thinking is rationalistic that arises from a basic faith in the self-sufficiency of reason. This is a faith I do not and cannot share, but I can respect and honor many of its great accomplishments.

It is only anti-traditional rationalism that I react strongly against, and one could not possibly accuse Whitehead of that.

And I agree so much with R.G. Collingwood on "magic." So many difficulties arise from the differing connotations that any particular basic word—words like magic, love, nature, religion, science, reason, etc.—has for the person either using it or reading it. But speaking of magic (a word with, for me, friendly and acceptable connotations), I remember some words of J.C.P. He wrote in, I think, *A Philosophy of Solitude*, that an immemorial rule of any mental magic is that it be practiced in sympathy with the traditional wisdom emanating from the deep earth on which we happen to live—or something to that effect. I think it is in this sense I cling to tradition. I have always thought J.C.P.'s magic was at bottom a "Christian magic," using the word "Christian" in its widest sense. And his magic was a benevolent, compassionate magic, for all his talk of his "cold planetary heart." In this sense then I cling to and value

Christian tradition: it is the tradition—ancient, subtle, profound—emanating from the deep earth on which I was born, and lived, and moved, and had my being when I was young.

Because I value my own tradition, I can understand and value other ancient traditions as also life-giving, subtle, profound. My Christian vision, such as it is (many would no doubt deny me it in name), lacks all proselytizing fury in regard to other authentic religious traditions. I delight in their variety and difference. Any "fury" of a polemical nature I may have is directed against anti-traditional thought in general, for I am convinced that anti-traditional processes, if unchecked, lead to darkness and death. With a Hindu Swami or a Muslim Mullah I feel, in the depths, at one. I find that they understand me, and I think I understand them. From most of our contemporary Western rationalists I am grievously alienated. Common culture, society, forms, language, education, etc., cannot bridge the radical differences of values and insights—differences that cannot but issue in a profound antagonism on both sides, however smothered and hidden under polite social usage.

I think what distresses and angers me in this extreme contemporary anti-traditionalistic movement is that, for all its pose of superiority and enlightenment, it is death-dealing; or, to put it perhaps more moderately, that it is certainly not life-giving or life-enhancing, or even life-accepting. All the poignant strangeness and mystery of our lives on this planet, with all the poignant hopes and tentative insights into eternal significance that we try to mediate through our traditions to the coming generations, all in short that binds the generations together and so demands love and sacrifice and compassion, all this is little or nothing to such people. They "know better" and center their lives—and invite all of us to do likewise—in the most vapid and transient of notions, notions that have been rattling about inside men's skulls from the earliest times, always to be rejected as pitifully inadequate by anyone capable of thinking at all. And all this is served up anew as "enlightenment," an "alternative society," as the latest word in wisdom and insight into the ultimate mysteries of our existence.

It is true that we live in mystery, a mystery not to be plumbed by traditionalist or modernist. But against this background of mystery the tentative indications of possible significance, crystallized in long anguish through many generations, mediated to us through our religious traditions, mean more, go deeper, than any modernistic claptrap. And are worthy of all reverence. Even if they are illusions, they have a nobility and dignity in their illusion that is not without meaning. A nobility and dignity denied to all that denies them.

This anti-traditional "rationalism"—which is, as far as I can judge, the "religion" of our contemporary clever ones—proliferates like a cancer in a healthy body, with the same end results for individuals and society alike—death. Its more immediate results are plain in any society where its influence becomes dominant.

It seems dominant in our universities, the places that should be centers of all that is truly life-giving in our traditions. It inevitably generates forces and tendencies that affect us all; even the best minds of our time cannot remain untainted. We are all of our time, and we are all infected. But we can at least try to recognize the disease. I think my own (as it may seem, excessive) adherence to the broad influence of our religious traditions is my personal attempt to retain a corrective in my life and thought to this "sickness unto death"! Perhaps I react more strongly than many because I am more deeply infected. I had read shelf-fuls of publications of the Rationalist Press Association and its "Thinker's Library" before I was twenty. I thought I was being initiated into the arcana of all true wisdom! The rest of my thinking life has stemmed from an increasingly vigorous revolt against all the pretensions of these blind leaders of the blind. As far as I am concerned, "they have been found out!"—as Santayana said of the religious people *he* revolted against. I too have revolted against the pretensions of religious people, but I have always known that something remained after their pretensions had been rejected, something of immense and abiding significance. But once the pretensions of the anti-traditionalists have been exploded there is nothing left but a tawdry vanity. They are "the hollow men," stuffed with straw!

Well, I have "let myself go," as they say. But in very truth the results of what I so fiercely revolt from are not pretty to see, and one has not to look far to see them.

Darling Mary, when I started this letter there was a great thunderstorm stumbling and crackling over the hills. Each afternoon for the past week this has happened, but we get very little rain down here. Now I come to myself and realize the thunderstorm is over. You must attribute any extravagance of expression in this letter to the influence of the thunderstorm—well, it has at least cleared the air! You mustn't mind my occasional eruptions in this vein. I sense that you find my vehemence in these matters rather extreme. It may be so; there are of course, must be, balancing forces. But that does not make these malignant growths any more acceptable. They cannot but be rejected, if our civilization is to survive.

So much for what I reject. As for what I accept, well, I rejoice with a great rejoicing to find a man of Whitehead's calibre writing those words, so eminently acceptable to me, that you quote: "The essence of Christianity is the appeal to the life of Christ as a revelation of the nature of God and of His agency in the world... can there be any doubt that the power of Christianity lies in its revelation in act of that which Plato had divined in theory?" Thank you for bringing these words to my notice, words I had forgotten. Would that more of our intellectual leaders could find it in them to repeat and supplement these words.

To move to another aspect of these matters, I do not think Collingwood's remark that "we are already living outside our tradition when we begin to examine it" is true in more than a very limited sense. It is true of course if the examination is made in a mood of detached indifference, or of hostile rationalism: in either case we were already "outside" before the examination started. Apart from these cases, the moment we begin to examine our tradition with sympathetic attention is the moment we begin to live consciously and decisively *inside* it and start moving to a deeper understanding of it, and grow more able to respond to all its supreme power of healing magic.

Yes, magic has its place in all true religion, and as you say, J.C.P. reveals this in his own masterly fashion in *Porius*, which is a magical book written by a great magician. My own particular Christian vision (and in this I feel close to poets like Blake and Smart, and the poet of 'The Phoenix and the Turtle'— not to mention Tom O'Bedlam) has always felt at home with and understanding of and rejoicing in J.C.P.'s great, compassionate, and benevolent "magic for all beings." I have always understood those (usually simple) people who as often as not had not read a word of his books, but who could see in John something not little of the true saint, something which of course our clever contemporaries cannot see, and will never see.

But John never did and never could move outside the influence of his tradition in any radical or effective sense. Anything *less* like an anti-traditional rationalist than J.C.P. it would be hard to imagine. At the most he mildly revolted against some of the nonsense and humbug that inevitably accompanies any great human tradition that involves vast numbers of human beings over great periods of time. And with the kind of rationalism whose only aim is to rid us of humbug and nonsense I am in complete sympathy. And when I think of his endless, *awed* rummaging into remote reaches of the past, of his loving attention to Homer and the Bible and old Welsh legend, and of how his way of interpreting and reacting to these ancient writings was exactly my own (of course he taught me in these things), of how profoundly "pious" and traditional in the best sense he was in all these things (and taught me to be so too)—well, in view of all this, I feel no hesitation or doubt in claiming his blessing and understanding in depth for my own particular vision of things! The differences are not radical. John's basic vision was poetic and sceptical, but sceptical in a profoundly "pious" way. My basic vision is religious, and certainly not less sceptical than John's, as far as most manifestations of cleverness in our modern world go. My religious basis is trust, faith if you like, but that cannot be otherwise. True religion is basically trust—trust in God, trust for the past, for the future, for all men, for all beings, however grim the terrible doubt of appearances. Trust in God, as the unconditioned creative divine source of all our being. But I must stop.

> Love always,
> Gerard

I went out after finishing the letter and, on coming in, the thought came to start another sheet, as there will be room in the envelope within the postage. Just a little now. I will add more tomorrow after seeing Will. When I went out the sky was covered with an immense cloud, a huge blue-black wing across the world. It is strange weather. I visited the waterfalls. At the Driftwood Falls was somehow comforted and reassured to see a pair of wagtails come to roost for the night on a thin branch of a marera tree stretched across and very close to the falling water—wet and moving leaves in the spray. Then, going in to the Wagtail Falls, saw a long row, perhaps a dozen, of rock rabbits sitting still and quiet, gazing out at me from the great cleft under the overhanging cliff. Home again in the last light under that curiously menacing cloud. Did not see the ducks at the stepping-stones. Back in the cottage and having my bath, the night wind that comes these nights rose suddenly. I thought of Will down there, his old man's eagle mind, "strong, alone, grown up now," as Richard Church has it in a poem of old age and the "purification" of old age that I read a little while ago. After my bath went out, the sounding wind had cleared the black cloud from the sky: multitudinous stars, far-flashing lights across the cosmos; Simangwa, black, numinous, yet friendly; lightning flickering over the horizon; the thought again of Will, "strong, alone, grown up now"; the thought of my dear Mary, hidden over the curve of the world under the northern constellations—all this added up to something I wanted to try to say, yet cannot say. I can only add up the moments, detail them in failing words... as I wrote these words I heard a heavy roar of water coming down from the forest; the night is full of the sound, the river has come down in full spate again; that cloud poured down in rain on the high country. I wonder about the wagtails on their thin branch in the dark so close to the waterfall...

Morning

I visited the waterfalls again and found the wagtails happily busy over a great mass of driftwood brought down by the spate. A flock of red-winged starlings were dashing in and out of the spray. The clouds have already begun to gather over Simangwa for the afternoon thunderstorm. Springy has come to graze in the little field next to the cottage. She looks very well, though the men say she has no teeth now.

Bonny, Kamila, Jenny, Jack, and Jill are all living down here at the moment. They came down for their horse-sickness vaccinations. Bonny is very sleek. I came across an amusing passage in Herodotus yesterday that reminded me of Bonny's reaction to the sight of a donkey whenever we happen to meet them in our rides: "Most strange it is to relate, that what aided the Persians and thwarted the Scythians in their attacks on Darius's army was the braying of the asses and the appearance of the mules. For, as I have shown, Scythia bears no asses or mules, nor is there in the whole of Scythia any ass or mule, by reason of the great cold. Therefore the asses, when they brayed loudly, alarmed the Scythian horses, and often when they were in the act of charging the Persians, if the horses heard the asses bray, they would turn back in affright or stand astonished with ears erect, never having heard a like noise or seen a like creature."

Describing another battle, between Cyrus and Croesus, he tells of how the Lydian horses bolted from the field on catching sight of the Persian camels, for, as he says, horses that have never seen camels "fear them and can endure neither the sight nor the smell of them." These are the kind of asides I delight in in Herodotus, and he is full of them. There is no pretension to fine writing, nothing portentous; the style is that of easy courteous conversation, but how extraordinarily vivid at times. One sees the Phoenician seamen in the southern ocean with the sun to the north, one sees the Ionian ships off Sardinia sinking into the waves with all their women and children on board, one sees the great Scythian warriors crossing the frozen Don with their women and children, moving across into the great steppes of Sind in central Asia... It is hard to trace the source of the power of Herodotus' style: the intellectual vision is dry, unperturbed by the fanaticism, the horror, the cruelty that abounds; it is, it seems, simple reporting of things seen and heard without any reflective comment, and yet what a tremendous comment on men on the earth and their ways it all adds up to! His towering theme is just this "men on the earth and their ways," and this is why this supreme historian—Collingwood would claim that Herodotus was not a historian at all, only a "chronicler"—so fascinates me. I too am fascinated by his theme, "men on the earth and their ways," and it is for this reason that I am fascinated by that deepest and strangest revelation of "men on the earth and their ways"—their *religious traditions*—just as Herodotus was. No peculiarity or quirk in their traditions, however seemingly cruel or obscure or superstitious, does he fail to mark and record with a seeming detachment that yet reveals an intense intellectual curiosity. Yet to me he is the supreme historian just because he never imposes his own notions, his own historical "doctrine," his own interpretative schemes onto history, as does Gibbon, who was Collingwood's ideal of a great historian, or as, in a lesser degree than Gibbon, Thucydides does.

I find I have started speaking of Herodotus and suddenly have the sense that in doing this I may perhaps make clearer in some degree my attraction to "tradition": it is that to me tradition in the widest, deepest sense most poignantly reveals the strangeness and mystery of "men on the earth and their ways." I am not really attracted to traditional doctrines as philosophical abstractions, but as revelations of men. It is for this reason that I am as interested in Vedic or Buddhist or ancient Egyptian traditions as in Christian tradition. Of course Christian tradition has for me, inevitably, a more inward interest in that it is the tradition that has molded my own civilization. Yet I find that I practice my own kind of mental magic as effectively (in some senses, *more* effectively) from my readings in Homer or the Vedic Hymns as from the Bible. It has become clear to me, by slow degrees, that the epoch in world history that most absorbs me and from which, as from far headwaters, arise and flow the great streams of spiritual tradition and insight that have come to have most significance for me, is the age of Abraham in the Middle East—the age Homer writes of in the Mediterranean, the age the Vedic Hymns reveal in India: three great ages that are in a broad sense roughly contemporaneous; in fact, three faces of *one* world age. I find I have the same basic reaction *away* from the scholastic and academic philosophies that arose in medieval India out of the old Vedic tradition as I have from the scholastic philosophies that arose in medieval Europe out of the ancient biblical tradition; and as I have from the academic philosophies of Greece and modern Europe, which have their earliest roots, when all is said and done, in the age of Homer and the Greek *religious* tradition—which latter interests me at a much profounder level than the Greek scientific and philosophical tradition that rose out of it. My deepest inner affinities are with ages reflecting simpler, more elemental, life forms and reactions: ages and ways of life that, as it seems to me, reveal in their elemental simplicity the strangeness and mystery of "men on the earth and their ways" more poignantly and profoundly than do later ages that are at once more complex and (at least at the level where philosophical discussion and doctrine is born), more *protected*. It is, at least in some degree, not untrue that extremely subtle rationalized academic scholastic thinking arises among groups of men or classes of men who are leisured, privileged, protected—in that the flow of history, in all its chaotic and disturbing rush, has left them, if only briefly and relatively, at peace. This kind of thought, the thought that arises out of such life-situations, is legitimate and immensely valuable; indeed, all higher forms of civilization are born from it, but it is not what most attracts me. I think too it always carried with it certain limitations of insight, certain (in its position) enormous over-simplifications of basic human situations. It reveals enormous and ever-proliferating complexity and subtlety at relatively superficial levels, concealing an equally exasperating naiveté and over-simplification—even lack of awareness—at more elemental levels. Something of all this, some sense of all this, lies I think at the root of my reaction against granting too easily all the claims—often pretensions—of academic philosophy. I always have a very lively sense that there is more, often, in existence "than is dreamt of in their philosophies."

Yet this "more"—so unfathomable, so poignant, so infinitely significant—is just what cannot be verbalized, or rationalized, or reduced to logical categories; what cannot be caught up in an abstruse dialectic and elaborated in an academic doctrine. This "more" only mediates itself to us through utterly simple elemental human situations or through records of such situations in the hands of great poets or artists. Rembrandt's 'Death of Jacob,' for example. Or a record like this:

> And they journeyed from Bethel; and there was but a little way to come to Ephrath: and Rachel travailed, and she had hard labour.
>
> And it came to pass, when she was in hard labour, that the midwife said unto her, Fear not; thou shalt have this son also.
>
> And it came to pass, as her soul was in departing (for she died) that she called his name Ben-oni: but his father called him Benjamin.
>
> And Rachel died, and was buried in the way to Ephrath, which *is* Bethlehem.
>
> And Jacob set a pillar upon her grave: that *is* the pillar of Rachel's grave unto this day.
>
> And Israel journeyed, and spread his tent beyond the tower of Edar.

This passage, especially in the Hebrew with the meanings, so poignant, of all the names, is tradition mediating itself in all its unfathomable depths through how many generations hurt and sorrowful, yet longing in hope and trust.

Or to move to another ancient writing: Odysseus is moving over the battlefield "through the black night, amid the slaughter, amid the corpses, through the arms and the black blood...." He hears a heron hard by on the right, "...saw it not for the darkness of the night yet heard its cry... and Odysseus was glad... and made prayer to Athene...."

How many men in all generations have found themselves, by the dire necessities of life and living, on battlefields at night amid "the slaughter, the corpses, and black blood" and found themselves praying to Athene, the

Virgin. One remembers all the men out at night on all the terrible battlefields of our own time. "Odysseus" here is all men, any man, on a battlefield at night; and when we strip away all our protective illusions, are we not all "on a battlefield at night"? And in our extremity do we not all pray to Athene, to the divine power or powers invoked under whatever name by our fathers and fathers' fathers... unto all generations?

Something of all this, something of the prayer of the Vedic priest to the divine fire "at the heart of all the worlds" to carry the dead to the "highest heaven of our forefathers" to "rest in everlasting light"—something of all this shines for me through what I mean by tradition, something beside which academic philosophy seems to me uncomprehending, anaemic, cold, ineffective. I do not say it *is* these things but only that, for a man of my temperament and insights, it does seem so. It has, for me, little power, in the depths.

Yet this morning at the Driftwood Falls a thought came to me—a possible glimpse into understanding of what Whitehead perhaps is driving at in his doctrine of "objective immortality." I say "perhaps" because, at least in *Process and Reality*, he expresses himself in terms of such extreme abstraction that I find it difficult to get the drift of his ideas in, shall I say, living existential terms.

I had an experience I often have. For a brief moment, as I watched the wagtails on the floating driftwood, it seemed to me that I was not "I" watching the wagtails, but *you* were watching the wagtails through my eyes. Now this experience often comes to me as my eyes turn from the wagtails to see the patches of wet moss growing on the black wet rock face under the falling water. For a moment it was not *me* watching that moss, but *J.C.P.* Yet J.C.P. is, as we say, dead. But his vision relives itself in some sense momentarily through my eyes—one who knew him and loved him. What I am trying to express is more than a passing affectionate fancy, as when we say "how John, or Will, or Mary would love to see this." "That is not what I mean at all," as Eliot says. No, it is that one is momentarily emptied of oneself and as it were possessed by the spirit of an absent or dead friend. Now could it be something like this that Whitehead is hinting at in his doctrine (which he stresses so repeatedly) of "objective immortality"? One thinks of course of the kind of immortality that, say, the spirit of Jesus has had through so many generations of Christians; or the kind of immortality of Father Abraham among Jews— Jews dying in endless tortures and persecutions and pogroms and concentration camps. The kind of immortality of many great sages in their devotees. The devotees of Ramana Maharshi are convinced that the spirit of Ramana in some sense passed into their spirits at the moment of his death, so that they were nearer to him than ever. One thinks of the immortality of all men after death in the hearts of those who loved them. We all know and share these feelings, yet what do they signify? Affectionate remembrance only, as many would say? Or do they signify an actual living indwelling objective immortality of all who have loved and been loved in the hearts of all who have loved them? Speaking in Christian terms, we have in this one side of the Kingdom of Heaven—of God—realizing itself eternally out of the sorrows and conflicts of time and our life in this world. One side only, but a side that necessarily implies the existence of the other side, though I do not know that in this Whitehead would agree. The other side is the continuing "subjective immortality" of that which realizes itself as "objective immortality" in the hearts of others. But to move to the source of this present thought: is my thinking about this doctrine of Whitehead's and my trying to understand it in the only terms that interest me—in terms of ultimate religious insights—is my thinking these thoughts and trying to capture them in a letter to you, and then your in turn thinking them (and of course also all those who read and try to understand Whitehead sympathetically), is all this, at one level, passing process in reality rooted in the living "objective immortality" of Whitehead's spirit? If so, this in its turn necessitates its corresponding "subjective immortality," that is, Whitehead in his own essential unique individuality as rooted in his own eternal essence (and not only as reflected in others as an "objective immortality")? I am not sure about this. I find Whitehead obscure and difficult to read, but he seems at times in other passages to see what he calls "objective immortality" as the only true immortality? But I may be wrong here.

Yet to move on to what all this has been leading up to. Granted something like this as Whitehead's doctrine, then I would define what I mean when I speak of tradition as the crystallized *reflection in time of objective immortality*. Here of course the term "objective immortality" would be taken as meaning objective immortality *in its totality for all beings* that have existed and will exist, *and loved and will love*, in time. The condition as it were under which a "potential" objective immortality can actualize itself in eternity is *love*, love here meaning the seeing of eternal value in another. If this is so, it would mean that the incapacity to love would signify the incapacity to realize "objective immortality," amounting to the possibility of an eternal state of deprivation, of being "lost"—a possibility ever-present to the deepest Christian vision. But that leads me too far away from my present theme. I would like Whitehead's comments on all this, but alas! "objective immortality," whatever else it may mean, seems to exclude that particular possibility. This range of intuitions seems to me summed up into marvelously brief and memorable expression by Blake in his three great utterances: "The Ruins of Time build Mansions in Eternity"; "Eternity is in love with the Productions of Time"; "Time is the Mercy of Eternity."

But to return to what I have tried to express throughout this letter. I see the moss with J.C.P.'s eyes when I see the wagtail with Mary's eyes; this is something received by me in love from outside myself, yet out of my past! It redeems the pain of separation of time's all-severing wave by transcending time into a timeless repetition made possible in love. But in the simplest terms, something precious, "immortal," is given to me that transcends the onflow of time. This is *tradition*. It redeems the time and fulfils the time. Again, when I see, or try to see, a particular human situation in simplicity and humility of heart—through the eyes of Jesus, or Buddha, or Abraham, or any of my forefathers, as his vision is mediated to me through my tradition—when I "see," or try to "see" in this way, I accept tradition, and transcend my isolation and solitary weakness in the present. Tradition is in its essence the irruption of eternity into time. It is actualized through what I take Whitehead to mean by "objective immortality." The obscurities and cruelties that cling to traditional forms in history are also truthful reflections of our human condition unredeemed by the grace of tradition. In the profoundest sense tradition, insofar as it reflects objective immortality into time, reflects the Kingdom of God into time. It is only possible through God's Grace—*is* God's Grace redeeming the time.

But I *must* stop.

With all my love,
Gerard

[On envelope] Just in from seeing Will. Had a happy evening with him looking at old books and drawings. Sorry I bent the sheets of the letter into different shapes trying to get it into a smaller envelope. Will showed me an old Greek school exercise book of Littleton's with some translations from Thucydides—1892! At Sherborne!

Spring Cottage
10 September 1971

My darling Mary,

I have just come in under the zodiacal light from being with Will. He is delighted to have the head of Homer, and so am I—"the uttering head, the mouth that groweth not old of the whole world!"

Three splendid letters from you, and this noble head! I have had my supper and my bath and then it came to me to send you a word—instead of going straight to bed.

I had a happy surprise this morning in Nanyuki, just after posting off an airmail letter to you. I was having coffee and a cheese roll in the Marina when a voice greeted me, and there was Gilfrid's Patricia, with Gilfrid and the two little girls in the Land Rover outside. I went out to speak to them—the children immediately asked for you! They both look very well, Marian very like Gilfrid now. They had spent a night with Will and been down his new road past Tony's salt-lick. Will this evening said he is worried that Gilfrid does not have regular meals.

I am pleased to read these lines you send me on Plotinus by Yeats. I read somewhere, in one of Yeats' letters I think, that at one time he passed through a phase of strong reaction against Plotinus as in some degree undervaluing *this* world. I think I told you of how I found two volumes of the Loeb *Enneads* in the library at Nairobi with the dates for lending stamped in them, showing they were being taken out regularly! I was pleased too to find them standing on the bookshelf beside Radhakrishnan's edition of the *Brahma Sutras*, also regularly borrowed. This made me think the borrowers were perhaps mostly Asians.

As I left the library and was coming down the steps between the huge stone lions I saw two small boys, one black and one brown, each snugly ensconced between the lion's paws on either side of me, both utterly absorbed in a book! There was a timeless quality about the two little figures oblivious of all—the crowds, the traffic, the bland afternoon sunlight—intent still faces over their books, and the massive stone visages above them. I had felt rather emptied and defeated going into the library. But coming out, having held in my hands copies of the *Enneads* and the *Brahma Sutras* and then seeing the reading children, came a sense of reassurance and a knowing that the great creative traditions are always, along innumerable channels—often secret and devious—renewing their life-giving flow among men.

I was thinking too of Cornford's book, which you are reading—*From Religion to Philosophy*—and how difficult and teasing these great basic works are! So encrusted with all the ambiguity that bedevils our dialectic on these subjects. I wondered how Cornford approached these matters, thinking of Kirk's work on Heraclitus, and *his* approach. In Kirk's hands how this very title would, as it would in the hands of most of our philosophers I fancy, already assume, or at least hint at, the assumption of a whole array of highly questionable presuppositions! Philosophy as the love of wisdom, yes. But there is a scientific wisdom, a religious wisdom, an aesthetic wisdom, a humanistic wisdom, and so on—all acceptable facets of a supreme Wisdom. There is philosophy rising from intense religious vision, from intense aesthetic vision, from widely-ranging scientific vision. But *From Religion to Philosophy* seems to imply a "progress" from...? to ...? Usually, on these terms, religion is understood as early science or magic that has not come to an understanding of itself. But religion is not in its essential nature primitive science or magic, or speculation. In the complex vision of living men involved and struggling in history it is indeed always found mixed up, entangled, in these other elements; but in its eternal, unwavering essence, in which is no shadow of turning, it is none of these things. In its first stirring it springs from the sense of the indwelling presence of the Holy. In its consummation it is the Vision of the Holy. The Holy, how express this mystery in terms other than itself? How express the sense of Beauty to one devoid of all response to it? How speak to the unmathematical of the truths and harmonies of higher mathematics so beloved by Bertrand Russell? These intuitions are rooted in ultimate primordial visions rising out of τὰ βάθη τοῦ θεοῦ.

Each such vision issues out of its own primordial integrity and may find fruition in its legitimate philosophical vision. The ultimate religious vision is the Vision of the Holy. From this, and only from this, issues religious philosophy: the love of religious wisdom, uttered by men like Plotinus, Boehme, Ramanuja. Yet one comes across so many works by men of a predominantly scientific or aesthetic cast of mind who can only understand religion as a primitive phase of their own basic vision, a basic vision that is, as often as not, deficient in any living sense of the Holy—a deficiency that deprives these men of any genuine understanding of religious vision. How to mediate a sense of the Holy to one deficient in it I do not know. Any more than how a musician can mediate his sense of the glory of great music to one who is radically unmusical.

The Bible is the supreme religious Scripture in the West because it is saturated with a sense of the Holy. This sense of a *tremendum mysterium*—

unutterably sacred, utterly unapproachable on any but its own terms—has given this book its immeasurable power over the hearts and minds of many generations of men—this sense of the Holy hidden in and springing out of the uttermost depths of suffering in existence. What does it reveal of the depths of spirit in Western man, that he has so obstinately, so irrationally, so desperately clung to the Gospels for close on two thousand years?—in spite of, as J.C.P. would say, all the "experts," of all persuasions, who would attempt to wean him from it, or explain it all away. How explain it away? Explain the sun away, the splendid silent sun with his many beams full dazzling?! But in spite of all the explanations the sun shines on.

Religion, however debased, confused, or superstitious, springs from man's sense of the Holy. If we pass from religion to something else devoid of the sense of the Holy we pass to something radically different. Religion is not an *ancilla* of any other perspective. It is itself inalienably rooted in its enduring sense of the Holy. It can clarify, purify, deepen itself... but it cannot, without ceasing to be itself, resolve itself into a preliminary process "progressing" to visions rising from other world views, even though those other world views be ultimately supplementary to its own vision.

Religion intuits the Holy as inescapably involved in the mystery of death. When Plato speaks of philosophy as the study of dying he is speaking as a truly religious philosopher. All religious rites are death rites. Rites that help the individual man build his ship of death—the ship that will carry him to "the other shore." From the point of view of religion, the spiritually creative movement in the life-movement is the death-movement. It echoes Heraclitus' words, "the name of the bow is life but its work is death!" Religious doctrines and rites are only interested in birth and life insofar as they lead on to death. An Indian tradition offers, as so often in these matters, an expression that goes to the root of the matter: the religious life, the life of spirit, is, they say, *brahmanah parimarah*, "dying round the Holy Power." The supreme sage lives and dies as a "dying round the Holy Power." His living is a continuous dying. The quality of living determines the quality of dying; and dying is a return into the Holy Power and the possibilities of spiritual destiny hidden in that Power. Religion attempts to symbolize this truth in innumerable ways, striving to initiate the creative death-movement in all men, whatever their circumstances or capacities. Religion seeks to realize in all its fullness and mystery the meaning of death. It is therefore always eschatological and apocalyptic in its ultimate symbolism. The theological trends in modernistic Christianity, or in any other authentic religious tradition, that seek to ignore or discredit or move away from apocalyptic symbolism are movements away from genuine religious insight. Apocalypse symbolizes the utterly hidden unfathomable possibilities latent in the divine creativity, the creativity that brings all being through death to restoration, to ἀποκατάστασις. The ends—individual men's ends, ends of cultures, civilizations, planets, worlds, universes—are hidden, but hidden subject to divine apocalypse, to the final unveiling of meanings and destinies. Religion seeks to elicit creative response in the depths of spirit to ultimate ends, the ends hidden in the creatively responding depths of the divine—the Holy Power. All religion, or rather all *in* religion, is secondary and derivative that does not serve and flow from this ultimate concern. Yet men like Kirk understand, or seek to understand, religion as primitive science, as simple-minded attempts to understand the processes of nature. But the religious man knows very well he can never "understand." He sees clearly too that the claim of science to understanding amounts to no more than ever more detailed and elaborate descriptions of process. This kind of mental activity is so basic to the scientific consciousness that it finds it very difficult to conceive that the fundamental drives in religion are not concerned with this kind of research or interest—or only in a very secondary sense. Philosophy can clarify religious vision but cannot take its place. There is a movement from primitive religion to fully developed religion clarified by philosophy, but religion sees philosophy, at least the rationalized thought processes given the name of philosophy in the West, as the *ancilla*. Some such thoughts as these Cornford's title brings to me; they are perhaps, from his point of view, not relevant, so I must stop. It is late now, very still and quiet; "what saith deep midnight?"

Today Collingwood's autobiography arrived back with the little note enclosed. I'll add a few words in the morning. I've just looked out—Scorpio sinking over Simangwa. Now to bed!

Morning

Back from a visit to old Kibrono, whom I found bathing in the river at the Fig Tree Drift. I saw a herd of oryx near Michael's Mount and two groups of gerenuk. I like to think of you watching the heron and to know I have one of his feathers in my *Iliad*. I will watch both Antares and Mercury.

Spring Cottage
23 September 1971

My darling Mary,

Three very welcome letters from you yesterday and the card of Rousseau's Waterfall. I took the card down to Will last night and he was very interested in it. I have an idea Rousseau did spend some years overseas with the French Colonial Service as a Custom's Officer. I took the review of the book on Karen Blixen down to Will as well. He has been reading one of her books lately and has spoken about her several times. I saw John Chart, who looks well and is cheerful but has his jaw bandaged and has gone down to Nairobi today to go into hospital for another operation.

Yes! I do understand Lucy's reluctance to leave home and travel so far. She will be snug and quiet in her cottage and safe and sound to greet you again in the Spring. You must pretend she is a stay-at-home robin while you are a willow-wren flying south to Africa for the winter.

Thank you so much for sending on to me this moving fragment found among Valentine's papers. I like to think it may perhaps be an echo of a few lines I sent her on sudden impulse not long before she died, which I called 'The Growing of the Lily'. I had in mind Boehme's Three-headed Lily. Perhaps too Valentine heard at the last the "heavenly music" sounding ever more clearly that Boehme heard as he lay dying, and that he called his son to listen to and share with him. Prayer too resolves itself into a supreme music in ultimate vision. I like the words on prayer you sent me. They bring to my mind the definition of prayer I learnt from my catechism as a child: "Prayer is the lifting up of the heart and mind to God."

Yes! It is true that the word "religion" has unhappy associations, and for this religious people are responsible. Yet I fancy the basic objection to it among anti-traditional minds is close to the true mark—they object to being "bound," whether "back" or "forward" or in any direction. The traditionalist finds true freedom, a creative freedom, in recognizing and accepting that he is "bound back" to God, and through God to all others. In doing this he shares in the creative power that brings him into existence. The negative freedom of an attempted rejection of this bond can only dissipate itself in a self-destructive nihilism, as among our contemporary atheistic existentialists, such as

Sartre and Genet. Yet in spite of all denials man is in very truth "bound back" to the creative Holy Power that brings all the worlds into being, and can only realize his spiritual destiny in acceptance of this fact.

You ask about the corresponding Sanskrit word. All that our Western traditions cover by the word "religion" is covered by two words in Sanskrit, two words reflecting the double aspect of the binding. The binding back to the divine Source is *yoga*—literally "yoking," from the same Indo-European root. This corresponds to all we aim at in our mystical doctrines. The binding to each other of all members of a community is *dharma*, from a root meaning "to grip, to hold"; and this covers all the social and moral duties that hold a society together and save it from disintegration. This corresponds to our institutional religion in its care for society as a whole. The *dharma* seeks to preserve social forms and strivings that make *yoga* possible for those potentially capable of it. What is striven for is that as many members of the community as possible should share, each in his degree, in the vision of the Holy. The word most closely corresponding to our "philosopher" is *parama-artha-vid*: *parama*—"beyond, transcendent, supreme"; *artha*—"object, aim"; *vid*—"seeing, θεωρία." So, *paramarthavid*—"a seer of the transcendent," or "one who aims at the Supreme." Indian tradition would have no hesitation in accepting, say, Plato or Plotinus as *paramarthavid*, but would have many reservations about bestowing such a title on our empirical philosophers and logical positivists. I think though that Indian (in fact Eastern in general) tradition would say that all our philosophical tradition tends to over-emphasize the importance of διάνοιᾶ at the expense of contemplative techniques aimed at the deepening and widening of the basic consciousness, which they seek to bring into a state of clarified stillness; whereas διάνοιᾶ, discursive reasoning, implies and encourages the continuance of a state of mental activity. I suppose all of us in the West find this Eastern insistence on stilling the mind the most difficult and demanding side of their traditional approach to supreme Wisdom. We pay our respects to the demand in words, but to realize any enduring state of mental stillness seems beyond our powers. I think this difficulty arises from the radically objectified orientation of our Western consciousness, which we cannot overcome, and probably should not even try to overcome: we would be being false to our own traditions to do so. I do not myself now believe that Eastern modes of metaphysical realization offer accessible paths to Western men; at best they do perhaps to only a few very exceptional men. But they provide a necessary complementary support in the total balance of the human world, which we ignore or attempt to destroy only at our peril.

I was just interrupted, happily, by a visit from Rose on her way down to see Will. She was delighted to see our three baby goslings on the lawn with their attendant train of fiercely hissing protective big geese!

Yes, I went this morning to one of the school committee meetings. I find all the talk rather exhausting, though it is little enough to do to show some interest in their problems. Tomorrow we have the company meeting, but may not achieve much, as Christopher has so far not replied to our letters and we do not know whether he will be there. I hear he still rents the house on the Beale, but very rarely comes there.

No need to bring the Yeats poems. I'll look forward to reading them next spring when I am back in Mappowder.

With love always,
Gerard

Spring Cottage
28 September 1971

My darling Mary,

Your good letter with Yeats' poem is with me. Yes, I know the poem. The whole subject brings up so much that I feel I can't comment just now. Religion, I'd say, senses a mystery in death for man, a mystery that is not exhausted or penetrated by understanding man in a purely biological sense. Yeats' poem cuts deep, as all his finer poems do, and is of a very deceptively ambiguous simplicity. No, I don't immediately get the drift of the second part of the poem, which I have not seen before; but the last two lines must echo for you your time on Chesil Beach. Yes, I know those tamarisks very well; I used to walk by them when I lived at Greenlease in Punknowle before the war (1937).

Yes, I too like those early essays of John's, and also *Suspended Judgements*. I think our new friend Cathy was a trifle unlucky that the first book of J.C.P's she came by was *The Brazen Head*—not, I think, one altogether calculated to rouse great interest in a reader unacquainted with the rest of his writings. But I may be wrong—it certainly made a dent on Christopher Gibson.

I often see in my mind's eye that wide sea-horizon from Chesil Beach, and hear in my mind's ear "the rattle of pebbles on the shores under the receding wave" as we cast J.C.P.'s ashes along the edge of the gray sea that day. And I have too our special Chesil Beach pebble here beside me.

A day or two ago I was thinking of Yeats imaging himself to himself as a honey-buzzard seeking his honey—"Honey of Thunder, Thunder of Honey"—in the ever-recurring, yet ever-changing world cycles: "perne in a gyre"; "many times he died, many times he rose again." The dying of the honey-buzzard, a circling back to his eyrie out of the fathomless and infinite sky; a "circling back," yet imaged elsewhere as "the sudden thunder of the mounting swan." How saturated with Upanishadic vision in all this Yeats is! Or, if you like, how Pythagorean, how Empedoclean—for I find it difficult to see the preoccupation with the mystery of death as "un-Greek." All that we know of Greek esoteric religion, of the Eleusinian Mysteries (which were Death Mysteries), of the tremendous imagistic hints irrupting into the plays of Aeschylus, of Odysseus' voyage in his Black Ship to Hades, of the funeral rites of Hector that close the *Iliad* (Aeschylus in trouble for revealing the mysteries—image to the inner eye of our imagination—in that haunting funeral song over the slain brothers Eteocles and Polynices in *Seven against Thebes*), of the Black Ship swiftly, swiftly speeding its way to "the other shore"—all this belies the picture we have so often brought before us of the "sunny, naturalistic" vision of the Greeks. The Greeks were far too profound not to be preoccupied with the central mysteries of our existence. But to get back to Yeats and his honey-buzzard: such a widely-circling bird would be a fitter life-companion for you, for my dear Mary—who might be imaged as one of those marvelously swift yet intensely hovering nectar-sipping Honey Birds—than a sore-headed irascible Honey Badger-Bear, that has to mooch and scramble through thickets, and dig his way to his honey—staying his hunger pangs meanwhile on slugs and worms and beetles, such lowly creatures; yet too there is the symbiotic relationship between the Honey-Badger and the Honey-Guide to be remembered, which is not without meaning; and all—Buzzards, darting Honey Guides, and Birds, Badgers, and Bears sore-headed—all seek the Honey, "Honey of Thunder, Thunder of Honey!"

I was with Will yesterday evening. A long silence fell as Will held his toast to the fire—then:

"Did you know your grandfather?"
"Yes, both of them took me for walks."

Another long silence—then:

"Did he have a beard?"
"No."

Another long silence.

He was very pleased with the gloves you sent him, trying them on and examining them minutely. I came back later than usual, with Jupiter and Scorpio slipping down over Simangwa into the Zodiacal Light, and Cassiopeia rising in the north-east. I watched for the occultation of Antares by the moon a few evenings ago, but as far as I could tell the moon didn't pass very near Antares at any time. One evening it was very close to Jupiter.

I often see baby rock rabbits sitting on their mothers' backs in the rock cleft beside the Wagtail Falls. They remain perfectly still, peeping out between their mothers'—or I dare say fathers'—ears. Tradition again?

With lots of love to you
and Lucy,
Gerard

Morning

A scarlet-chested sunbird just arrived at the scarlet verbena outside the window.

That great procession of all the Athenian citizens to participate in the Mysteries of Eleusis shortly before the Sicilian Expedition comes to my mind. Preoccupation with "death as mystery"—un-Greek?

Yeats too is voyaging in his Ship of Death to a Mystery in what is perhaps his greatest poem—'Sailing to Byzantium'.

Spring Cottage
20 August 1972

My darling Mary,

I have just come back from supper with Will. The half moon is sending down quite a bright light on the sunflowers and moonflowers and cosmos round the cottage. The thought came to me to pick a few of these moonlit petals and send them to you. Will gave me two pullovers to darn. I said I didn't have a darning needle, so he produced a fine big wool pack needle. I'll try my hand at it tomorrow afternoon when I get back from Nanyuki. He is busy doing paintings. Did I tell you he trapped the leopard that used to grunt round the cottage, near Lizard Hill?

I think your 'Transfiguration' is very fine. If it is ever printed it should be with the excellent quotations from Newton, Plotinus, and Whitehead as part of the poem. What makes this poem so moving and powerful is that it expresses a whole theology of divine transfiguration; the underlying thought gives it a validity and strength often lacking in poetry on religious themes. The poem has been running through my head most of today. You are gradually writing a number of poems flowing from religious insights of great beauty: and I feel it a wonderful thing to be able to share them with you. How I wish they could be more widely read and shared!

It has been a quiet gray day; the sky over Simangwa grew quite dark and boding during the afternoon. I had a good walk after tea along the river and saw the black duck on the Stepping-Stones Drift as I came back to go down to Will.

With my love always,
darling Mary,
Gerard

Spring Cottage
16 March 1973

My darling Mary,

Here are a few letters from you.

I will jot down on this sheet when the mood takes me and send it off to you from Nanyuki next Monday.

Yesterday evening I went for a long walk across to the hills and climbed a high rock and rested, looking out over the great landscape. How many rocks and trees and hills and valleys my eye touched on are haunted for me by memories of you, things said, things done, walks, rides, picnics, restings... during our long years together out here! Then, as all the ways grew dark, I came back to the Stepping-Stones Drift just in time for the down-gliding splash of the black duck on the pool. This morning I've replied to Sally's letter, which I am putting in with this. She has certainly replied in some detail to my question on bird-migrations in that part of the world!

As I was lying still and quiet in bed last night waiting for sweet sleep to fall on my eyelids, I found myself reciting to myself 'The Phoenix and the Turtle' as a special poem for you and me, and it seemed to me that this mysterious and wonderful poem does in some way utter a word not without meaning for us. It seemed too that the words were limned in a darkness long after we were both dead—both "long long ago dust"!

I hardly know how to reply to Christopher Grey. I would like to respond, but am not very keen on India in the hot season. I'm never very good at enduring great heat. If I do go it should be in the cooler time. But I do feel always a curious sense of a strange link and even some curious sense of responsibility for Christopher. Well! I must think. But I could of course go to see him at Delhi I suppose.

17th

I had a wonderful walk to the great split rocks above the bay by the Pink Place. It is the first time I have been right up to them, a very exciting place with a fine evergreen tree standing over the rocks and throwing them into shadow. There were so many rock rabbits there that were extraordinarily tame. They paid very little attention to me or the dogs. Sitting under the tree

I could see through a narrow gap right up to Loru Moru and Bugi-Ngai. I had the feeling it was a lonely place not often visited by men; no klipspringers, which I thought I might see there.

After my bath I went out on to the lawn in bright moonlight. Two rabbit hares were tumbling and playing close to Slate, who was quite unconcerned; they too were unworried by me and moved only a little way off.

The hadadas are going over with a great commotion.

19th

Down to Will last evening and got badly stuck in the mud near the red gate on the way back. A sudden heavy rainstorm fell while I was with Will. He gave me one of his old "baranas" to darn. I must try to find darning needles in Nanyuki this morning. Will seems rather more tired in the evenings these days, I fancy. But he enjoyed his visit to the Samburu Park.

Now to getting the car out of the mud!

Lots of love always,
Gerard

Spring Cottage
25 March 1973

My darling Mary,

I enclose a copy of a letter I've just written to Winona. She gave me some notes from a thesis done at the Jung Institute on the *Odyssey*, which I only looked into this morning. They started this ferment in my head, as I felt I was saying things in some sense important to myself as well as to Winona. I thought I'd keep a copy. I have always wondered why the Cyclops episode moved me so deeply, and think I may have caught at something in these comments. The notes Winona left me stress mainly Cyclops as a threat, to law, civilization, etc., and Odysseus as the Hero who meets this threat; but I have always felt this oversimplifies.

Will and I had a good day together on Friday—a breakfast picnic at one of his dams watching birds (spoonbills, egrets, geese, wood ibis, etc.) while he did a quick water-color of the mountain. When we got back just before lunch Will was told that a lion had killed near the bottom of the Timber Track, so the rest of the day was spent preparing a guntrap—quite a job, as neither of us had made one for so many years, and it was necessary to find or make all the paraphernalia. Then we sat up over the trap to guard the gun. A lion came about eight—not quite dead, so we shot it, pulled it from the trap, and set the trap again for the lioness. But she didn't come and we gave up about midnight. Will was delighted, as he thinks Blackwell isn't keen enough on hunting or sitting up for them. The trap idea was partly done, I think, to goad Blackwell into greater efforts—unfairly of course because I feel sure he (Blackwell) does his very best, but is run off his feet trying to keep up with everything.

I saw Gilfrid in Nanyuki last Monday. He looked to me not well and in pain, though he said he was fine except that it is too painful for him to sit in his airplane. How one longs for him to be more careful with himself.

Your good card of Macillacuddy's Reeks for my birthday has come. It does catch the feeling of that part of Ireland very well I think!

I have just finished Byron's letters, feeling very friendly to Byron as a result—a brave man, absolutely honest about himself. I understand now something of Goethe's admiration.

With much love always,
Gerard

[To Winona, same date]

Dear Winona,

I've carbon-copied this letter to Mary as she too is excited by Homer.

Winona, shall we say that for some reason, like Pallas Athene, I have been thinking of other things?—I did not look at your notes from the thesis on the *Odyssey* until this morning. Well, these notes did start off a whirlwind of fancies and actions in my skull (the skull, as old J.C.P. would say, of a baby giant); so much so, that I thought to try to jot some of them down and send them off to you, because when you come up again I would so much like to read the Cyclops episode from the *Odyssey* (the episode these notes are for the most part concerned with) to you. And this letter will give you some glimpses into my Cyclopean Vision. Not for nothing was Homer the supreme poet of the subtlest and freest minds and people ever to appear on this wild planet of ours. Not for nothing was Homer the "Bible" of the Greeks. Not for nothing have the great poets of our Western world, from the Greek Tragedians down to our own time, been so busy quarrying the inexhaustible mines of Homer!

But first of all you must remember how Hiawatha avenged his mother, Wenonah, against his father, the West Wind—a Wind of Storm and Danger in Homer! For the Cyclopean Vision is not for children, not even for grown-up children, although of course a grown up child *can* go on living in the pretense that the Cyclopean Vision does not exist, does not exist at least for good sensible people such as most of us no doubt are! As these notes remark, the Cyclops is "dangerous for human beings." He is wild and cruel and unjust and lives alone among the windy mountains, his heart set on lawlessness; so we meet him, this one-eyed monster. Well, so be it; yet there are those among us who "identify," as they say, with this lonely monster in his solitary cave. Let us even say we all, every manjack of us, identify with him when all the masks are off! He is the man in all of us, the uncouth Giant companion of the Great Mother, with his solitary heart ever set, ever unchangingly set, on "having his own way," on looking out on the world through the one-eye in the middle of his forehead to his own one-eyed freedom. He is the most moving and gigantic and disturbing symbol in the whole of the *Odyssey*. He is any man, every man in his utter aboriginal essence. Aye, and of course the two-eyed crafty Odysseus, he who knows so well all the ways of men, of all us two-eyed twice-born time-servers, we who *always keep tight-shut our Cyclopean Eye*—Odysseus, I say, in his obsessive concern to return to the ways of the rest of us and the cities of men, comes up against this huge and lonely savage that would devour him and all his companions, and all their eyes; aye, this Odysseus, this crafty one, if he is not to be swallowed up, if he is ever to return to "the ways of men," can only escape by *blinding the Giant of his Eye*. And what a Blinding is there! The Blinding out of himself of *his own aboriginal freedom*! This is the price he pays for his return to Ithaca. And even with that, before he achieves this blinding he loses half his companions, the comrades he so recklessly led into the monster's cave to confront him. Odysseus in his childish cunning thought to receive from the Giant "gifts of hospitality," but finds that he brings instead human sacrifices, and *still* has to go on to that dread act of blinding in order to escape. Better had he steered clear of that island, better never to have sought out that one-eyed one in his cave!, better never to have brought upon himself the wrath of the Earth-Holder, the Earth-Shaker, the Father, the Tempestuous Begetter of that Giant.

And Polyphemus, this huge aboriginal being living alone with his flocks and herds and cheeses and milk-pails in his cave, a law unto himself—this free, unimplicated being, is *sought out* by Odysseus, the eternal meddler, the curious crafty virtuous one who fears the Gods in his thoughts; is sought out and blinded of *his One-Eye*, so that the trickster, the clever one may return in safety to his own little ways! The ways of No-man!

Odysseus the much-enduring, he who suffers as a man, is forced to become a "no-man" if he is to blind the Giant of his Eye. And what more ghastly, more dreadful symbol of man, man mutilated of his utter essence in freedom, than Polyphemus standing at the edge of the unresting sea, stretching forth his hands to the starry heavens, praying to Poseidon his Father for vengeance on Odysseus the No-man, his One-Eye now but a blinded empty bloody socket: "Hear me, Poseidon, Earth-Enfolder, thou dark-haired god, if indeed I am thy son and thou declarest thyself my father...."

So he spoke in prayer and the dark-haired god heard him.

And the Cyclops lifted on high again a far greater stone, and swung and hurled it... putting into the throw measureless strength....

Well! What to make of all this? A scene, it always seems to me, central in world literature in its poignant and terrible significance, for those who can understand; an elemental aboriginal significance for any who can open even for a flicker of flickering second their own inner Cyclopean Eye to glance upon it—if we have not already become No-men, and blinded ourselves of our own One-Eyed Freedom. In us all is Odysseus the man of many woes, in us all is No-man, the crafty dissembler, in us all is Polyphemus, this huge suffering blinded Giant standing at the edge of the unresting sea, praying to his father.

And what of Odysseus, shrivelled to No-man, as he taunts Polyphemus in answer to the Giant's prayer to Poseidon to heal his Eye?: "Would that I were able to rob thee of soul and life, and send thee down to Hades... as surely as not even the Earth-Shaker shall heal thine eye!"

So mocks Odysseus from his shrivelled no-man heart. All this a vision from (tradition has it) a blind wanderer! What depths below depths of dark ambiguous vision stir in our hearts as we contemplate this tremendous symbol come down to us from the ancient world. To utter any word of "interpretation" on it is to castrate it of its terrible power. But we may be sure of this, it is a grim warning sign on the road to freedom. Once in the cave, we pay the price, we blind the Giant of his Eye or are swallowed up by him. Swallowed up by him? Perhaps to be vomited out again like Zeus from the Belly of Cronos? For after all Zeus *was* the Stone! Perhaps to become flesh of his flesh, to look out through the Eye of the Cyclops, through the Eye of his primordial freedom? But that is to be alone, alone looking through One-Eye out on the world of multiple, related beings who consent to live not a law unto themselves... ready to devour these beings at one's pleasure, or certainly at necessity, when the "hateful belly" bids. So then this aboriginal freedom is solitary, unimplicated, relationless... loveless, for love always abides in relation to another; love rejects, cannot but reject, unconditioned freedom—it abides rather in a freedom conditioned by its own necessities... oh, how go on from here! *Can* the Cyclops enter freely into the conditioning of his own freedom? To mutilate him of his Eye is to rob him of his freedom and the very possibility of free relation—which is love. And he the Giant Solitary has—even he—been moved to love his favorite ram. Who can remain unmoved by his words to his ram, as the great creature carries out Odysseus from his cave tucked up and hidden under his belly? Who dares to answer such questions? Odysseus had been wiser, we were all wiser perhaps, to heed the voices of others, and dodge the visit to the cave of the Cyclops—after all, it *may* be we can reach our dear native land without taking on this terrible adventure and being forced to this terrible decision. Whom shall we invoke as we come to the way branching off from our familiar road to this cave? Hecate?

And then again that eye—that One-Eye in the middle of the forehead—to what abysses of thought it leads us. We think of the single eye sometimes appearing in Buddhist images of *Prajnaparamita*—the Perfection of Wisdom, Supreme Gnosis—this single eye in the forehead of the Image symbolizing Sivaistic creatively-destructive intuition or transcendent Intellect, the Hagia Sophia of ultimate Christian Vision. So this Giant is possibly—*it may be, certainly*—possessed of a Sacred Wisdom in his aboriginal freedom as he gazes out through his One-Eye? A wisdom threatening devouring destruction to little No-men? Who can only save themselves, or lose themselves, by putting out that One-Eye? That one eye in the middle of their own foreheads that they keep so tightly shut? Does this eye in very truth gaze out of an unrelated loneliness, empty of all love, or does it relate rather to a transcendent relation in love, a love that glares destruction on all but the transcendent? Can little No-men know the answers to these questions? Perhaps only through surrendering to destruction—to being swallowed up?

Perhaps in timeless truth that Eye shines out as a Morning Star: "Father, Oh, Father, what do we here in this land of unbelief and fear? The Land of Dreams were better far, above the Light of the Morning Star?" So at least thought William Blake. A Morning Star of Joy shines from the foreheads of all men who wake up into and cling to their utter freedom in God.

So the Cyclops in his Cave gives us furiously to think, or not think! He is indeed dangerous to men. Dangerous whether with his Eye blinded or not, it seems.

Something of all this came tumbling through my head as I looked through these notes from that thesis, and the impulse to scribble these pages to you with the hope that we can, it may be, dive a little under these waves when you come up next week. I sat up with Will last night and with him trapped a lion to its end; to me there has always been something Cyclopean about Will.

Gerard

*Spring Cottage
12 May 1973*

My darling Mary,

This morning I should have been traveling down from Waterloo to Dorchester! I have started going for short walks now along the river morning and evening. The leg is almost back to normal though there remains a slight swelling and hardness, but no pain! I still have a week's supply of the drug, the anti-coagulant.

Last evening I was out when Will came. He left an album of colored photographs of most of his bigger paintings, done by Tony. Tony seems more successful than Francis in bringing out the colors. I am to bring this album to Mappowder with me for Lucy to look at. Rose also called in yesterday with Charles—both well and happy.

Winona writes that she is tackling a thesis on *Faust*—that is, writing one herself. An ambitious project. With both you and Winona writing to me of Goethe I feel I must pay more attention to him myself some time. I have been re-reading Boehme's *Signatura Rerum*, and find a number of references to "the Mothers" that I had forgotten. Was this perhaps Goethe's source for these mysterious deities? Boehme in places seems to personify *Ungrund* as the *Mother of All Beginnings*, but has other references to the three Mothers who seem to be reflections, or rather sourceless sources in *Ungrund*, of the Three Persons of the Trinity! Certainly the Mother of all Beginnings, the pure unconditioned creative potentiality verging to the nothingness of utter non-being, is, in Boehme, the sourceless source of the Trinity—the Mother of God, the Eternal Feminine, which he more often calls *Ungrund*. But from

Ungrund itself the first faint shiver to creative manifestation arises as a threefold "feminine" source to the "masculine" Trinity; and this source he sometimes refers to as "the three Mothers," sometimes as just "the Mothers." All this seems to me a more likely source for Goethe's "Mothers" than Plutarch. I remember that Goethe seemed deliberately evasive when pressed on *this* point by Eckermann. He muttered something to the effect that "I can say no more," wrapping himself up in "an air of mystery," as Eckermann says. But from what I remember of *Faust* and *Wilhelm Meister*, there is every evidence Goethe had been deeply interested in and involved in the esoteric religious fraternities—with all their alchemical and astrological symbolism—that influenced Boehme. And with his penchant for wrapping himself up in "an air of mystery," or perhaps from a genuine desire not to "divulge the mysteries" (although I suppose he would not, like Aeschylus, have got into trouble for this), he hesitated to name his real source! But of course I may be very wide of the mark in all this speculation. Yet it is certain that the *Behmenites*, the religious fraternities deriving from Boehme, exercised enormous influence in Germany in the centuries before Goethe, even making, I have read, a deep dent on the mind of *Spinoza*!

Here are two letters, one from Sally, one from Christopher. Christopher's letters are growing franker, I think.

Give my love and very special regards to Mrs. Jackson when you see her. I've had a good letter from Reggie and must write to him.

With my love always
and to Lucy,
Gerard

Spring Cottage
9 January 1974

My darling Mary,

I am starting this letter to you here to finish off in Nairobi, as I may find it hard to write of matters brought up in your letters there. Mugambi has been into Nanyuki today taking money from cattle sales to the bank, and has brought back *five* letters from you! So my head is buzzing with notions—theological and otherwise—stirred up by your letters. But I am off to see Will in about an hour, so haven't much time now to offload them. "High-thundering" Zeus has just let out a warning growl from over Simangwa!

But what I am excited by is this splendid essay you have sent me from the *Times Literary Supplement* on Martin Buber, whom Muriel at Woodbrooke is immensely devoted to, and of whom Redwood used to speak, and to whom Berdyaev is so friendly. Strangely, I have never read him although I've always felt intensely interested in him and friendly to what I have heard and read of him. And this article helps to confirm my sense of something in him hugely relevant to our time and problems. And what an enormous question mark he puts against Barth, and, to be fair to Barth, to Pauline Christianity as a whole. And I have always been aware too of this question mark. And yet too—such are the ambiguities of our human situation—what a terrible and disturbing question mark Barth, and Paul, put against this noble Buberian humanism, which has always so attracted me, yet which at deeper levels of theological perplexity I see as perhaps too simple, too involved in wishful thinking. Zeus has just growled again, more angrily and warningly. So perhaps I must for the nonce move to lighter matters. But there does remain in me the sense that, as far as I can tell at this very second-hand acquaintance, there are in the Divine Nature, and in human nature, dark and tragic and ambiguous—even horrifying—depths that are not to be plumbed by such holy simplicity. Old J.C.P. could, I fancy, whisper a word or two in Buber's ear not easily assimilable to this vision! My own simple response as a simple human being to the New Testament has always been to the Synoptic Gospels, rather than to John or Paul; and I gather Buber would share this response (at least to the Synoptics); but I suspect the dark and anguished negations of Paul and Barth are not without meaning, and plumb depths—τὰ βάθη τοῦ θεοῦ—untouched by simpler minds and easier visions. Yet all that said, with whatever validity the saying of it holds, what a grand and likeable, aye loveable old prophet the Jews have again brought to birth in our time in the person of Buber.

The next exciting thing in your letters is the lovely poem from Valentine's hand come to you through Sylvia, and your equally fine and moving response to it. Lucky Sylvia to receive such a response, and I like to think this poem of yours will bring about possibilities of understanding so far not realized.

Then the third thing I rejoice in is this dear letter from Katey. Oh and what a happy thing to receive so open-hearted a message, so far removed from the caution and reserve, even emotional timidity, of her brother Christopher. Christopher is I suppose still "pondering in the deep of his heart" over my last letters to him—long barren silence squares with his desire at this time, it seems. A touch of Buber would do him the world of good!

And now I must off to W.E.P. and will finish this letter in Nairobi. But enclose at once a letter come today from Sally in Australia.

Evening

Just back from W.E.P. with letters from him to Rose and Lucy to post in Nairobi. Tony came in by plane to spend the night with Will, so I left a little earlier than I'd expected. Will's foot looks very bad, angry and inflamed and very painful, almost as bad as the other was, and I feel it unlikely there will be much improvement. It is hard not to think the only remedy is as for the other. Like Rose, I feel Will has had enough. I would like to see him out of it now. His spirit is wonderful, but one can't see anything else for him than increasing pain and misery. I feel the only thing I can say about it is what is in my mind. I somehow feel too this particular kind of end should not be in Will's fate. But there it is. For me now to know he was out of it all could only bring joy. As Theodore said to me once, "Death is always a mercy." But this death especially and supremely so. And that there should ever be another like him is not even remotely possible. All this is in my mind and heart when I insist on the mystery and utter value and uniqueness and wonder of realized personality. The "impersonalists" can keep their wisdom as far as I am concerned. On this Buber and Berdyaev are absolutely on the mark. And it is on this supreme mystery that Christianity is centered. And I find no truly profound and living and urgent sense of this mystery *anywhere* outside of the Christian Tradition. Here even Buber's sense of its significance is, as far as I can judge, inadequate. He as it were hovers at the outer edges of the Christian mystery, which lies, in spite of all the dread and negation and fear and trembling, at the heart of Pauline Christianity—and is to be found nowhere else. Curiously, Will said to me this evening as I wheeled him back from the office, out of the blue as it were and certainly apropos of nothing then being said (though my mind was full of Paul after reading the essay on Buber)—Will said, "I am a Paulite"—and didn't enlarge on the theme. But I emptily wondered what J.C.P. and Llewelyn, each from his own angle, would have made of this word from the last and greatest of the sons of Mary Cowper Powys. Buber's lack of final comprehension is revealed by his tragic attempt, or trust, that the Kingdom is in some sense now realizable in this world, and not an utterly *eschatological* glory. So I stand with Barth as I see Will moving to his death. But this too is said out of a sense of the utter mystery and *incomprehensibility* in which we are all—great and small, best and worst—caught up.

With love always to Lucy
and to Mary,
Gerard

P.S.

These remarks on Buber are not meant too seriously. I don't know enough about him really, but this essay does provide some very revealing information on his theology. As he is a Jewish thinker, it is not surprising that he misses the depths in Christian vision. The temptation to bypass Paul in favor of the "simplicity" of Jesus in the Synoptics is a temptation even for Christians, much more so for a Jew. But I don't think it bears examination from the Christian point of view, which can only be eschatological if it is to remain itself.

Nevertheless men like Buber can shake us up a lot, as we should be—most Christianity is a pretty tepid affair.

The Trinity of Rublev

'I appoint unto you a kingdom'

on them falls not the light
as earth turns towards day
the light that falls as weight
on our opaque clay

on them does not fall
the dark that hides all
the mate of untold pain
the hold of dayworn brain

the kingdom appointed for them
is not of the light
or the dark of our sight
toil begins not nor rest ends for them

for those three who bend
with dwelling and aureoled head
with suffering hands that bless
with celestial and luminous dress

although they have entrance here
their presence and being is there
by grace of this cup they show
the kingdom appointed we know

MARY CASEY

When word came the letters were about to go into print I was reading *Iconostasis*, by Pavel Florensky. This prompted the thought that Mary Casey's poem 'The Trinity of Rublev' should appear here [G.C.].

The communication of the dead is tongued with fire beyond the language of the living

POSTSCRIPT

...the immensely subtle composition of things, which always and everywhere include an actual infinity.

LEIBNIZ

'Two Women teaching a Child to Walk'
Rembrandt, c. 1635-7

> Waiting for the restitution of all things
>
> ACTS 3:21

> But through such strange illusions have they passed
> Who in life's pilgrimage have baffled striven—
> Even death may prove unreal at the last,
> And stoics be astounded into heaven.

These lines from the Epilogue of Herman Melville's poem *Clarel* have recurred often to my mind as I reread these letters written many years ago. They reflect stages on life's way in the way of a pilgrim. I would express myself now with more circumspection in some directions, but in others in a more radically challenging manner, in the case of currently accepted modes of "correctness" in the fields of theology and philosophy. It is as though one met with an old friend after many years and became aware of changes in his outlook not until then realized.

With passing years I have come to an ever clearer recognition of deep-seated aberrations corroding wide areas of outlook in our time. Crude "scientific" mythologies centering on "big bangs" and "black holes" reflect the violence and nihilism inherent in the rejection of traditional values. It seems many have become incapable of understanding even the simplest of metaphysical insights. However, this incapacity is not the real culprit; it is rather a matter of will, of perverse *choice*. Once this is recognized as such, a way is opened for the individual to be "astounded" into the freedom of the divine Truth.

I recall another poem by another American poet, Emily Dickinson:

> From Blank to Blank—
> A Threadless Way
> I pushed Mechanic feet—
> To stop—or perish—or advance—
> Alike indifferent—
>
> If end I gained
> *It ends beyond*
> *Indefinite disclosed*—
> I shut my eyes—and groped as well
> 'Twas lighter—to be Blind—

The italics are mine. They stress for me the key insight in the poem. Such utterance at the limits of thought loses itself in the apophatic. However, if one is to speak in clearer terms one has to attempt more direct communication. We seek an end *beyond* the *indefinite disclosed* of our contemporary culture with all its multitudinous ramifications—especially in the realms of art and science.

This being so, I would say the need is upon us in the Western world to wake up from the dogmatic slumbers our "rationalist" friends seek to share with us to our endarkenment, and their own. What if their light be but darkness? That, I venture to suppose, is in some degree at least possible? However that may be, St. Paul remains central to my thinking and to the thinking of all truly penetrating religious thought in the authentic Christian tradition; and so I would like to consider briefly Paul's doctrine of the redemption of the whole creation in the context of Spinoza's doctrine of God.

Margaret Wilson, a close contemporary student of Spinoza, has judged that "for better or for worse Spinoza is not a modern thinker." I agree and understand him rather as a watershed between the "God-centered" Middle Ages and the "man-centered" modern age. He had a foot in both camps and was happy in neither. This was at the root of his love/hate relationship with the thought of Descartes, whose approach to philosophy—as "corrected" by his many and vociferous followers—was largely influential in initiating "modernism."

Spinoza (in some ways a forerunner of Nietzsche) was a Jew and a close student of the Bible; he established the modern critical approach to the Bible and announced the "death of God," at least of the God of Abraham, Isaac, and Jacob, Who was to be replaced by an impersonal force operating in splendid isolation: a supreme solipsist. Yet this impersonal force was in fact chosen as a doctrine by the very personal choice of the philosopher in contradiction to his own theological first principles as stated in the definitions opening *Ethics*. Choice is the ineluctable essential element in all human action (action here including thought). This contradiction was, it would seem, conditioned by his understandably hostile reaction to the long history of outrageous persecution directed at free intelligence by the ecclesiastical devotees of the God of Abraham, Isaac, and Jacob. It was by no means the cool dispassionate insight claimed by his followers. This central confusion in his thought led to the confusion discernible on close examination in his subsequent ethical and theological discussions. Recent essays by Garrett and Donagan, both scholars profoundly sympathetic to Spinoza, have indicated some of these *non sequiturs* and confusions.

For my part I wish to consider some of the implications of Spinoza's basic definitions in the opening of *Ethics* and to place the doctrine of St. Paul on cosmic redemption in that context. Spinoza was one of the most searching metaphysical intelligences to appear in the West since Plotinus. Christian ecclesiastical theologians should pay closer attention to both these thinkers. The tendency to evade the problems raised by philosophical theology has weakened and restricted purely Biblical theology. Problems are never solved by pretending they do not exist. Biblical theologians should overcome their fear and opposition to the "God of the Philosophers"—Pascal's reactions in this field do not bear serious examination.

Spinoza's doctrine of God, in the initiating definitions of *Ethics*, as free (*causa sui*), infinite all-possibility excluding negation expresses in his terms that "with God all things are possible." In this it must be realized that some of us grant Spinoza the courtesy of taking in full seriousness the basic implications of *causa sui*. Infinity that seeks to exclude all-possibility is no true infinity. The two terms are absolutely identical in meaning and implication. The refusal—overt or implicit—of so many students of *Ethics* to accept *causa sui* in its full rigor is in the interest of their commitment to determinism. Yet it remains in itself a free choice and acts for them as a protection against authentic metaphysics. This choice has characterized the Western "rational" mind for centuries. It remains what it has always been—an evasion. The signs of the times however indicate that it is growing uncertain of itself in spite of its advantages in buttressing the determinist position; the "rational" mind of the West now gives evidence of waking up and obeying the Scriptural admonition to us all: γρηγορεῖτε! In his penetrating study of necessity and freedom, *The Multiple States of Being*, Guénon has helped clarify thought in these matters. Inexplicably however (in one of the intemperately caustic asides that mar his writings) he seems to share Dr. Johnson's incomprehension of Spinoza. Dr. Johnson in his dictionary presents Spinoza as incapable of distinguishing between God and the physical universe. Dr. Johnson was not a gifted metaphysician. But it is surprising that a mind as lucid as that of Guénon at its best should share the great lexicographer's difficulties in understanding Spinoza.

It must be admitted that Spinoza wavers in a baffling way between his God-centered insights into freedom and his man-centered acceptance of determinism. This is of course a difficulty we all share in every moment of our lives. However, the insistence of Spinoza on viewing the whole cosmic process *sub specie aeternitatis* brings in the theme of transcendence as underlying his whole thought and can be interpreted (and has been by powerful minds: instance Hegel) as bringing Spinoza's ultimate vision to a pantheistic acosmism parallel to the Vedanta of Shankara: a mode of thought profoundly congenial to Guénon. Guénon did not see this and it remains difficult to believe he ever made a close study of Spinoza.

It is clear that the determinist interpreters of Spinoza distort his thought in the interest of their anti-metaphysical notions. The philosopher Joachim, in his studies of Spinoza and in his fine work *The Nature of Truth*, has produced a powerful corrective to these distortions. Nevertheless, his final caveats and his failure to acknowledge adequately the intractable problems (for his own approach) of time and history remain disappointing and amount to no more than an expression of the incapacity of the finite to grasp and, as he would wish, to rationalize the infinite. All attempts to rationalize the infinite leave us with Emily Dickinson's "indefinite disclosed," one manifestation of which is contemporary science.

"Back of beyond," if one may be allowed the expression, lies Revelation rooted in the unconditioned freedom of, to use Boehme's term, *Ungrund*: the limit of all possible thought. It is just here that great religious art and imagination emerge as mediators of Revelation. At this level Spinoza, unlike his contemporary Leibniz (the last truly universal, philosophical mind to appear in Europe), cannot respond, for he allows his obsessive rationalism to reduce art and imagination to "confused thought." Vision that transcends "rationalism" is not allowed. Spinoza's *Deus sive Natura* excludes the mystery of transcendence. "Nature has no outline, imagination has," warns Blake. Thomas Aquinas adds "*imaginare est creare*." What is the whole creation but the image-making of God? "Rationalism," as the illusory tyranny of the finite over the infinite, cannot accept Revelation.

Let us take two examples that spring to mind immediately. Rembrandt's drawing 'Two Women teaching a Child to walk' and Van Gogh's painting 'Wheatfield with Reaper.' In the first we are invited to share Rembrandt's immeasurably profound understanding of tradition: an understanding that marks all his work. In the second we share the incarnational vision of Van Gogh: a vision that challenges and transcends all abstract rationalisms. In the words of Sedulius Scotus, we see "Christ the Sun rising from the Dark over the harvest fields of God." To see in these works nothing more than "confused thought" is ludicrously inadequate. The mind boggles, to put it mildly, at the attempt to subsume in such a category artifacts of incalculably more complex structure as, for example, Chartres Cathedral, Bach's Mass in B Minor, Dante's *Divine Comedy*, or the Blue Bird Fresco that appeared in Knossos about 1600 B.C. springing from a marvellously delicate and profound world vision. Any confusion present lies in the mind of the "rationalist" critics rather than in the mind of the artists. Our "rationalists" need, let us put it quite bluntly, to wake up. When they indulge their assumptions of superiority in fields outside their competence we invite them to reflect on the words of Descartes: "it is of the nature of a finite understanding not to comprehend many things, and of the nature of a created understanding to be finite...." There is a need and a place for Revelation, a need well understood and explicitly accepted by two of the most seminal thinkers in the Western philosophical tradition: Descartes and Leibniz. One cannot but be struck, on reading and listening to many comments on religious and philosophical themes from "rationalists," by their ignorance of the great philosophical and theological traditions of Western civilization. These are the very traditions that underwrite all that is valid in their own researches: an underwriting of which their work stands in need, unaware though many of them are of this debt. It is patent to all who are not philosophical illiterates that modern Western science owes its very existence to a historical process following on from these intellectual traditions. True scientists acknowledge this fact. Yet many of their more thoughtless and vocal spokesmen often convey an impression of a radical incapacity to grasp the intellectual significance and necessity of disciplines other than their own. They should go back to school and seek to become aware of the questions philosophical theology seeks to answer. As Collingwood has pointed out, one can never understand a thinker until one recognizes the question he is seeking to answer. In these fields our "rationalists" remain sleepwalkers.

The striving to rationalize the infinite so characteristic of our times in the West is distinguished by its concern to exclude the dimension of possibility from final perspectives. Some brief comments on Guénon's doctrine of universal possibility as identical with the infinite may be ventured here, for Guénon defined (as did Leibniz, to whom he owed so much) the possible by the absence of internal contradiction.

For Spinoza the possible is disallowed as only implying lack of knowledge of cause. All is in fact determined. The "possible" is that which confusedly seeks to deny determinism. The freedom of the spirit as rooted in the unconditioned *Ungrund* in both man and God is denied. Man can only be understood as a mode of God and God determines and is determined by nature.

Deus sive Natura excludes all freedom. The absolute infinity of God is denied in that universal free possibility is denied. Spinoza is uneasily aware that he has ratted on his own first principles. This retreat leaves God in the domain of the absurd—a notion congenial to the Biblical fool. Clearly Spinoza cannot mean this. Yet insofar as he excludes possibility from the infinite he seeks to limit the infinite and to deny the freedom of God. Spirit realizing itself in freedom is personality, and this necessitates understanding God as Person.

Freedom is realized in personal relationships. It is a personal category which cannot but be empty of final meaning in the context of the solipsism inherent in unqualified monism. This accounts for Spinoza's indifference to visions of the end: to eschatology. Only a pluralistic theism can give true (eternal) significance to freedom realizing itself in personal relationships, that is, in friendship. Christ said to his disciples, "I call you friends." The Christian vision of God as a Trinity of Persons bringing into being a world held in transfiguring relationships meets this need. Christianity remains unmoved by the claims of a monism that evades the realities of the life of the spirit, a monism that for all its talk of the infinity of God seeks to impose limits on the freedom and power of God. The denial of personality to God is a limitation. It is a negation specifically excluded in the definitions "Concerning God" given in *Ethics*, Part One. God, we are told, cannot bring into existence beings other than Himself to share His freedom and eternity: such a childish notion defies the necessities of mathematical logic! Stuart Hampshire, in his persuasive study of Spinoza, remains, with his philosophical master, caught in this dilemma. The contradiction arises from a personal choice: an act of will parading itself as pure intellectuality. The mystery of the will as "free" is not recognized. The choice here is conditioned by the modes of thought inherent in a monism that seeks to exclude the transcendence of God as not "rational." Yet always the sense of and necessity of admitting transcendence returns to haunt their minds. *Aeternitas* is invoked: an *aeternitas* in some inexplicable manner not transcendent. Yet *aeternitas is* the transcendent: what else can a timeless order beyond the spatio-temporal processes of nature be but transcendent? The verbal "mathematical/logical" gymnastics adduced to deny transcendence are but (to echo Wittgenstein) *word play*. The power of pure (discarnate) transcendence to reduce the whole cosmic process to a ghostly charade, as Hegel noted, is dreaded and evaded. Equally, the real presence of *aeternitas*, with its power to take up into itself and redeem a cosmic process that remains isolated in futility until it is fully admitted and welcomed, is likewise dreaded and evaded. "What then?" sings Plato's ghost! The problematics inherent in any attempt to "rationalize" the infinite remain threateningly offstage. God, we are told, can only be conceived as an impersonal force reflecting the impersonality of pure mathematics—a conception that, bafflingly, needs a "person" to conceive it! On the altar of this impersonal "God" all the measureless depths of interacting creative relationships between free persons, both human and divine, are sacrificed. Yet these personal relationships make up the whole of life as lived in the freedom of the spirit. Even mathematical metaphysicians, we suspect, cannot escape them. However that may be, it is certain that Pascal, Descartes, and Leibniz, men of outstanding stature as mathematicians in their time, judged they could not escape them and held firmly to the conception of God as a Trinity of Persons.

In this connection two propositions in *Ethics*, Part Five, are of exceptional interest. Parkinson translates them as follows: "In God, however, there necessarily exists the idea which expresses the essence of this or that body under the species of eternity" (Prop. XXII) and "The human mind cannot be absolutely destroyed with the body, but something of it remains, which is eternal." (Prop. XXIII) In the explanatory notes to these propositions the usual caveats are advanced, such as "eternity cannot be defined by time nor have any relation to it." The contradiction is patent. The "sensing" and "experiencing" of the eternal takes place in time, which "cannot have any relation to it." We become aware in this sequence of reflections of a certain troubled wavering of the will. There is a weakening of the customary resistance to the possibility of understanding *aeternitas* as at once both "immanent" and transcendent. This is a moving and critical moment in the discourse: this involuntary revelation of the painful perplexity of a powerful mind poised in an instant of crucial transition. Spinoza's consciousness glances at and immediately turns away from the possibility of divine restitution as he intuits that neither mind nor body (which constitute in his understanding a single reality) can be destroyed by death. He is but a hair's breadth away from accepting the possibility of resurrection as within the power of God. Has he not intuited an absolutely infinite reality that will admit no negation as—God? A sceptical imp advances in mockery. He hesitantly turns away from the traditional religious insight that the power of God cannot be limited by man. Given the extraordinary power of Spinoza's thought to influence the subsequent thought of the West we realize we are at a decisive turning-point in the history of Western thought. This turn to metaphysical scepticism reinforces the already crystallizing scepticism of the West. More radical sceptics such as Hume and Kant arise to rationalize his fatal surrender. "Post-Christian" man is launched on his continuing attempt in self-deception to isolate himself from the infinite: from God. The onflowing current of scepticism persuades itself it has superseded the "blind faith" of the past. Three centuries pass and the mischievous imp moves on to mock the "certainties" of "scientific" humanism as the modern world moves into acute crisis. Its vaunted "splendid isolation" from ultimate truth loses its splendors and starts to look... well... not so splendid after all. The slide into metaphysical scepticism gathers momentum in its power to emasculate the deeper virilities of a disintegrating culture. The world assumes aspects more and more threatening... Among the "voices off," the poet Yeats, always aware of Jacob's Dream threatening, warns:

> Now his wars on God begin;
> At stroke of midnight God shall win.

The contradiction in Spinoza's thought (resulting in the ultimate metaphysical scepticism we have noted) arises from a lack of clarity in his approach to the enigma of possibility. Freedom, as defined by Guénon, resides in the metaphysical instant of passage from cause to effect. This can only be fully realized in and by God as traditionally understood. Finite being may, in its degree, share in it by centering on and in God. This is the traditional definition of prayer. Prayer as free response by man to the infinitude of God remains the only horizon not lost in the night of John 13:30. The divine freedom is not limited by determinations issuing from causal links in process. It transcends these links in the spatio-temporal, rooted as it is in the timeless. In his flickering consciousness of these issues Spinoza continually wavers. So do we all. It is for this reason Spinoza remains so fascinating to all not entirely given over to and acquiescing in the lack of the eternal that marks the secular humanism of our time. Kierkegaard saw lack of the eternal as despair: the sickness unto death. Despair marks our modern culture at every level insofar as it seeks to deny eternal values. However, as humans made in the divine image, we remain conscious of all that hangs on our choices. These choices are inescapably woven into our deepest existence. It is the focused intensity of these issues in the consciousness of God and traditional man that makes it legitimate to understand God as a Person. Any attempt to deny this is another vain attempt to limit the infinite. Spinoza must have been aware of this and it explains his paradoxical, desperate insistence on viewing all *sub specie aeternitatis*. That indeed saved him from despair but he seems not to have grasped all the implications.

It is in an intuition of the divine as the realm of universal possibility that faith, in the religious sense, is rooted. Clear metaphysical insight confirms the validity of that intuition. It is the basis, albeit understandably weakened in the conflicts of history and cultural diversity by confusion and superstition, of all the authentic religious traditions of man. I suggest that, given the dominant pretensions in our time of "scientific rationalism," it is the fear of appearing naïve rather than intellectual scruple that militates against the widespread acceptance of this intuition among our contemporaries. Insofar as religious, philosophical, and artistic approaches to truth are shrugged off, as they all too often are, this "scientific realism" evinces a distorted mentality that is not genuinely scientific or rational in that it fails to recognize the endless complexity of the real in process. It should not need saying that these critical comments are not in any sense directed at true science, which cannot but remain aware of the validity of perspectives that lie outside the field of its own enquiry, as demonstrated in the Platonism of A.N. Whitehead, the friendly approaches to Vedanta of J.B.S. Haldane, and the uninhibited open vision of Erwin Schrödinger, who in a late essay on the subject here under discussion wrote that "an elimination of metaphysics requires taking the heart out of *both* art *and* science, turning them into skeletons incapable of any further development." John Polkinghorne and David Bohm have expressed similar judgements.

The redemption of the whole of creation—a thought that St. Paul reaches out to in Romans—is within the power of God as conceived in the first part of *Ethics*. The definition of God put forward by Spinoza has been translated by G.H.R. Parkinson as follows: "By God (*Deus*) I understand a being absolutely infinite, that is, a substance consisting of infinite attributes, each of which expresses eternal and infinite essence." Spinoza adds in an explanation: "to the essence of what is absolutely infinite there appertains whatever expresses essence and involves no negation." This explanation has inevitably aroused widespread analysis and comment ever since its first appearance over three hundred years ago. In my own understanding of it I urge, in agreement with Guénon, that the absolutely infinite is identical in God with universal possibility. Universal possibility is necessarily involved in the definition, and necessarily involves *causa sui*, rooted in the creative unconditioned freedom of all-possibility. We meet this doctrine elsewhere, more particularly in the *Ungrund* of Boehme and the *Gottheit* of Eckhart. For both Spinoza and Paul this God is πάντα ἐν πᾶσιν, all in all.

I agree Spinoza did not see all the consequences I have elicited from this doctrine. However, it remains the basic formulation of his doctrine of God and is also acceptable to the doctrines of traditional Christianity. It is doubtful whether he himself was fully aware of all its implications. I would urge that this doctrine fully underwrites Paul's acceptance of it as a basis for his prayer for the redemption of the whole creation: ἀποκαταστάσεως πάντων, as put forward by Peter in Acts 3:21. It could not arise as a problem for Spinoza's monism. Christianity's pluralistic theism does not find it in any way problematic (see Ward: *The Realm of Ends*). In his study 'Christianity and the Metaphysics of Logic,' Philip Sherrard has advanced a challenging defense of Trinitarian metaphysics as over against the monistic logic of Guénon. It commands close attention from those not altogether bemused by unqualified monism. A number of questions are posed, not open to easy answer by those who assume the superiority of the impersonal over the personal, of monism over pluralism.

We are under no duress to take the eschatological nightmares of Augustine and Calvin over-seriously, rooted as they are in Manichean dualism rather than in the Gospels. With Peter and Paul we endure in hope, in eternal hope for all in the Christian vision that shaped the insights of Gregory of Nyssa, of Origen, of Julian of Norwich, and of uncounted Christians throughout the last two thousand years: the ultimate hope of the restoration of all things in God. At the present time the sophistries of the hollow men—those masters of self-deception and shallow scepticism used as a mode of evasion, who see themselves as our instructors—need cause us no deep disturbance. Our sufferings pass, rooted as they are in separation from God, and are in their degree largely illusory. In the presence of God, of the redeeming reality we move in and towards at each moment of our lives, they are accepted as birth pangs into eternal life.

Let us recall the counsel of Plotinus and look, "here" and "there."

"Here" (by the determinate counsel and foreknowledge of God), the victims of all manner of affliction: of selfishness, greed, cruelty, famine, war, plague, slavery, imprisonment, self-sown inner corruption; of evil men, of the Holocaust—all, yes! each and every one of them return in their time and place to God.

But "here"—where is there an end of it, the soundless wailing?

Repetition...

By the determinate counsel and foreknowledge of God.

Death, as my old African friends and old Dorset friends always reassure me, is but going home.

And "there"—at home—all is well.

All creatures formed in the image of the divine freedom, fallen into unfreedom, caught in the inane of "this world" cannot but mourn...

Blessed are they that mourn, they shall be comforted.

Unlike Leibniz, Spinoza's wariness in the face of teleology and his detachment from emotion and imagination reflect his tendency, in defiance of his own first principles, to limit the powers of God. Even God's power to love is limited to Himself! This introduces a degree of coldness into Spinoza's ultimate vision. He tries hard to save the appearances under the unacknowledged influence of incarnational revelation; yet it remains that men, and beyond men all possible worlds, pass like shadows across the face of Spinoza's God. Resurrection, as within the will and power of God, is denied.

Spinoza's unknown attributes of God, Wordsworth's unknown modes of being, the order of the unmanifested of Guénon, lie hidden, but potent for realization in the divine infinity. In Christian terms they lie hidden with Christ in God.

The unimaginable touch of time, the end-touch of time implicit in each passing moment of time that brings time to an end, lies for us, caught up as we are in history, in the future. Waiting we realize Time's final meaning in prayer.

A Poem for Robert Davis[1]

under the white clouds[2]
a wind blowing
gently breathing to the heart speaks

now
even now

here
even here

flute notes sound
to primal unmemoried birth

beyond the window
in the garden
birds are singing

morning sun rising
reaches out
touches
the ancient tower

re-assuring home
to calling bells...

ἔρχου Κύριε Ἰησοῦ

---

1. See 'A Note on the Headstone'.
2. See Wang Wei's poem 'Lament for Yin Yao' (*Poems of Wang Wei*, G.W. Robinson, trans., Penguin Classics, page 61): "Your bones are there under the white clouds until the end of time/ And there is only the stream that flows down to the world of men." See also *The Clear Shadow*: 'Good Friday' and 'Four Meditations for Easter'; *Echoes*: 'Easter Morning' and 'Nightfall.'

Appendix

All Truth is a Shadow except the last. But every Truth is Substance in its own place, though it be but a Shadow in another place. And the Shadow is a true Shadow, as the Substance is a true Substance.

ISAAC PENNINGTON

Jacob Boehme

Jacob Boehme, a speculative and devotional Christian mystic of the highest order, was born in 1573 near Goerlitz in Germany. His parents were poor peasants, and Boehme was acquainted with poverty from birth to death. He received as a boy only the barest initiation into the rudiments of a formal education—a little instruction in reading and writing and the customary elements of religious teaching. He was from the beginning introspective and withdrawn, and was—perhaps as a consequence of this—put to more than his share of solitary work herding sheep and cattle in the fields around his village. At this time the visionary element in his makeup became apparent. On one occasion he told his father that he had found and climbed to the top of a mountain. There on the summit he saw four red stones leading into a cave that was filled with light radiating from a golden vessel. At this he was seized with fear and ran away. Later, accompanied by other boys to give him courage, he attempted to return to the cave but could not find it again.

JACOB BOEHME
Sutor Gorlicensis
1575-1624

His physical strength was not great. For this reason, in his fourteenth year, his parents apprenticed him to a shoemaker rather than send him into the heavy work done by his father on the land. A story has come down to us from this period of his life. One day when he was alone in the shop a stranger came in and asked for a pair of shoes. The man paid for the shoes and returned into the street—but suddenly turned back and called to him: "Jacob, come forth." Surprised that the stranger should know his name Jacob obeyed and ran out to the man, who took both Jacob's hands in his, and, looking at him earnestly, said: "Jacob, you are as yet only small but the time will come when you will be great. You will suffer much misery and persecution, but be brave and persevere. God loves you and will be gracious to you." This experience induced a deep restlessness in him, and so he left his master and set out as a journeying cobbler. This led to a time of hardship and insecurity and agonizing inner conflicts that was brought to an end when he found and was accepted by another master. Soon after entering the service of his new master he records that one day, as he bent over his last, he was lifted up into a condition of blessed peace. He was lit up within by a divine light for seven days. "The triumph that was then in my soul I cannot describe. I can only liken it to a resurrection from the dead." But outwardly there was nothing particularly noticeable about him. A friend wrote later: "His bodily appearance was somewhat mean. He was small of stature, had a low forehead, prominent temples, an aquiline nose, a scanty beard, a feeble voice. He was modest in bearing, unassuming in conversation, patient and gentle-hearted. One mark drew attention: quiet gray eyes suddenly sparkling to a heavenly blue...."

In the year 1594 Boehme returned to Goerlitz, and some years later he married a girl of the town. The marriage was a happy one. His wife bore him four children and proved herself a thoughtful and considerate woman not unaware of the value of the unusual man she had married. For the next ten years he practiced his craft, was attentive to his household affairs, was kindly to all who approached him. During this period he had two visionary experiences that were to prove the source of the God-intoxicated wisdom revealed in his writings. One day his eye fell upon a pewter dish reflecting back to him in marvelous splendor the morning sunlight. He was immediately rapt into a profound inward ecstacy in which—as it seemed to him—he could see into the deepest heart of things. He was to call his first writing *Morning Glow.* Some years later this vision was completed by another, in which all that had remained in some degree chaotic and fragmentary became coherent—a perfect whole.

The intervening period however had been one of deep psychic disturbance and disequilibrium. The light at times faded into an anguished inner darkness: times when he could do nothing but cling to the memory of his vision as he labored in "the mystery of iniquity as a child goes to school." Yet the vision went on "breeding within, gradually unfolding like a young plant." He entered into the vision of the "Three-headed Lily." He knew the bliss of "breathing the scent of the lily." He was able to cry out with the poet, "behold the cohesion of all: how perfect." For Boehme, his vision of the Three-headed Lily was his vision of the Blessed Trinity.

And now he began to record something of his inner visions. Writing in the evenings and at odd moments away from his last, he wrote his first work, *Morning Glow*, whose title he changed later, at the suggestion of a friend, to *Aurora*.

Boehme was living at a time of intense and bitter religious controversy in Europe. The tides of Reformation and Counter-Reformation were flowing strong and fast. Cruelty and violence in the most extreme degree were weapons men did not hesitate to use in their attempts to impose their own religious doctrines on others. Boehme's writing began to circulate among friends, and all who were interested; for it was an age of extraordinary interest in religious matters. Very soon a manuscript was discovered and seized by the Lutheran pastor of Goerlitz. He denounced it as heretical—a charge carrying with it in those days the grimmest possibilities. Boehme was summoned before the city council and at first sentenced to exile from his native town—a hard enough matter for a poor man. This sentence was however quickly reduced under pressure from the more moderate members of the council, and the shoemaker was ordered instead to "stick to his last," keep his ideas to himself, and write no more. For a time he obeyed, but his opinions were known and brought him "much ignominy, shame and reproach, budding, blossoming from day to day." His business no longer supported him. The pastor, Gregorius Richter, continued to denounce him publicly from the pulpit. He was sneered at and insulted in the streets: "He smells overmuch of cobbler's pitch" went the cry. At length he was forced to sell his shop and set out as a wanderer. To live he sold woolen gloves from door to door through the villages and towns. For five years he obeyed the command to write no more, but at last could no longer resist the inner imperative to share his vision with other men, and he started to write again. Privately the manuscripts began to circulate which were later to earn his work a unique place among the spiritual writings of the world. He had in the meanwhile been gaining more friends, many of them learned and influential men. Early in 1624 his friend Abraham von Franckenburg published a selection of his writings under the title *The Way to Christ*. Richter acted immediately. Boehme was again charged and banished. He was not even allowed to see his wife and children. He found refuge with a friend in Dresden. Soon he was summoned before the Electoral Court on a charge of heresy. He made a profound impression on the board of theologians and divines called to examine his case by the Elector. The charge was dismissed, but Boehme was again warned to be careful.

He was by now mortally ill. Meanwhile his implacable enemy Richter had died and it was found possible for him to return to Goerlitz. He was carried back to his home and there died shortly after midnight on November 21, 1624. Shortly before his death he urged his son Tobias to "open the door wider that he might hear more clearly that heavenly music." A little later he said, "Now I go to paradise," and so died. He was in his fiftieth year.

Boehme's opponents in Goerlitz tried to prevent him receiving a burial service. His friends set over his grave a wooden cross with the inscription:

Here rests Jacob Boehme, born of God,
died in Christ, sealed by the Holy Ghost.

❧

Boehme's metaphysical, mystical, and religious doctrines are so searching, detailed, and penetrating, so vast in their scope and implications (often too, it must be admitted, so obscure in their expression), that his thought could well occupy the study of a lifetime. He became known as the father of German philosophy, and his influence has been traced and acknowledged in the work of Leibniz, Kant, Fichte, and Schelling. Hegel spoke of him as "that man of mighty mind." Schopenhauer confessed he could not read him without awe and tears. In the fields of theology and mysticism his work has been even more profoundly seminal. Names like William Law, von Baader, Oetinger, St. Martin, Maurice, and, in our time, Berdyaev, bear witness to this. Goethe used Boehme's unfathomable intuitions into the metaphysical significance of the feminine in his *Faust*. Sir Isaac Newton closeted himself for months to study Boehme, fascinated by his doctrines of motion and force, as well as his theology. All this being so, we can only give the briefest outline of some aspects of his basic thought here.

Boehme differs from the Christianized Platonism of Origen and Eckhart—two other Christian visionaries who have transcended the congealing limitations of Christian ecclesiasticism—in that his vision is more radically Biblical. His gnosis is expressed for the most part through traditional myths and symbols rather than in intellectualized concepts. This corresponds to its more searching quality.

Let us look at his Three-headed Lily: the Blessed Trinity rooted in the mystery of *Ungrund*. No comprehending approach can be made to Boehme by readers who cannot—whatever may be the reason—share in some degree, however limited, his intuition of the mystery he calls *Ungrund*, the 'ungrounded'. Reflecting some of Boehme's own expressions, we may say that *Ungrund* is the primal source, the unconditional freedom, the uncreated root of all—of both God and world. It is symbolized by Boehme as the Dark. It is the aboriginal No-thing, Vacuity, Void. Yet it is utter, unconditioned creativity and freedom. It is a Womb teeming with all the infinite potentialities of creation. As pure source, potentiality, he calls it the Mother; and at times, insofar as it reflects the Three-headed Lily in the Dark of *Ungrund*, as the Three Mothers or the Essence of All Beginnings, All Mothers. It is probably the aspect of Boehme's thought that most outraged Richter, but one profoundly congenial to the Catholic doctrine of the Mother of God. I have given it emphasis here because it is essential to all Boehme's thought, and must always be kept in mind. In Boehme all is the manifestation of *Ungrund*—proceeds from it, returns to it. Yet *Ungrund* is in itself No-thing, the "nihil" out of which both God and Creation spring.

In this unutterable mystery of otherness beyond all possibility of definition—in this Abyss beyond the Deity—lies the source of all, the "ungrounded Ground" of the very Godhead itself. With the Godhead we arrive at the barest possibility of definition: it is the Essence of all essences, the Life-giving Root of all existence. This eternal Godhead co-exists in the Father, the Son, and the Holy Ghost: a Trinity of Light manifesting out into Existence the potentialities inherent in the "Feminine" Dark of *Ungrund*. The Father generates the Son eternally, and the Holy Ghost eternally "proceeds" from both Father and Son. The Son as Divine Word eternally "creates" out of the nihil—the nothing of *Ungrund*—in the ever-dawning morning of an ever newly created Day: Eternal Nature. Eternal Nature flows out in a triple manifestation called the Fire-World, the Light-World, and the Dark-World. These three worlds interpenetrate at all levels and are modes of a single living whole in the manner of the three *gunas* of Vedanta in the manifested world. From this Eternal Nature flow all possible worlds in every possible mode of succession—temporal or non-temporal—imaginable to us, or beyond our imagining. Eternal Nature is the Plenus or Fullness in which all created elements, essences, principles, and potentialities of all possible worlds are contained, among them our particular world. Eternal Nature is the reflection in the created order of *Ungrund* in the uncreated order.

In his cosmology Boehme reveals affinites with the thought of Heraclitus and Empedocles. "In Yea and Nay all things consist." "Strife is the father of all." The cyclic fires of the cosmos flow from the creative *fiat* of the ever-living Divine Fire which in good and evil, love and hate, is inherent in the very substance of Eternal Nature and consequently in all the structures of the Cosmos. Cosmos is the Chaos of Eternal Nature striving to realize the Forms and Harmonies of the Eternal Archetypes: here the thought is Platonic. Within the circles of the Cosmos this conflict is inescapable—it is woven into the fabric of creation. Boehme rejects all thought of God as evolving in time, in the Cosmos. God transcends creation. God's act of creation is not a temporal act. Creation is "other" than God. Nevertheless creation reflects the hidden life of the Uncreated that brings it into being. The Dark-World in creation is a reflection of *Ungrund*. The Fire-World is a reflection of the uncreated Fire of the Father. The Light-World reflects the "truth, beauty, and goodness" of the Son. The Son is the Uncreated Light that shines out into the darkness of *Ungrund* and the Dark-World of creation. The Holy Spirit "proceeds" from this creative interplay of the Divine Fire and Light, and in the Holy Spirit arise the Divine archetypes of creation, which flow out into temporal realization in Eternal Nature. The Uncreated Fires of the Godhead are the source of the Light Fire and the Dark Fire of Eternal Nature—of good and evil alike.

Let us turn from Boehme's doctrine of God and Nature to his doctine of Man. Man is a created being in Nature. He is other than God. Yet he is created in the image of God. Here Boehme's Christology comes out as central to his whole vision. His doctrine of Christ is essentially orthodox. Christ is the God-Man, the Mediator, the Bridge across the gap between the uncreated eternal and the created temporal. Christ is the Universal God-in-Man. Individual man wills to become "at-one" with God in Christ, or moves into the outer darkness—and returns to *Ungrund*. That he can make this choice, that he has this freedom, is a mystery that cannnot be rationalized, or rationalized away. Man, like God, is rooted in the ultimate, undifferentiated freedom of *Ungrund*. Freedom is the uncreated, and even in the circles of Eternal Nature man shares in this freedom. Man as Divine Image reflects the mystery and ultimate freedom of the creative interplay between Light and Dark in the Godhead Itself. In this mystery lies the source of all the baffling enigmas in the spiritual life of man. For this freedom is experienced by man as "nothingness" until it freely receives into itself the Signature of the Trinity. This means that freedom cannot be realized objectively in the objectified world of "fallen" man. Man is fallen insofar as he wills separation from God. One factor in this equation our modern nihilistic existentialists, such as Sartre and Heidegger, understand very well. That is the human factor. The Divine factor is for them non-existent, as they are willing—or at least trying to will—separation from God. But separation from God means return to *Ungrund*, to nothingness—a word with which they make much play.

Boehme is always intensely aware of the mystery of the will. He resists any attempt to rationalize away this mystery, be it in God or man. He equally emphasized the orientations of the will in man necessary to secure his entrance to the Divine Light-World—that is, to salvation. These are faith, hope, courage, patience. These virtues all involve each other. Taken together they conform the will of man to the Will of God as revealed in Christ, the Son. Boehme's vision of the world, and man in the world, is endlessly dynamic, caught up in the mysteries of the will in both man and God. For him creation is a vast process of birth and rebirth: of life freely returning or freely refusing to return to its source in God—or, beyond God as Triune Person, to *Ungrund* itself. This last possibility is however to Boehme—as it must be from the point of view of the created person—a state of Eternal Loss. It is Eternal Death. Eternal Life—Resurrection beyond death—is in God and in God alone.

Within the categories and distinctions Boehme makes, this position is incontrovertible. For Boehme the rest is silence. However his doctrines taken in their fullness, in the fact that they rest on his affirmation that "the Eternal Good is the Eternal One" (a Plotinian note that brings him into harmony with Eckhart) seem to imply an unuttered acceptance of the ancient Christian doctrine of the "restitution of all things" (of *apocatastasis*, as the Greek Fathers had it), that is, of Universal Salvation. This seems an inherent necessity, a consequence, of his thought. That Boehme hesitated to make it explicit can be understood, I think, as flowing from his intense awareness of Freedom as an ultimate mystery that cannot be rationalized. For Boehme the last word could not rest with an "inherent necessity." He was in any case content to leave the issue—where it should be left—with God.

For myself as a Christian I would say that, in Boehme, I find all the elements of a fully Christian theosophy that does not shrink—as so many Christians have done—from a truly universal vision of man and his destiny in God. Yet this is achieved on a genuinely Biblical basis, which means it is more in harmony with the real roots of Christianity than the metaphysics of Eckhart, owing so much to Neo-Platonism, or the theology of St. Thomas Aquinas, with its Aristotelian basis. Boehme's work may therefore become the instrument of a more real understanding of Christianity among the non-Christian traditions of the world.

JACOB BOEHME

Extracts from the Writings of Jacob Boehme

as a Gloss, or Mirror,

to throw light on the themes discussed

I add these extracts from Boehme's writings, which may serve to convey something of the unique personal quality of his utterances—so different from that of any other writer, and so immediately recognizable as his, and his alone:

O hear me—for I know well what melancholy is. I have lodged all my days in the melancholy inn.

When I beheld and contemplated the great deeps of this world, the sun and stars, the clouds rain and snow, and considered in my spirit the whole creation of this world... and found in all things good and evil, love and anger—even in wood, stones, earth, and the elements, as also in men and beasts—when I considered the deep beyond the earth... I fell, child of the stars and elements as I am, into deep melancholy and heavy sadness... and was in darkness... and in the darkness was God....

God has set light and darkness before every man: choose that which thou wilt! But what storms must the soul endure and undergo....

Where wilt thou seek God? In thy soul that proceeds out of Eternal Nature.

The source whirls within itself.

The first fire was but a beginning and not a constant and lasting light.

Out of one beginning many beginnings are born.

God is in thy dark heart. Knock and He shall come out within thee into the light.

Love gives essence; God gives Himself to every essence; the dear lovely child Venus is in us all.

God Himself is so near thee that the geniture and the signature of the Holy Trinity is being continually wrought in thy heart... wilt thou but have it so....

The greatest understanding lies in the signature. By their external form all creatures, as by their voices and action, by their desires and inclinations, make their hidden spirit known. For nature has given to everything its own language according to its inmost essence....

The Son, the Divine Word, is the Maker of the formings: in Him is the true golden sevenfold[1] man, the seer and knower of the wonders of God, the man of heavenly essentiality, the inward holy one generated from fire and light....

The wrath and anger-fire of God is cause of the divine joyfulness... life grows in death, but if the light goes out in the essence it is eternal death....

Man is a chaos, a complexion of great wonders... but within this Chaos is a wonder-eye: God Himself, the Being of Beings Who manifests Himself in particular beings as the Eye of Eternity....

The Day holds the Night swallowed up in Itself—even as the Night dwells in the Day.

But the Night is not Manifest: Yea, Day and Night lie locked up in each other as one Essence....

---

1. Sevenfold "Man" reflects: *Ungrund*, Godhead, Father, Son, Holy Ghost, Eternal Nature, and Universal Man. Note that the "Son" is central.

Ramana Maharshi

There is a Light which is flowing and darkening every Light

ECKHART

As a man rooted in the Christian faith, I wish to offer a few considerations that seem to me to spring from a Christian understanding of, and devotion to, Sri Ramana Maharshi. I begin with some general observations that will, I hope, provide a background against which such a Christian approach will be revealed as fraught with meanings that transcend any purely private and personal significance.

It is at this time common ground among thoughtful men and women the world over that humanity has entered into a period of extreme crisis and danger. This crisis reveals itself at every level of human striving, but most acutely and painfully in the depths of men's religious consciousness. Among men of all religious traditions there is a need to reach out to deeper understandings of both their own tradition and traditions native to cultures and civilizations other than their own. For men rooted in great and ancient forms of the spiritual life, the differences in emphasis and perspective between what we have come to call "East" and "West" remain the most urgently demanding of understanding and acceptance.

In the West, the religious spirit has crystallized, in Christianity, into the form most expressive of the peculiarities of the Western mind. In the East, Hinduism presents the form perhaps most difficult of access to Western understanding. As a Christian who has been for many years fascinated and attracted by Hinduism—approached through wide reading and some devoted study of the great Sanskrit Scriptures—I confess that the figure of Sri Ramana has come to hold for me a place of central significance, both in my own spiritual life and in my attemps at understanding Hinduism. It is from this point of view that I write what follows. I concentrate on the "death-experience" in his youth which initiated for Sri Ramana his supreme spiritual realization, and which was the source of his extraordinary power.

As I am writing for devotees of Sri Ramana, there is no need to recapitulate in detail what is known of this experience, but I would like to quote briefly from the account given by Paul Brunton: "He was sitting alone in his room one day when a sudden inexplicable fear of death took hold of him. He became acutely aware he was going to die, although he was outwardly in good health.... He began to prepare for the coming event.... He fell into a profound conscious trance wherein he became merged into the very source of selfhood, the very essence of being...."

He emerged from this trance "utterly changed": Bhagavan was born.

Insofar as we can understand or attempt to express our understanding of this experience in words, it seems true that it involved in some quite radical sense the "death" of the seventeen-year-old Venkataraman: a "death" which yet left the eternal "Self" incarnated in the still living body of the youth.

It is known that the "conscious death" experience that brought about this final realization of the Spirit had been preceded in the foregoing months by incursions of deep dreamless sleep from which the youth could not be roused and from which he emerged only with difficulty. We may intuit that in these sleep-states—so profound as to be close to death-states—the psyche withdrew to the deepest sources of its being—to the primal *Ungrund* spoken of by the Christian mystic Boehme, a state of unconditioned freedom—and returned from the death-trance to the fully conscious realization of the divine essence: a radiant formless glory.

All the known facts of the Maharshi's long subsequent life seem to bear out the truth that he remained unchanged in this state until his *mahasamadhi*.

A short time after his "death" Sri Ramana disappeared, leaving his family and the home of his childhood with the farewell message: "I have, in search of my Father and in obedience to His command, started from here...." His distraught mother found him two years later near the great temple of Arunachala. His response to her importunities that he return home with her was to the effect that "I must be about my Father's business." Those not familiar with the Christian Scriptures will find a close parallel to this event in Sri Ramana's life in the New Testament (Luke 2:41-52).

It is, from the Christian point of view, of special interest that Sri Ramana in his earliest expression of his understanding of his spiritual destiny used simple, personal terms: "I have, in search of my Father and in obedience to His command...." Such terms are entirely consonant with the Christian doctrine of Grace, which is experienced by the Christian as a Divine Person-to-human person communication of the Divine Presence. Without this Grace, revelation, which illuminates simultaneously a past outer event and a present inner awareness, is not possible. Only some similar operation of Grace makes explicable the devotion to the Maharshi which becomes a living experience of the spirit in the deepest reaches of its freedom to many who have never seen him, have never been to India, and, in some cases, have very little acquaintance with or knowledge of Hindu religion.

Christianity, in its attempts to provide a theological account of similar facts in the life and influence of Jesus, evolved the doctrine of the Trinity; and a Chrisian will naturally think in terms of this doctrine in any attempt he may make to understand Sri Ramana. There is the claim of "Sonship" to a divine "Father" who makes a "personal" demand of obedience "even unto death." There is the inflow of the Spirit which made obedience possible.

For readers unversed in orthodox Christian theology I should explain that the Greek word "ho theos" (God) is used in the New Testament of the first Person of the Trinity: the "Father." The Son is not God in an absolute sense but God as Christ: the Universal Man Who is revealed for Christians in Jesus. The Divine Son becomes Man. The Father, while one with the Son and incarnate in the Son, yet remains transcendently "more" than the Son. The way for the Christian to the realization of Sonship in all its fullness lies through death in Christ, the Universal Man.

It is with the centrality of death in this Christian "way" that I am here concerned. The Christian seeks to realize and accept in his life the meaning of death. Death is the limit to life in time and seems to threaten extinction. Yet only through death of the ego can his full relationship with God be realized. Life is—religiously understood—a birth through time and death-to-time into eternal life. Insofar as a man centers himself in God as the source of his being he finds the meaning of his existence and his true Self: the Divine Image.

It is clear that these fundamental Christian insights are of immense value and importance to a Christian understanding of Sri Ramana Maharshi and of his death-experience. The life of the spirit for all men always involves, in some degree, a dying-to-time while still in the body. At the very headwaters of European thought, Heraclitus said: "The name of the bow is life, its work is death." For Plato, philosophy is "the practice of dying." For Jesus, "the Father raiseth up the dead." In the case of Sri Ramana there was an abrupt and radical completeness about his death-to-time—while continuing to live physically in time—that commands astonished attention. The psyche in its sleep-return to *Ungrund* seems to have, in that unconditioned freedom, broken from bondage to time into the full reconstitution of its Divine Image—and then freely returned into time full of grace and truth. To the grace and truth many have witnessed: men and women from the most varied backgrounds and religious persuasions—witnessed too to the extraordinary numinous power radiating from the personal presence of the Maharshi.

In the present age, when purely contemplative modes of the religious life are, if not entirely discounted, yet little understood or valued in the West, the presence of a supreme contemplative sage in the East, who elicits devotional response and faith in men nurtured in diverse religious traditions throughout the world, is a fact full of hope and meaning for the future. In most expressions of devotion to Sri Ramana—even when issuing from those intellectually sophisticated in the highest degree—there is patent a childlike joy and trust in Bhagavan. Those who find such trust inexplicable should recall the saying of

Heraclitus: "The Kingdom is of the Child," and the words of Jesus: "Except ye become as little children, ye shall not enter the Kingdom of Heaven."

We know that Sri Ramana himself revealed throughout a long life a child-like innocence and gaiety of heart, coupled with an awe-inspiring majesty at all times, and more expecially at the end, through a lingering and painful illness, in the face of death.

A Gloss on the Preceding Essay

After a reading of Eckhart's Sermon number Thirty-Seven

When a man is in true possession of his eternal self pay good heed. Such a man is very hard to recognize. When others fast, he eats; when others watch, he sleeps; when others pray aloud, he is silent. In short whatever other people practice seems indifferent to him. He needs nothing for he is in possession of his eternal self. He knows none can take from him his birthright which is his eternal self. That cannot but remain eternally his own. Such a man reflects into the finite world the infinity of God.

Blessed is the land in which even one such man is born and dwells...

Three Meditations on Prayer

These meditations are an attempt to recapture words spoken at a meeting for worship at Woodbrooke, an institution run by The Society of Friends. A friend who was present has urged the attempt. The writer should perhaps say that the time was just before Holy Week, and understanding will be deepened insofar as the Christian mysteries "remembered" at that time are held in mind and heart.

Prayer is one of the mysteries at the heart of the Christian faith. Meditation is itself, in Christian teaching, a form of prayer: prayer through the use of images and discursive thinking. Meditation leads on to contemplation, which is, as image falls away and mind and heart grow still, pure prayer: the silence growing out of the divine word: "be still and know that I am God."

Prayer is the lifting up of the mind and heart to God.

It may happen that a time of suffering and dereliction in a man's life may again bring him, one who has forgotten how to pray, to lift up his mind and heart to God. Then the divine response may be to the man as the falling of rain after long drought.

We read of times of drought in India and Africa. Such a time is now being lived through by the men and animals who live along the Webi Schebeli river in Somaliland. The herds of elephant are forced each day to graze farther out into the wilderness of dry thorn-bush that lies along the course of the river. Each day they have to return to the river to drink. Each day they grow weaker as the distance between food and water increases. Some will die of thirst when they are no longer strong enough to return to water. Some will die of hunger when they can no longer reach grazing. All other creatures in the bush suffer the same struggle. The camels and cattle grow thin, provide no milk, start dying. The small cultivated plots in the patches of good soil on the river banks dry up. Each day the effort to carry water from the river grows heavier. Men, women, and children grow thin, start dying. At some time—no one knows just when—men find themselves praying. No longer the formal daily prayer at set times of the world of Islam: rather a continual inward urgent prayer slowly emerging into consciousness as the days go by, with the sense of its presence having long preceded conscious awareness. Clouds gather at times, promise rain, disperse again. One senses now that all men, all creatures, the very land itself, are praying for rain. At last—on a stifling night, perhaps—one hears the rain: a gently persistent falling in the darkness. Of this there are no words to write for those who have not lived through the drought.

But the people have learnt to pray. They have learnt the one thing ultimately needful: to enter prayerfully into the presence of God. They know other droughts will come. They know the suffering inherent in existence itself will not, cannot, pass. But the people know that in the presence of God all suffering is redeemed. They share a knowledge lost to those in more protected societies, who have forgotten how to pray.

Prayer is the remembrance of God.

"Our birth is but a sleep and a forgetting." Man, through his religious traditions, seeks to break into this forgetting: ever renewing for all men the remembrance of God.

In prayer man remembers God.

In prayer man remembers himself before God.

I remember traveling, some years ago in Africa, from before dawn, then through the heat of the day, over a plain encircled by horizons boundless as the sea. Soon after noon a huge hill of bare rock appeared, coming into view over the horizon many miles away. All through the afternoon we moved slowly through the terrible sun-glare towards the hill throwing its lengthening shadow to the east over the desert. On reaching the hill, before unpacking, we rested awhile in the cool shadow away from the sun-glare. And as a sudden blessing came the memory of ancient words half-forgotten, half-remembered:

"The presence of God is like the shadow of a great rock in a harsh land."

Prayer is the practice of the presence of God.

It may happen that a moment comes in a man's life when he finds himself facing the empty quarter, and the way lies ahead.

An explorer was some years ago seeking to cross Rus' al Khali—"the empty quarter": the vast and desolate area lying across the southern half of the Arabian peninsula. He made careful preparations and secured supplies, guides, and camels. As he moved south into the northern fringes of that frightful wilderness he met, staggering from the south through the sun-glare and mirage, the figure of a man weak and half-delirious from hunger and thirst. In those solitudes, so hostile to life, the meeting was a chance hardly to be believed. He received the man into his caravan and restored his strength with rest and food and drink. He recalls that later, before the traveler resumed his journey, his guides, speaking to the man, said, with all the grave courtesy of the Bedouin to fellow wanderers in the wilderness: "What necessity lay upon you, friend, that you journey alone over the empty quarter—a solitude so vast and so great that even the birds can scarcely pass over it in their flight?"
The stranger replied: "A necessity was on me to go as quickly as may be to my father, who dwells to the north. But I was not alone. God was with me."

A Note on the Headstone

The tombstone depicted on page xiii lies about twelve paces to the north from the base of the tower in Mappowder churchyard. It is referred to in my essay 'A Double Initiation', which appeared in *Recollections of the Powys Brothers*:

> Each afternoon too there was Compline in Mappowder village church—usually empty but for the Rector Dr Jackson and Theodore [Powys] saying the responses. Theodore would arrive half an hour early. There was a stillness in the church in that time of waiting. One sensed the strange numinous quiet of the long hours he sat there, day by day, always in the same pew at the back of the church, alone... in 'the waiting silence in us that is free.'
>
> One afternoon as we leave the church he pauses beside the grave of:
>
> *Robert Davis*
> *son of Robert and Mary Davis*
> *who departed this life August 24 1726*
> *aged 19 years*
>
> He reaches out with his walking stick almost touching the beautiful head carved reclining in the stone, the hair blown back from an ear—more deeply engraved or less worn by time—'cocked for the resurrection'—there is only the faintest hint of mockery in the words... "but always remember Gerard that death to whomever it comes, however it comes, whenever it comes, is always a mercy...." So the moods pass through him...

Some years earlier I had received another "emblematic utterance" (as a Chinese sage might say) from John Cowper Powys, 'the Old Man of Phudd' as he signed himself (living then at Phudd Bottom in upstate New York): "In the indrawn breath of matter is a word that may change all." These gnomic sayings from two brothers entered into a symbiotic growth in my mind over many years. The present book may perhaps (from one point of view) be understood as reflecting some of the meditations following from their influence as I thought on the meaning of the death of Robert Davis.

Biographical Note

Gerard Casey was born at Maesteg, South Wales, in 1918. Both his parents belonged to the Catholic Irish immigrant community there. His father had worked in the mines from the age of twelve, until he enrolled in the Welsh Fusiliers as a volunteer during the First World War. After the war he trained as a teacher. His quickly-growing family joined him first in Cardiff, a city which made an indelible mark on his eldest son Gerard, as witnessed in his "script for voices" *South Wales Echo*. Later the family moved to Aberkenfig near Maesteg, where Casey's father was a headteacher of the Catholic primary school for more than 30 years. Here his youngest son Patrick, the Pat of these letters, was born, fourteen years after Gerard.

As a young man Gerard Casey discovered in a local library the works of John Cowper Powys (J.C.P.), who was to have a lasting influence on his life as guide, philosopher, and friend. It was John who first introduced Gerard to his youngest brother Will (W.E.P.), a successful farmer in Kenya. In 1938 Casey joined Will Powys and his family as a farm assistant.

On Gerard's first leave in Great Britain after the Second World War (which he chiefly spent with the East African Army in Somalia and Ethiopia), he met Mary, his future wife. Mary was the only daughter of Lucy Amelia Penny, the youngest sister of the Powys family, which further counted among its eleven children the authors Theodore Francis and Llewelyn Powys, both also mentioned in these letters.

Gerard and Mary married in November 1945, before Gerard's return to Africa. By the end of 1947 the Caseys were established on their own farm, The Beale. The Beale stood on the slopes of Mount Kenya between two of Will Powys's larger farms, at Kisima and the Ngare Ndare.

In 1956, after the troubled years of the Mau-Mau movement for Independence, the Caseys acquired another farm lower down at Ndere, beyond an area of forest reserve. There they built two small cottages, one at Sirakoi and the other, Spring Cottage, close to Will's farm at the Ngare Ndare. They had about 5,000 sheep at The Beale, and about 1,000 head of cattle on the more spacious ground at Ndere.

In the late 1950s Gerard Casey suffered from severe encephalitis, an illness that recurred for over ten years and necessitated a reduction in his activities. In 1964 he entered into a partnership with a young man, Christopher Gibson, who undertook to grow crops on The Beale farm. The farm was finally sold to the African Land Settlement Scheme in 1972.

Gerard continued at Ndere, eventually turning the farm there into a co-operative. He handed over its general management to Mbui Manyara (Mlefu), his headman for many years, but remained one of the directors until the mid-1980s.

From 1963 the Caseys began to spend longer periods in England, at first staying with Mary's mother in Mappowder, Dorset. Later they were able to buy the adjoining cottage. In time Mary would become more and more reluctant to leave England for Africa, but Gerard continued to fly to and fro till 1990. Mary Casey died in January 1980. Gerard Casey still lives in Mappowder.

In view of the nature of the letters printed in this book readers may be interested to know that he is a member of The Society of Friends.

www.ingramcontent.com/pod-product-compliance
Lightning Source LLC
Chambersburg PA
CBHW081916170426
43200CB00014B/2739